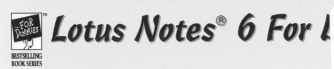

Lotus Notes® 6 For I

MW01000689

Navigating among Documents

To Go to This	Use This	Or This
Next unread document	Tab	F4
Previous unread document	Shift+Tab	Shift+F4
Next document	Up arrow	
Previous document	Down arrow	

Working with Documents

To Do This	Try This
Read selected document	Press Enter or double-click document
Delete selected document	Press Delete on your keyboard, drag the document to the Trash bin (in Mail), or choose Edit⇨Delete
Close document	Press Esc or choose File⇨Close
Edit document	Press Ctrl+E or choose Actions⇨Edit Document
Send a message	Choose Actions⇨Send Document or click Send or Send and Save button
Forward a document	Choose Actions⇨Forward, or click on Forward or Forward without Attachments button
Send a message when you're in another database	Choose Create⇨Mail⇨Memo or press Ctrl+M
Move from field to field in a document	Press Tab to go to the next field or Shift+Tab to move to the previous field
Update a view	Press F9 or choose View⇨Refresh

Selecting Text

To Select This	Do This
A word (in edit mode)	Double-click it
Next several words (Edit mode)	Ctrl+Shift+ right or down arrow key
Previous several words (Edit mode)	Ctrl+Shift+ left or up arrow key
All the text in current field	Choose Edit⇨Select All or press Ctrl+A
A large chunk of text	Position cursor at beginning of text and then Shift+click at end of text
From cursor to beginning of field	Press Shift+Ctrl+Home
From cursor to end of field	Press Shift+Ctrl+End

Lotus Notes® 6 For Dummies®

Cheat Sheet

Getting Help Quickly

To Do This	Use This
Get help on current task	F1
Find a help topic	Help⇨Help Topics
Get help on error messages	F1 when message appears

Using Bookmarks

Use This Bookmark	To Do This
	Open your Inbox
	Open your Calendar
	Open your Address Book
	Open your To Dos
	Open the Replicator
	Open Sametime*
	Open Favorite Bookmarks
	Open Database Bookmarks

You'll see the Sametime bookmark only if it has been activated by your administrator.

For Dummies: Bestselling Book Series for Beginners

Lotus Notes® 6

FOR

DUMMIES®

Lotus Notes® 6

FOR

DUMMIES®

by Stephen Londergan

Wiley Publishing, Inc.

Lotus Notes® 6 For Dummies®

Published by
Wiley Publishing, Inc.
909 Third Avenue
New York, NY 10022
www.wiley.com

Copyright © 2003 by Wiley Publishing, Inc., Indianapolis, Indiana

Published by Wiley Publishing, Inc., Indianapolis, Indiana

Published simultaneously in Canada

For general information on our other products and services or to obtain technical support, please contact our Customer Care Department within the U.S. at 800-762-2974, outside the U.S. at 317-572-3993, or fax 317-572-4002.

Wiley also publishes its books in a variety of electronic formats. Some content that appears in print may not be available in electronic books.

Library of Congress Control Number: 2002108100

ISBN: 0-7645-1649-3

Manufactured in the United States of America

10 9 8 7 6 5 4 3 2 1

1O/QR/RR/QS/IN

About the Author

Stephen Londergan has been on the Lotus Notes and Domino bandwagon since 1989, and this is his ninth book about it. He lives near Boston with his wife Robyn and three sons, Michael, Richard, and John.

Dedication

For Pat Freeland, who has been my colleague, collaborator, and teacher, and who is my friend. I wouldn't be in the writing business without you.

— Stephen Londergan

Author's Acknowledgments

Many thanks to Linda Morris, for making sure that I say what I'm supposed to say when I am supposed to say it; to Diana Ermini for making sure that what I say is accurate; and to Teresa Artman, for making sure that I say it all the way that I should.

Publisher's Acknowledgments

We're proud of this book; please send us your comments through our Dummies Online Registration Form located at www.dummies.com/register/.

Some of the people who helped bring this book to market include the following:

Acquisitions, Editorial, and Media Development

Project Editor: Linda Morris

Acquisitions Editor: Bob Woerner

Senior Copy Editor: Teresa Artman

Technical Editor: Diana Ermini

Editorial Managers: Leah Cameron, Kevin Kirschner

Media Development Manager: Laura VanWinkle

Media Development Supervisor: Richard Graves

Editorial Assistant: Amanda Foxworth

Cartoons: Rich Tennant, www.the5thwave.com

Production

Project Coordinator: Ryan Steffen

Layout and Graphics: Amanda Carter, Joyce Haughey, LeAndra Johnson, Jackie Nicholas, Brent Savage, Jacque Schneider, Betty Schulte, Julie Trippetti, Mary Virgin

Proofreaders: John Tyler Connoley, David Faust, Charles Spencer

Indexer: TECHBOOKS Production Services

Publishing and Editorial for Technology Dummies

Richard Swadley, Vice President and Executive Group Publisher

Andy Cummings, Vice President and Publisher

Mary C. Corder, Editorial Director

Publishing for Consumer Dummies

Diane Graves Steele, Vice President and Publisher

Joyce Pepple, Acquisitions Director

Composition Services

Gerry Fahey, Vice President of Production Services

Debbie Stailey, Director of Composition Services

Contents at a Glance

Table of Contents

Introduction

So exactly why did you buy this book, anyway? (And, hey, thanks for buying it, by the way.) Maybe you're here because your company just got Lotus Notes 6 (the latest and greatest version of Lotus Notes), and even though you've been using other, older versions of Notes for a while, you're suddenly faced with using this new release. Or perhaps you're grown accustomed to using a different program (such as Microsoft Outlook), but now you've decided (or been told) to use Notes, instead. Maybe you've never used e-mail before and you're starting your e-mail career with Notes. This book is for anyone who's using or planning to use Lotus Notes 6 and Lotus Domino 6.

Lotus Notes has been around since before 1989. It's no surprise, then, that it's so popular — and according to IBM (the company that makes Notes), over 85 million people use Lotus Notes.

In the first edition of this book, written way back in 1993, I had a lot of explaining to do — what e-mail was, why it was so much more efficient than (gasp!) paper memos, and why using a computer to communicate could make your life better, and so on. Now that we're in the 21st century, I'm making the leap of faith in this book that most people already get the whole e-mail concept, and that you have at least heard of things as varied as Web pages, e-mail return receipts, and modems.

Of course, you can use Lotus Notes for a lot more than just e-mail: It's a nifty tool to use for other good things. You can use Notes to help manage your calendar; you can use Notes to collaborate (big fancy word) with other people; and you can even use Lotus Notes with the Internet to get information from the World Wide Web.

So rather than leading you through what e-mail and the Web are, I want to focus on making your life easier. I'm guessing (hoping, actually) that you have better things to do than sit around and read computer books. Thus I try to make this book full of very practical, how-to information that shows you how to use Notes with a minimum fluff. Of course there are a few concepts that I have to explain, but I'll keep the hot air to a minimum, and that's a promise.

About This Book

I know that you're busy and that you hate to read computer manuals. So I designed this book to tell you just what you need to know to get rolling as quickly and as painlessly as possible.

Among other things, this book contains the following:

- ✔ How to send an electronic message to one person or to a group of people — forget the copy machine, interoffice envelopes, and the like
- ✔ How to read, reply to, and (occasionally) ignore all the e-mail that you receive
- ✔ How to organize, print, save, and forward messages
- ✔ How to send messages to your in-house colleagues and others through the Internet
- ✔ How to use Notes to collaborate, how to read and contribute to Notes databases, and how to store information in those databases so others can see it or interact with it
- ✔ How to hide sensitive and confidential information from potentially prying eyes
- ✔ How to create attractive and eye-catching documents
- ✔ How to communicate with the office even when you're away (at home, or perhaps in a hotel room)
- ✔ How to cruise the Internet without leaving your chair (or Notes, for that matter)

You have a choice — either read this book from cover to cover (not necessarily in one sitting!) or choose the particular topics that interest you and read just those parts in the order that makes the most sense for you. Both approaches give you the information that you need. In general, the concepts are straightforward, so you won't have any trouble jumping from chapter to chapter or even from section to section. And don't forget to check the index, which is sometimes the most direct way of finding an answer first.

I strive to avoid techno-babble and geek-speak as much as I can. If a particular term is unfamiliar to you, just take a gander at the glossary at the end of the book.

Foolish Assumptions

Without so much as a phone call, I make the following assumptions about you, dear reader:

- You want to know *what,* but not necessarily *why.* I leave the why to the computer nerds and concentrate on what's important to get you working with Lotus Notes ASAP.

- You have access to a computer on which someone has already installed Lotus Notes 6.

- You're willing to send a check for $221 (US) to your beloved *Lotus Notes 6 For Dummies* author. (Just kidding, although tips, checks, bank drafts, wire transfers, or even cash, are always appreciated.)

Conventions Used in This Book

If I want you to type something, I put it in bold, like this: **Type this** and then press Enter. (In this case, you type *Type this* but not *and then press Enter.* But you probably already figured that out.)

Sometimes I refer to text that you see onscreen. When I refer to a message just as it appears on the monitor, it looks like this: `Some words on your screen`. If the text is longer than a few words, it looks like this:

```
This is a computer message exactly as it appears onscreen.
```

I frequently tell you to make menu selections or use buttons. When I tell you to click a button, look for a picture of that button in the left margin. I also present menu commands, like this: Choose File➪Database➪New. You simply click the first menu and then, from the drop-down list that appears, click the second one, and so on. If you use a computer with Microsoft Windows, you can press Alt (on your keyboard) and also press simultaneously the underlined letter within that command word. For example, if File has an underlined F, press Alt+F for a nifty keyboard shortcut to open the File menu.

If a dialog box appears when you use a command, I reproduce it right in the book (in brilliant black and white) and tell you how to use it.

How This Book Is Organized

The arrangement of the chapters in this book reflects the order in which most people become familiar with the various aspects of Notes.

Part I: Get Rolling with Notes

In the first part of the book, I get the inevitable definitions out of the way and then jump right into getting Notes set up on your computer. Reading Part I is like finding out what all those dials on the dashboard do before you try driving a car.

Part II: It's a Mail Thing

The second part of this book deals with the things that you'll most likely use Notes for the most: sending, receiving, and working with e-mail messages. This part also is also where you can discover how to use Notes to manage your Calendar and To-Dos.

Part III: When It's Not a Mail Thing

Read through the chapters in the third part of this book for the skinny on how to get at your company's Notes applications, how to read and create documents in them, and even a little bit about how to create your own databases. You also find some other cool things to expand your already dazzling command of the program.

Part IV: Making Notes Suit You!

Eventually, everyone wants to type special characters (such as the copyright symbol ©), modify the style of paragraphs, customize and personalize the way Notes works, use Notes with other programs, search for information, or manage bookmarks. When that time comes for you, peruse Part IV.

Part V: Worldwide Notes

When you're ready to move into high gear and take your Notes knowledge with you into the 21st century, turn (without delay) to Part V. In this part, I show you how to take Notes with you on your business trips, how to hop from Notes straight onto the Internet, and how to get Notes talking to the other programs and places where you store information.

Part VI: The Part of Tens

Every *For Dummies* book has The Part of Tens — so why should this book be any different? In this part, I present an assortment of useful factoids. This treasure trove of tips includes ten things new to Lotus Notes 6, ten things you should never, ever do, and other useful tidbits. The Part of Tens in this book is nowhere near as exciting as The Part of Tens in Dr. Ruth's *Sex For Dummies,* but it'll hold your interest.

Part VII: Appendix

I finish up the book with a glossary of the terms and concepts that I explain throughout the book.

What You're Not to Read

I consider every last word in this book to be informative, insightful, and often quite humorous. Each word was chosen with considerable care and deliberation, and I can't think of a reason why you wouldn't want to read every one of the scintillating sentences contained herein. Because you indeed do have a life, however, and better things to do, I mark the especially trivial details with a special Technical Stuff icon so that you know what you can (and can't) skip.

Icons in This Book

I scatter scads of little pictures (icons) amongst the pages of this book. Read on to see what each kind of icon is about.

This icon alerts you to information that's especially interesting to, uh, *nerds*. You know, the kind of people who always kept your high-school math classes late because they were asking so many questions? In some high schools, this person was all too often the victim of something known as a *wedgie*, but that's a separate book. I'm not saying a bunch of football players will give you a wedgie if you read these sections, but then again. . . .

This icon tells you that some little shard of knowledge is coming your way to make your life with Notes just a bit easier. Tips are definitely worth reading.

As you stumble along the pathway of life, these little commandments are things that you should never forget. For example, you should always . . . well, it had something to do with, ummm. . . . I'll come back to this later.

Ignore these at your own peril. You've been warned.

This icon points out those features new to Lotus Notes 6, or tasks that you perform quite a bit differently in 6 compared to previous versions.

Where to Go from Here

Okay, get going; you have a lot of reading to do. Don't be afraid to experiment and remember to check out the Lotus Notes Help feature early and often.

Part I
Get Rolling with Notes

"He saw your laptop and wants to know if he can check his Hotmail."

In this part . . .

*W*hen you tackle a new computer program, the best thing to do first is to read the basic information about how the program works. (Of course, most people install the program, make lots of mistakes, get mad, and finally, after lots of sputtering and fuming and complaining, turn to the instructions.)

Lotus Notes 6 is a powerful and complex program. The chapters in this part prepare you to use Notes to its full potential without wasting a lot of time, developing bad habits, or cursing the program because you can't figure out how to do something.

So, here in the first part of the book, I present the information that you need to know before getting started. I've attempted to avoid technobabble whenever possible, but sometimes knowing the official terms actually helps. If you call your help desk and say, "The thingie next to the hinkyminky returns a box that says something when I clunk it," you can bet two things: you haven't been helpful — and therefore the help desk can't help you; and whoever answered the phone at the help desk is probably laughing at you.

Chapter 1

Just What Is Notes, Anyway?

*L*otus Notes 6 is a program that helps you communicate and work with other people. You can use Notes to send people e-mail and also to share other kinds of information, such as documents, spreadsheets, Web pages, and other good stuff like that.

If you're a loner who doesn't like to interact with others, or if you think that information is power and you'd rather not share, well, then, you probably won't like Lotus Notes. If, on the other hand, your work often requires you to collaborate with other people, and if you want (or need) to share information with co-workers, customers, and the like, you'll be a Notes jock in no time at all.

The really good thing and ultra-cool thing about Lotus Notes is that it's easy to use. You can make Notes sing with little or no knowledge of the messy underside of computers. If you find expressions such as *TCP/IP, remote access,* and *HTML* scary (or perhaps even downright boring), Notes is the program for you! Even if you still think *Java* always has something to do with coffee, you'll be able to use Notes.

With Notes, you concentrate on the important things — such as sending flattering e-mail to your boss, responding to your customers, and sounding lofty and knowledgeable at meetings.

And what's better, you don't even have to be at the office to participate in this aforementioned technological fiesta. If you have a modem or can connect to the Internet, you can do all your work from home, the hotel, or even from an airplane — although you better get the boss's permission first!

Care to Collaborate?

Collaboration is the word that IBM (creator of Notes) uses to describe what Lotus Notes helps you do. What that really means, in the simplest terms, is that you use Notes to work together with other people. Lotus Notes is different than a spreadsheet program like Microsoft Excel or a word processor like Microsoft Word. In programs like Excel and Word, the work that you do is yours and yours alone. You usually store the files that you create with these programs on your own computer, where no one else can see them. Sometimes that's good if the information is private or personal. But other times, you want to share.

When you use Lotus Notes, on the other hand, you share information by putting the information that you create in a place that everybody can get to. (Around since 1989, Notes is the oldest collaborative program of them all.) Notes certainly won't help your golf game, nor will it help you win friends and influence people (call Dale Carnegie for that), either. That said, Notes *will* help you do the following:

- Send e-mail messages.

- Create databases and fill them with information that you, everyone, or only people who you choose can see and edit.

- Be sure that the same information on a particular subject is available to everyone who needs it — regardless of where they are and without having to worry about what kind of computer or network they use.

- Allow people to communicate as quickly as possible, whether the communication is gossip, news, or vital corporate data. (And who can always tell the difference?)

- Be sure that the forms and documents that your organization uses are standard so that you and your colleagues all seem organized, even if you're not.

- Provide a central place to look for everybody's daily calendar of appointments.

- Keep information in a safe and readily available place, rather than in piles on everyone's desk.

✔ Prevent prying, nosy, unauthorized busybodies from rummaging around in places where they have no business.

✔ Save trees.

✔ Combine information, images, text, and tables from different places, such as spreadsheet programs, word processors, and even the World Wide Web and other parts of the Internet.

✔ Store information and e-mail for users who are only occasionally connected.

I mail, you mail, we all mail e-mail

Unless you've been living under a rock, you've heard of e-mail, and you probably know that the *e* stands for *electronic*. So, take away the *e* and you have *mail,* and that's about all there is to it.

Most people prefer e-mail to snail-mail (regular postal delivery) because e-mail is so fast. Plus, you don't need to hunt for stamps or walk down to the mailbox. (Of course, there is the *little* matter of someone buying a computer for everyone, connecting them all together, and then buying Lotus Notes. But that's somebody else's headache.)

In Lotus Notes 6, the messages that you send go to everyone who you address it to — and to *only* those people. If you write a nasty note about the boss and send it to a friend two floors down, you don't have to worry that the boss will see it — unless your friend decides to forward it to the boss or print it and hang it on the bulletin board. And as the old saying goes — with friends like that, who needs enemies?

With Notes, unlike other e-mail systems that I could mention, you can add text enhancements (such as boldface, italics, and underlining), change colors and fonts, and add tables and sections, hyperlinks (whatever that means), and even pictures. Instead of sending messages that make people yawn, your messages can make people sit up and take notice — just like the one in Figure 1-1.

And, barring the rare (and expensive) system meltdown, you're always confident that your Notes e-mail message will be delivered. Contrast this assurance with a memo slipped into a company mailer and left to languish in the quagmire of interoffice mail. In Figure 1-1, look at a message that's addressed to a group of people in the Sales Planning Department; also, a carbon copy is being sent to Mike Dempsey and Jeremy Dies. All these people will receive this message in time to act on the schedule changes that the memo discusses . . . ahem, assuming that the message was sent before the changes take place.

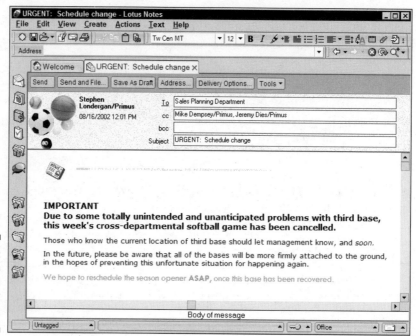

Figure 1-1:
Spice up
your e-mail
with colors
and fonts.

In this new millennium, more and more people around the world take e-mail for granted. By using Notes, you can send an e-mail message to your buddy working down the hall, a customer who works at another company, your cousin who's studying art in Paris, or even your kid who's at home using America Online. In other words, you can use Lotus Notes to send e-mail messages to just about anybody, anyplace, at anytime, whether they work with you or not. Any questions?

Databasically

The most important concept in Notes is the database. In fact, the entire program is organized around databases. A *database* is just a bunch of information that's been collected together. A printed catalog of holiday candles that you get in the mail is really a database — it's organized in a particular order, with the name, description, picture, and price of each item kept nice and neat. But when you want to place an order, the only way to find a particular item in that candle catalog is to turn the pages and let your fingers do the walking. That's when computer databases are much more useful.

When you use Lotus Notes, you create *documents,* such as e-mail messages, company policy statements, sales records, or listings of baseball statistics. These documents that you create are all collected and stored in databases along with other documents. You can find information in databases without ever turning pages or scanning long lists. Ask one of these databases to show you all sales contacts in Alabama, for example, and as quick as you can say, "Hey, how y'all doin'?" the list of Alabama's good ol' boys (and girls) appears onscreen.

Probably the most popular and common kind of a Notes database is a *discussion database,* which is the IBM electronic version of the backyard fence. It goes like this: You express your opinion on a particular subject by composing a main document in a discussion database. Because the database is shared and accessible by your co-workers, a colleague from the Singapore office might compose a reply to you, telling you that you're all wet. Someone else in Texas can compose a response to that response, telling the Singapore person to lay off. And so on. Others might sound off their opinions by writing entries to the discussion database. People anywhere and everywhere in your organization can respond to these opinions or just use them as a reference.

You can write your opinion by using Lotus Notes working in Windows, for example, even if one person's response is created on a Macintosh and others use Unix. Everyone can read all the documents, regardless of what kind of computer that the documents were composed on. You all share — not just your highly sought-after opinions, but also drawings, enhanced text, Microsoft Excel spreadsheets, and Web pages. You might even find that some people who are responding don't use Notes at all but are instead using a Web browser to access the Notes database.

Finally, in Lotus Notes, databases also contain *views* and *folders.* Views and folders contain *documents.* Documents contain *fields.* And fields contain individual pieces of *data.* (You see, the whole concept is based on data, and that's why they're called *data*bases.) Do NOT let all this jargon bog you down! In other chapters, I get into what these terms mean for you and how you can put them to good use.

You Can't Be All Things to All People

Notes has amazing e-mail, database, and Internet capabilities. But, for all its power and glory, Notes does have some limitations.

What Notes isn't

As I mention in the earlier section "Databasically," Notes uses databases. But it isn't a true *relational database*, if that term means anything to you. (Skip ahead if it doesn't.) *Relational databases* enable you to enter data in a field in one database and then use that same field in another database. Notes can't do that. Unless you're a database design jockey, you probably don't give two toots about whether a database is relational. But the fact that Notes isn't relational translates into some good news and some bad news for you.

The good news is that Notes isn't rigid. When you create a new Notes database, Notes doesn't make you set the size of a field and then limit entries in that field to your specified maximum size. *Fields* are the little bits of information, such as a person's last name, that make up a document.

For example, in other programs, you'd have to decide how many characters that a Last Name field could accept. Suppose that you allow 15 characters and then you hire John Jacob Jingleheimerschmidt. You'd either have to be satisfied with *J J Jingleheime* or go through the nail-breaking procedure of redesigning the database. With Notes, you just type away, secure in the knowledge that Notes will take anything and everything that you type.

Because it isn't rigid, Notes allows you to create rich text fields. A *rich text field* is a field in which you can add such fancy stuff as character formats (boldface and italics, for example), embedded word processing documents, bits of Web pages, or maybe even video clips and pictures of your (no doubt lovely) children.

So, what's the bad news? If you use your computer to track customer orders and you have 19,200,675 orders to track, using Notes is kind of like utilizing a screwdriver to bang a nail — it's not the best tool for that job. Applications that require the care and management of millions and millions of records usually *don't* belong in Notes.

Not only is Notes not a relational database, it's also not the program to use for *transaction-based systems,* such as airline ticketing. Imagine lots of travel agents in lots of different cities selling lots of tickets for a particular flight and recording the sales on their own copy of a reservations database on their own computers or terminals. Later, at departure time, a huge crowd of people appears, all with tickets for the same seat on the same plane. When companies need *immediate* sharing of information everywhere, they typically use a rig of terminals connected to a single gigantic computer somewhere, and they use a different kind of software, such as the IBM WebSphere Application Server. Lotus Notes allows periodic, but not immediate, sharing of updates to databases.

But don't worry — whether you use Notes probably isn't your decision, anyway. Let the geeks down in the IT department decide when to use Lotus Notes and when not to. Just make sure that you tell them to buy lots of copies of this book — whatever they decide!

What Notes is

Notes *is* an especially innovative and powerful program because of its capability to send e-mail and maintain databases of all sorts that every person in the organization can share, add to, and read. Sure, you can use other programs for e-mail, and some even let you share information. What sets Notes apart from the crowd is its capability to do both.

Rich text fields and other Notes fields have an advantage over those in regular databases: They don't have a field size limit. In other database programs, changing the size of a field in a large database can be a heck of a lot of work — and, if not executed correctly, can corrupt your database. Notes, on the other hand, doesn't care whether you put one word or a whole book in a field. And what you put in a field may not even be words at all — maybe it's a photograph from your digital camera.

Fields in other databases are, in a word, *blah*. No boldface, no variety in fonts, and no possibility for attachments or embedded objects. Not so with Lotus Notes rich text fields because they contain more than just information. Rich text fields can contain anything that your heart desires, setting them apart from the mundane; they educate and excite readers, allowing you to show yourself to be the creative genius that you are.

With Notes, you can use databases for

- **Reference:** Members of your organization seeking knowledge can find what they need to know, contributed by those who have knowledge to share — from each according to his or her ability, to each according to his or her need. (Kind of brings a tear to your eye, huh?)

- **Workflow:** Those charged with a broad task can record the individual assignments and proclaim the completion of each, documenting both progress and completion. "Well done, old chap!"

- **Calendars:** You and your colleagues can easily schedule appointments and meetings with one another.

- **Communication:** All the people in the organization can communicate privately or publicly with anyone they choose, whether via e-mail, fax, pager, cell phone . . . you name it.

- ✔ **World Wide Web:** People can browse a database containing Web pages and other types of information from the Internet even if they're not connected or don't have Web browser software.

- ✔ **Fax:** You and your co-workers can distribute valuable data stored in your organization's databases to a needy and grateful public.

This, then, is Notes. More than just software, more than just a database, e-mail program, or Web browser, Notes is a dynamic tool for sharing knowledge throughout an organization. And remember, knowledge *is* power.

What Makes Notes So Special?

A few additional features that distinguish Notes from mere e-mail programs or database programs are its capabilities to make compound documents and to replicate databases.

Compound documents feel the power

You've heard of compound fractures, right? Well, compound documents are nothing like them. That doesn't clear things up? Well, how about this: Normally, when you're busy using Notes, you're typing a memo or filling in a form or writing some text to be included with other similar entries in a database. Sometimes, however, you need to put more than just text in your document.

To emphasize a point that you're making about sales figures, you may want to include a spreadsheet that you created, a set of slides that you made in Microsoft PowerPoint, and even a related Web page that you found on the Internet. Just copy and paste all these items into your document.

The result is a *compound document* containing data, graphics, or other stuff from other places.

Replication explanation

Replication, a special process for making sure that two copies of a particular database have exactly the same contents, is what makes Notes the great program that it is. Oh sure, other programs allow you to send e-mail, but they don't replicate. Remember that your mail database is only *one* kind of database that you use in Notes. Chances are that other people in your organization have created other databases. *Replicas* (copies of those databases) might be on many of your organization's servers around the world. This magic is how your colleague in France can see what you've been working on.

He looks at a *copy* of the database in question that's available and close to him on his server in Paris while you look at a copy of the very same database on your server in, say, Chicago.

One example of this technological feat is a database listing each employee's name, employee number, location, shoe size, and other important data. At each location, these replicas are updated as people are hired or fired or change their shoe sizes. Obviously, employees at each location enter different information into the database. Replication enables Notes to include all the information on all the databases.

When the replication is complete, all replicas have the same information, so up-to-date information is available everywhere. Every so often, the server in France talks to your server in Chicago so that the two servers can synchronize their copies of the information. That way, the Chicago server ends up with all those documents that your French colleague has been composing; at the same time, the server *en France* gets the documents that you've been adding. Pretty cool, *n'est-ce pas?*

Replication is also the process by which disconnected workstations update their own, personal copies of databases. So when you take your laptop on a trip to Denver, you can replicate with the server back at the home office, too. That way you can keep working, even when your computer isn't connected to the network. You decide how often this technological feat occurs. In a database that has a rapid turnover of information, such as your e-mail or a database of news articles from the Internet, replicating several times a day might make sense. A database that doesn't change often, such as one listing corporate policies, might replicate only once or twice each week, or perhaps once a month. It's up to you.

Who's the Boss?

Notes uses computers all hooked together in a network. In some ways, a *network* is like a department in a corporation because it has individual workers and someone in charge. The individual computers need to be connected to a sort-of *boss* computer to be able to work together. No doubt your boss serves the same vital role in your department.

Servers with a smile

The computer in charge of a Notes network is the server. The *server* acts as a central, shared computer for the others, storing the mail databases for all the people whose computers are hooked to it and regulating the flow of information. (It usually stores other databases, too, besides just e-mail.) In fact, most companies end up storing so much of their information in Notes that they end up having lots and lots of servers. (Your faithful author's employer, for example, has hundreds of servers and thousands of databases.)

Right around 1997, Lotus started calling its servers by a new name: *Domino* (as in "We just got a new Domino server" or "Domino servers are really cool").

The server is usually a very powerful computer with a lot more memory and storage capacity than the ones (like yours) that are connected to it, and it's usually housed in a physically secure and remote location. Is this beginning to sound like your boss — powerful, having the best equipment, remote, and in charge? The server might also be like your boss in that it's not where the regular work in Notes is performed. The actual work is performed on the individual computers connected to the server.

In large organizations, many Lotus Domino servers (all around the world), each with their own bunch of attached computers, are connected together over the company-wide network.

Down by the workstation

In the wonderful world of Notes, your computer is known as a *workstation*. (Fair warning: Sometimes you might hear someone call it a *client*.) Workstations, where real people perform real work, usually contain the Notes program files for each individual user and also any databases that the users create for their own personal use.

Not all workstations are always connected to a server. For example, if you go on a business trip and take your laptop with you, you would need a pretty long network cable to connect directly to the office unless your business trip takes you to only the parking lot. When you use your computer to connect to the server by phone line and modem, your computer is a *remote workstation*. Some workstations are both local area network (LAN) and remote. If you have a laptop, you can hook it to the LAN when you're at the office and then use its phone modem for a remote hookup when you're on the road.

No matter how fast your modem is, using Notes on it will be slower than using Notes at the office where you're connected to the server through the network. So plan on taking extra time when using a modem and be sure that your teenager won't need the phone for a while.

User ID — Your Key to Notes

When you were born, the hospital gave your mother a copy of your birth certificate. When you graduated from high school, you got a diploma. And when you learned to drive, you got a driver's license. Similarly, when you start using Notes, someone gives you a *user ID*.

Don't expect to get a copy of Lotus Notes, install it on your computer, and then be able to tap into the nerve center of your company. Even if you're the company president and have a fistful of Notes disks, even if you *do* lunch rather than eat it, and even if you have the fanciest car in the parking lot, until you get that user ID, you don't have a prayer of being able to use Notes.

Your user ID is the key that gives you access to your own mail database and other databases in the company. To you, a user ID might look like only a series of numbers and letters. To the servers, however, it's what makes you a legitimate user of Notes in your organization, and it's what establishes your authority as an employee/member in good standing.

Your user ID makes you a member of *your* organization. For example, you can't sneak into your competitor's offices down the street and use your user ID in its Notes network because your user ID is created by and recognized only by your own organization.

Keep a copy of your Notes user ID on a floppy disk so that you can copy it back to your hard drive if you accidentally delete your Notes program files or if you experience the heartbreak of computer failure, theft, or mishandling by that luggage handler back in Denver. Remember, if your computer breaks down, your user ID can be used to access another person's computer as if it were your own. For this reason, you should keep your Notes user ID in a secure place (literally under lock and key). If you're lucky, the folks down in IS might have a back-up copy, but check with them before relying on them!

When push comes to shove, your user ID is just another (small) file on your computer. You need your user ID each and every time that you use Notes. Most folks keep their user ID file on their hard drive. If you want to use your computer at home to do some work, you'll have to make a copy of your user ID file and bring that copy home with you. You can't use Notes without that user ID. Never, ever — no fooling.

Chapter 2

Getting Acquainted with Notes

In This Chapter

▶ Starting and stopping Lotus Notes

▶ Facing the Notes interface

▶ Getting smart about toolbars and bookmarks

So, your company just got Lotus Notes 6, and you're all excited about using this powerful, state-of-the-art program that you've heard so much about. Or maybe you aren't so thrilled because your boss announced that you had to start using Notes, and you're not exactly overjoyed at the prospect of cozying up to yet another software program. In either case, the good news is that figuring out how to set up, start, and stop Notes isn't all that difficult.

I assume in this chapter that your Lotus Notes software has already been installed on your system; contact your administrator (in a hurry) if that's not the case.

Starting Notes

First things first: To start Lotus Notes, just double-click the Notes program icon. And just where is this mysterious Notes icon? Well, that depends on where the person who installed the program put it. The icon that you're trying to find looks like the image that appears after this paragraph. I can't say exactly where it appears on your computer because its location depends on whether you're using Windows, Macintosh, or whatever. If you're using Windows XP, for example, you can find the Lotus Notes program icon in the folder named *Lotus Applications*, which in turn is found in the All Programs menu, all of which is available through the Start menu (phew!).

Understanding the Welcome Page

After you get Notes running, you should see a screen that looks something like Figure 2-1. This is your *Welcome Page.* Although it might take a minute to get here from when you start Notes the very first time, this screen is what you'll see from now on whenever you start Notes. You need to know about the following main elements of the Welcome Page. You can see all these components in Figure 2-1.

If you get lost, you can always get back to the Welcome Page by pressing Esc until everything else disappears.

- ✔ **Menus:** In just like every other program you've ever used, use these to control the way that the program works and to make things happen.

- ✔ **Toolbars:** These contain buttons that you click to easily do things.

- ✔ **Bookmarks:** These are an easy way to open a particular thing, such as your Inbox or a favorite Web page.

- ✔ **Task buttons:** These are context-sensitive buttons that make it easy to do things.

- ✔ **Welcome Page:** This is what you see when you first start Notes — sort of a homepage for the program.

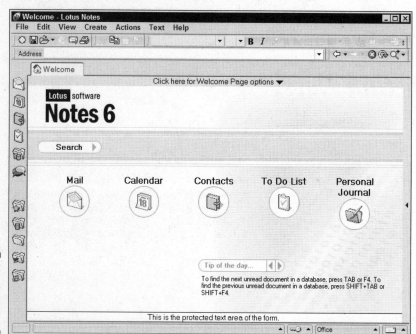

Figure 2-1:
Welcome
to Lotus
Notes!

Using the Welcome Page

As you can see in Figure 2-1, the Welcome Page has a bunch of buttons and things that you can click. Most of these are shortcuts to bookmarks and menus. They're always available, and you'll probably find them helpful.

The Welcome Page shown in Figure 2-1 is the default page that you get when you install Notes. As you can see, it provides access to the five basics in Notes:

- **Mail:** Where you read and send e-mail messages
- **Calendar:** Where you can create and manage your meetings and appointments
- **Contacts:** Where you can store the e-mail addresses, names, phone numbers, and addresses of friends and colleagues
- **To Do List:** Where you keep track (and don't forget) all that stuff that you promised that you'd do
- **Personal Journal:** Where you can keep a Notes-based diary of sorts

You can customize the Welcome Page so that it shows you exactly what you want. You can even replace it altogether and see your Inbox, instead. Take a look at Chapter 16 to discover how to do that.

The Notes 6 Welcome Page also includes a new Tip of the Day feature, which gives you little hints and various insights into how to use the program.

What's on the Menu?

The Lotus Notes menus work exactly how you'd expect them to. Many of the options available here are the same as the options in other programs. For example, you save a document in Notes the same way that you save a spreadsheet in Lotus 1-2-3, which is the same way that you save a document in Microsoft Word or a presentation in Microsoft Visio by choosing File⇨Save.

If you're a mouse user, just click any menu item to open it; you should get a drop-down list of menu choices. If you don't like to use the mouse (some people downright refuse to), you can press Alt and then use the right- and left-arrow keys to select the menu that you want. Then press Enter when the item is selected. You can use the same strategy to choose an item in a menu; use the arrow keys to select the item that you want and then press Enter.

Note that some menu choices are gray while others are black. You can choose only the black items; menu options that appear gray aren't appropriate for whatever you're doing. For example, if you're in the middle of editing a document and you take a look at the Edit menu, you find that the Select by Date option appears dimmed, indicating that you can't select by date (whatever that means!) while you're editing a document.

Wise Up with Toolbar Buttons

A new feature in Lotus Notes 6 is the toolbar buttons, such as the Stop and Next buttons, which you'll find at the top of the Welcome screen (refer to Figure 2-1).

In case you're a veteran Notes user, you should know that these new toolbars buttons replace SmartIcons.

Toolbars come and go, depending on what you're doing — in other words, the toolbar that you see when you're editing a document will be different than what you see when you're reading your e-mail. Those in the know call this flexibility *contextual*, meaning that menus, buttons, and toolbars change depending on what you need at the time.

Almost all toolbars have buttons, which you click to perform some kind of action, such as making a word **bold**, or printing a document, or what have you. Truth be told, these buttons are really, really easy to use, and spending too much time reading about them or thinking about them will make them out to be more complicated than they really are.

To use a toolbar button, just click it. You can do everything with toolbar buttons that you can do via the Notes menus. Using toolbar buttons, however, might save you from having to learn the ins and outs of all the menus. Clicking a button compared with accessing menus can save time, too. Consider this: The top 87.3 percent of the things that you need to do is covered by some toolbar button.

So the only challenge, really, is figuring out which button does what. Some, such as Print, are pretty obvious, but others are less so. (On the Welcome Page, any guess what those big white arrow buttons do, for example? Or how about the one that looks like a pad of paper with a pencil?)

Fortunately all toolbar buttons come packed with a hint, which you can see if you put the mouse pointer on the button in question and let it sit there for a second. Check out the upper-left corner of the Welcome Page in Figure 2-2 — look for the little box that reads *New*. That's the hint for its icon. The bottom line? You don't have to remember which does button does what because you can always get that little hint.

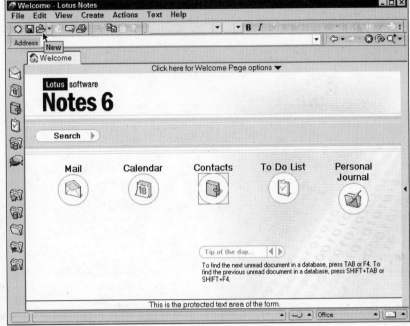

Figure 2-2:
Point to a toolbar button to find out what it does.

Notes has more toolbars up its sleeve than it appears — in fact, probably more than you'll ever use. The buttons that you use when you read a message, for example, are probably not the best ones to have around when you compose a message. So don't be surprised if you notice the toolbars changing. The buttons that you see in one context — such as reading your e-mail — are different from the one that you see in another context, such as setting up your modem.

Betting on Bookmarks

Bookmarks are your way to remember a particular Web page, document, view, or database. Notes is preloaded with a bunch of bookmarks for you, such as your Inbox and Calendar. They appear on the far-left side of your Notes screen, and they're always visible. As you use Notes more and more and as you develop your own favorite places to go, you can add your own personal bookmarks, too. Figure 2-3 shows some of the bookmarks that you get by default. Use bookmarks to quickly and easily go to some place that you've been before.

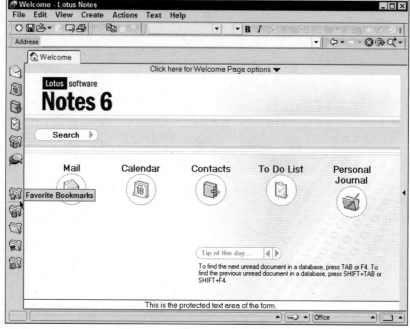

Figure 2-3:
Use
bookmarks
to get from
place to
place,
quickly and
easily.

Opening a bookmark

When you want to visit a bookmark, just click it. For example, if you, Jane Q. Public, want to read your mail, click the first icon (Mail) in the Bookmark bar. Presto, there's your mail.

What happens when you click a bookmark depends on what kind of bookmark it is. Clicking some will open a particular Notes database, such as the one for your mail. Clicking others will open a particular document within a Notes database. Some will open a Web page; and still others will open a list or folder of even more bookmarks. To discover how to organize your bookmarks, read the upcoming section "Creating bookmark folders."

If you're not sure where a bookmark is going to take you, treat it like it were a toolbar button — hover your mouse pointer on the bookmark without clicking it. Refer to Figure 2-3: Look at the mouse pointer and the hint that pops up to see that the bookmark is for your Favorite Bookmarks. Notes always shows you a hint about what the bookmark is going to do or where it's going to take you.

When you click a folder in the Bookmark bar, a menu of its folders slides out, as you can see in Figure 2-4. You can use this to more easily move amongst the items on your Bookmark bar; this list slides away after you find (and click) the bookmark that you want to visit.

Many people prefer to have the Bookmark bar slide-out tray available all the time. To activate this, just open any Bookmark folder and then choose Pin from the View menu. Now the tray stays open all the time. Figure 2-5 shows what it looks like when you choose to leave the Bookmark tray open. To make the Bookmark tray slide back in, just choose Pin from the View menu again.

Creating bookmarks

Suppose that you open a Web page or a Notes database that's really cool, and you want Notes to remember it for you so that you can easily get to it again. In Figure 2-6, you can see how to start this process. (**Hint:** Notice where the mouse pointer is in figure.) In Figure 2-6, I'm creating a bookmark for the Q3 Surveys - Customer List database.

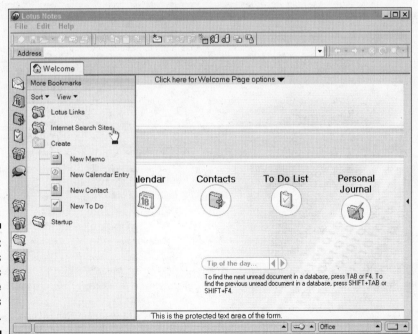

Figure 2-4: Sometimes bookmarks have more than meets the eye.

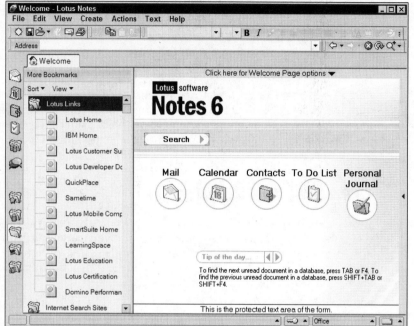

Figure 2-5:
Pin the
bookmarks
to your
screen so
that they're
always
open, if you
prefer.

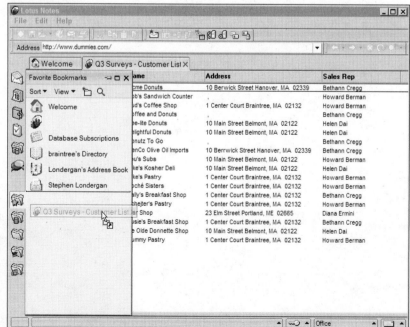

Figure 2-6:
Add
bookmarks
to your
Bookmark
bar.

1. Open the thing — Web page, database, folder, whatever — that you want to bookmark.

2. Point to the task button for the window you just opened.

   The task button in Figure 2-6 is the tab that reads Q3 Surveys - Customer List.

3. Click and drag the task button over into the Bookmark bar.

   You can also right-click an object (such as a document) and then select Bookmark from the pop-up menu that appears to create a new bookmark.

Removing a bookmark

Use the following steps to remove a bookmark that you no longer need:

1. Point to the bookmark that you want to delete.

2. Click the right mouse button.

3. Choose Remove Bookmark from the pop-up menu that appears.

4. Click the Yes button in the dialog box that asks you whether you're sure that you want to delete the bookmark.

Creating bookmark folders

To organize your new bookmarks, simply create a new bookmark folder. Use the following steps to do so:

1. Point to a folder on the Bookmark bar.

2. Click the right mouse button.

3. Choose New Folder from the pop-up menu that appears.

4. In the Create Folder dialog box that appears, type the name of the new folder in the Folder Name text box.

5. Find a home for the new folder in the Select a Location for the New Folder tree list.

6. Click OK.

7. Your new bookmark appears where you had Notes place it.

Moving bookmarks

Suppose that you're unhappy with a bookmark's location. You can easily move it to another place on the Bookmark bar or into one of the your bookmark folders. Use the following steps to move a bookmark:

1. **Point to the bookmark that you want to move.**

2. **Press and hold down the left mouse button to drag and drop the bookmark to its new location in the Bookmark bar.**

Deleting bookmark folders

When you no longer need a bookmark folder that you've created, use the following steps to remove an entire bookmark folder:

1. **In the Bookmark bar, point to the bookmark folder that you want to delete.**

2. **Click the right mouse button.**

3. **Choose Remove Folder from the pop-up menu that appears.**

4. **Click the Yes button in the dialog box that asks you whether you're sure that you want to remove the folder.**

Think long and hard before you delete a bookmark folder because doing so also removes all the bookmarks inside the folder, too.

Trying Out the Task Buttons

Have you noticed that when you open different databases, documents, and Web pages, you get a task button for each? Figure 2-7 shows what my screen looks like after I open several different things.

Use these buttons — officially called *task buttons* — to switch from one window to another or to close a window altogether.

Switching windows

Switching from one open window to another is easy because all you have to do is click the task button that you want.

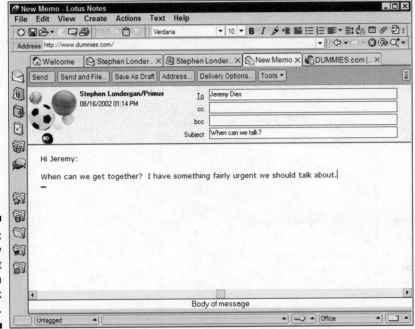

Figure 2-7:
Every
window that
you open
gets a task
button.

Closing a window

Closing a window is just as easy. Just click the little X in the right corner of the task button for the window you want to close, and it's history. You can also close an open window by pressing Esc or by choosing File⇨Close.

You don't have to switch to a window before you close it.

Going to Places Where You've Never Been

Bookmarks certainly provide an easy way to open documents, databases, and Web pages. But the day will come when you want to navigate to someplace where you haven't been before. Maybe your company has a new Notes application that you need to check out, or perhaps you want to open a new Web page. It's easy to do, but how you do it depends on where you're trying to go.

Opening a new database

To open a new database, choose File⇨Database⇨Open (or press Ctrl+O), and then use the Open Database dialog box to tell Notes which server and database you're after. See Figure 2-8.

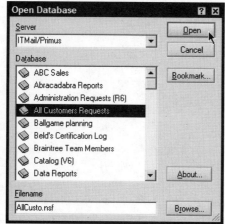

Figure 2-8:
Finding and
opening a
Notes
database
is easy.

After you find the database that you want to open, select its name in the Database list and then click Open.

Click the Bookmark button in the Open Database dialog box to add the selected database to your bookmarks for future reference. Doing so adds the database to your bookmarks *without* opening the database at the same time.

In Chapter 12, I discuss the finer points of opening a new database and dealing with the ins and outs of the Open Database dialog box.

Opening a new Web page

To open a new Web page, type the Web page's address in the URL field in the Action bar. Press Enter, and Notes opens the Web page that you request.

Notes R5 users will be happy to see that you don't have to click that little globe any more to open a Web page.

Although Notes automatically bookmarks any database that you open in the Bookmark bar Databases folder, you have to add a bookmark manually for any Web page that you want to remember. You can, however, click the History bookmark to revisit Web pages that you've been to before.

When the Time Comes to Say Good-Bye

When you're finished using Lotus Notes (time to go home already?), exit Notes just like you exit any other program. The easiest way to tell Notes that you're finished is to choose File➪Exit Notes. Depending on your operating system, you may have other, snazzier ways to end the program. For example, with Windows, you can press Alt+F4 to exit Notes. (To get really fancy, just click the X in the upper-right corner of the Notes window.)

Part II
It's a Mail Thing

By Rich Tennant

"...so if you have a message for someone, you write it on a piece of paper and put it on their refrigerator with these magnets. It's just until we get our e-mail system fixed."

In this part . . .

When you know what Notes is and what it isn't and you're confident when using random bits of Notes terminology in a conversation (to the amazement of your friends and co-workers), you're ready to actually send a message. Maybe you can already read a message that someone sends you. Then again, maybe you have like 50 important messages crowding your Inbox, the boss is drumming her fingers, and here you are reading this little introduction.

Within the chapters of this part, I explain the e-mail functions of Lotus Notes 6. When you finish here, you should wonder why the heck any office ever bothers with photocopies and phone calls these days.

Chapter 3

Gotta Get My E-Mail

In This Chapter

▶ Opening your mail

▶ Rearranging your e-mail messages in the Navigation pane

▶ Reading and sorting your e-mail in the View pane

▶ Discovering what all those icons mean

▶ Glimpsing the Action bar

▶ Closing your mail

Your regular mail arrives in a mailbox, but your Lotus Notes e-mail arrives in your Inbox on your computer. (Actually, although you read your e-mail while sitting at your computer, your e-mail messages are usually saved on the server computer and aren't stored on your own system right there at your desk.)

This chapter is a big jump-start into the wonderful world of Notes e-mail. By the time that you're done, you'll know what you need to know about what's in your mail, how to use the views and folders, and how to use buttons in the Action bar. Notes 6 has made some subtle changes in the way that mail works, so Notes R5 users will want to watch for them.

A rose is a rose is a memo is a message! The words *memo, document, message,* and *e-mail* are used interchangeably. In Notes, they all mean the same thing.

May I Have the Envelope, Please?

The most direct and easy way (although you have many other ways) to open your Notes mail is to click (just once) the Mail icon in the Bookmark bar (far-left side of your screen). Up springs something that looks very much like Figure 3-1. There, in a list, is your very own, personal, for-your-eyes-only e-mail.

Action bar

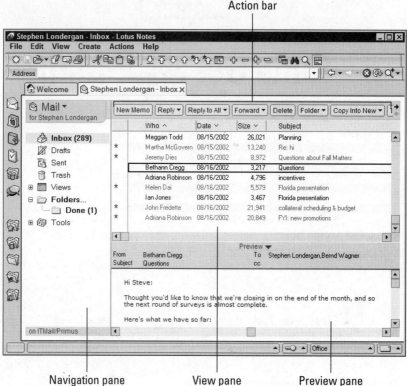

Figure 3-1:
Your Notes
mail has
four parts:
the
Navigation,
View, and
Preview
panes; and
the Action
bar.

Navigation pane   View pane   Preview pane

Nobody but you can open *your* mail database. (And you can't open anyone else's, either. Not that you would even think of doing such a thing.)

Actually, as you can see in Figure 3-1, more than just your mail is onscreen when you open your e-mail. In fact, the screen is divided into four parts. When you open your mail, think of your screen as a window that you're looking through. As such, the four parts of your mail are called *panes*, as in window panes:

- ✔ **Navigation pane:** The first pane (left side) is called the *Navigation pane*. In this pane, you move amongst the folders and views in your mail.

- ✔ **View pane:** On the right side of the screen is the *View pane*. This pane provides a summary of the messages in whichever folder you select from the Navigation pane.

- ✔ **Preview pane:** Beneath the View pane is the *Preview pane*. You can choose to enact this view or hide it. If this view is active, you see whatever message you have highlighted in the View pane. (A message is highlighted when you see it sporting a black border, or a *selection bar*.)

You show or hide the Preview pane by choosing View⇨Document Preview⇨Show Preview. Or, you can click the triangle next to the word *Preview* on the bottom Navigation bar.

✔ **Action bar:** Last, but not least, is the *Action bar*, which is just a bunch of buttons that let you do things to your mail, such as Reply and Delete.

Onward, upward, and e-ward! Get ready to see how you can adjust the panes, rearrange your messages, and (most important) read your messages.

Navigating the Navigation Pane

You use the Navigation pane to sort, navigate, and otherwise rearrange the messages in your mail. For example, the Inbox folder shows you all the messages that have been sent to you (not the messages that you've sent to other people); the Drafts folder shows messages that you started to create but never bothered finish and to send; and the Trash bin is where messages go when you don't need them anymore.

To open a folder and see the messages that are in it, simply click the folder's name. For example, to see what (if anything) is in the Sent folder, just click it.

You can also see in Figure 3-1 that some items in the Navigation pane — such as the Inbox and the Done folder — have a numeral next to them. This indicates how many messages are in that folder.

And check out Figure 3-1 to see that some of the items listed in the Navigation pane have a little plus (+) or minus (–) sign next to them. They're just Notes' way of telling you that there's more than meets the eye. When you click these plus or minus signs, you either expand or collapse (respectively) the associated folder. In other words, you click the plus sign to show or the minus sign to hide whatever Notes has up its sleeve.

Refer to Figure 3-1, where you can see a + sign next to the heading Views (in the Navigation pane). That's your cue that there's a little more information to do with that heading . . . but that it's hidden. In Figure 3-2, you can see what the screen looks like when you click the plus sign: The plus sign toggles to a minus sign; more importantly, Views has expanded to show the names of all the views.

When you want to hide (collapse, actually) that list again, you just click again.

The bottom line: These little buttons in the Navigation pane of your mail are used to show and hide information, and you just click them to go one way or the other. That's it!

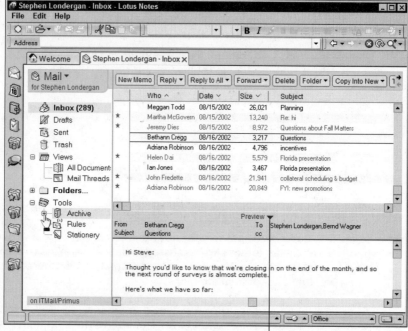

Figure 3-2:
Click the
plus sign
next to an
item in the
Navigation
pane to
expand it;
click it
again to
collapse it.

Click the twisty to expand or contract.

If you root around in the Navigation pane and expand all its twisties (which you should try, just for practice), you'll find 12 things, which I explain in loving detail, right here in Table 3-1. *Twisties* are the little arrows that appear next to headings. If they're right facing, then the heading is collapsed. If they're pointing down, then the heading is expanded.

Table 3-1	Twelve Important Folders in Your Navigation Pane	
Folder Icon	*Folder Name*	*What the Folder Contains*
Inbox	Inbox	Messages that have been sent to you
Drafts	Drafts	Messages that you've started but not finished
Sent	Sent	Messages that you've sent to someone else
Trash	Trash bin	Messages that you're going to delete
Views	Views	The All Documents and Discussion folders

Folder Icon	Folder Name	What the Folder Contains
All Documents	All Documents	Every single e-mail message that you have
Mail Threads	Mail Threads	All your messages, organized by topic
Folders	Folders	Your own folders, which you create to help organize your messages
Tools	Tools	Includes Rules and Stationery (see listings in this table)
Archive	Archive	Helps you store and organize old messages
Rules	Rules	Helps you organize your mail by automatically filing certain kinds of messages in certain folders
Stationery	Stationery	Forms that you create to help send the same message over and over again

To see what's in a folder, just click it. To discover how to put a message in a folder, read Chapter 5.

When you open your mail, you see the contents of whichever folder you were in the last time that you opened your mail. For example, suppose that you were reading your messages in a folder you created called *Status Reports*. When 5:30 p.m. rolls around and it's time to go home, you close your mail. When you come back to work tomorrow morning and open your mail, you'll find yourself in the same folder that you were in when you left — Status Reports, in this example.

Because *new* messages are always delivered to your Inbox, you probably want to work in that folder most often.

Click the Inbox folder in the Navigation pane to find your new e-mail messages.

Traversing the View Pane

The View pane presents you with a summary of the documents in a given folder. When you press the up-arrow and down-arrow keys ($\uparrow$/$\downarrow$), the selection bar moves from one message to the next. (The *selection bar* is that big black outline that highlights the active message in the View pane.) And, when you press $\uparrow$ or $\downarrow$, you also see a preview of that document in the Preview pane *if* you have the Preview pane enabled.

Each row of information in the View pane represents an individual message. Each message is divided into columns of information:

- ✔ **Who:** The name of the person who sent the message
- ✔ **Date:** When the message was sent
- ✔ **Size:** How big the message is
- ✔ **Subject:** The message's subject

Aside from just looking at the View pane to see who sent you what messages and when, you can do a few other things, which I describe in the following section.

Changing the column width

Sometimes the contents of a View pane column are wider than the column itself, which means you can't see all the information about a message. This problem (unlike world hunger) is easily remedied by simply changing any column's width, as shown in Figure 3-3.

This pointer allows you to change column sizes.

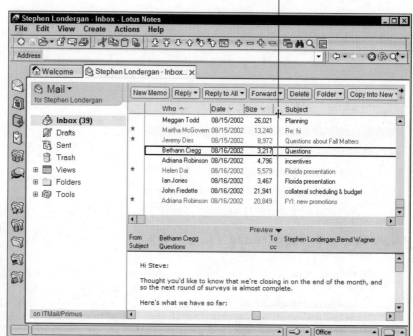

Figure 3-3: You can change the size of any column in your mail.

To change a column's width, simply go to the top of the View pane (where you see the Who, Date, Size, and Subject column headings) and move your mouse so that the pointer is on the vertical line representing the right side of the too-narrow column. When you get the mouse right where you want it, the pointer changes to a two-headed monster, as you can see in Figure 3-3. Then all you do is click (and hold down) your mouse and drag the column to the right to whatever size you want. Easy, huh?

Sorting your mail

Take another gander at Figure 3-3 and check out the headings for the Who, Date, and Size columns. Note the little triangles in each of these? Columns with triangles are set up to sort *on-the-fly,* which is a fancy way of saying (no, this doesn't involve an airplane) that you can re-sort the documents by clicking the column heading.

For example, if you want to rearrange the documents in the Date column so that they're listed from newest to oldest, click the word *Date* in the column heading. Before your very eyes, the documents rearrange themselves. Click the word *Date* again, and the documents shuffle into the opposite order of receipt. Do the same thing with the Who and the Size columns to either re-alphabetize the documents based on the message senders' name or to sort by document size, respectively.

Sorting your mail by the person who sent it makes it much, much easier to find a message from that particular person. This is especially useful if you've been using Notes for a while and have lots and lots of messages. Notes has lots of different ways to search for and find information, but usually the easiest way to find one particular message is to just re-sort your mail so that all the messages from a particular person are listed together. Find a lot of good information on searching in Chapter 13, if you're interested.

Anytime you that see a little triangle in any column heading in any database, you can click the heading to rearrange the documents listed in that column.

Reading your mail

When you press the ↑ and ↓ keys to move the selection bar in the View pane, the Preview pane (if enabled) changes to give you a preview of what's in each message.

To read a message in its entirety, you can either double-click the message in question or highlight it with the selection bar and then press Enter. Bye-bye, panes; the document that you selected now fills the screen. After opening a document, use the ↑ and ↓ keys (or the vertical scroll bar) to move through the body of the document.

Closing a message

When you finish reading a message, you can close it and return to the View pane by doing one of the following:

- ✔ Press Esc.
- ✔ Click the little *x* in the document's Task button at the top of the screen.
- ✔ Press Ctrl+W.
- ✔ Choose File⇨Close.

Or you can move immediately to another message:

- ✔ Press Enter, and the next message appears.
- ✔ Press Backspace, and the preceding message appears.
- ✔ Press Tab to move to the next unread message or press Shift+Tab to move to the previous unread message (if you have one).
- ✔ Press F4 to see the next unread document or press Shift+F4 to see the previous unread document.

If you're getting a little worried about remembering all these options for moving from message to message, don't sweat it. Choose the one that works best for you and forget the others. Enter and Backspace are pretty easy to remember.

If you're especially observant, you may have noticed that before you open a message, it has a little star next to it in the View pane. And after you open a message, its star is gone. You may have noticed also that the name of a message in the View pane changes colors after you open it. It used to be red, but now it's black. What gives?

Notes 6 keeps track of which documents you've read and which you haven't. If a document in the View pane has a red star next to it, you know that it's brand-spanking new — or at least that you haven't read it yet. On the other hand, if the message in question doesn't have a star and it's black, you *have* read it.

R-E-D documents haven't been R-E-A-D.

Deciphering all those icons

Gaggles of little icons inhabit the View pane. Use them as guideposts because each icon tells you something about the message beside it.

Some icons appear because certain things have happened to a message. For example, when you include a file in a message that you send, the message in the recipient's Inbox bears a paper clip icon in the View pane.

Other icons appear when someone who sends you a message selects a special Delivery Option to mark the message as being particularly important, or as a question, and so on. You can read in Chapter 4 how to apply these whimsical icons.

(Not everybody knows to do this, and even those people who do know how to do it don't do it to every message, so don't be surprised if most of your messages don't have this.)

Table 3-2 shows all these little Delivery Option and View pane icons as well as what they indicate.

Table 3-2	Icons in Your Notes Mail Database
Icon	*What It Means*
	A message that you sent.
	A message that you've saved but haven't sent yet.
	A message marked with High Importance. (Read me now!)
	A message marked as Personal. (Just between us . . .)
	A message marked as Confidential. (Your secret's safe with me.)
	A message marked as Private. (Keep it to yourself.)
	A message that's a thank you. (You're welcome.)
	A message marked as a joke. (Or at least funny.)

(continued)

Table 3-2 *(continued)*

Icon	What It Means
★	A message that tells you that you did a good job. (Atta-boy!)
	A message with bad news or a complaint. (Harumpf.)
	A message marked For Your Information. (Heads up!)
?	A message marked as a question. (Say what?)
	A message marked as a reminder. (Nag, nag, nag.)
	A message with an attached file.
	A message that's incomplete.
1	A high-priority task.
2	A medium-priority task.
3	A low-priority task.
✓	A task that's been completed.
	An invitation to a meeting.
	A meeting that's been rescheduled.
✗	A meeting that's been cancelled altogether.
	An invitation that's been accepted.
	An invitation that's been declined.

Icon	What It Means
	An anniversary.
	An all-day event.
	An appointment.

> **TIP** Newsflash from the You've Got Better Things to Worry about Department: Don't tell anyone that I told you this, but you can be pretty successful with Notes 6 even if you don't memorize all these little pictures and what they mean.

Taming That Distracting Preview Pane

If you have the Preview pane enabled, it shows you at the bottom of the View pane the beginning of whichever message you've highlighted with the selection bar. (The active message is surrounded by a solid black outline.) You really can't do much with the Preview pane other than read the document that displays there. That said, it's nice to have because it tells you what's in the message before you open it.

> **TIP** Maybe you want to see more than just the opening of a message. Assuming that your Preview pane is open, choose View⇨Document Preview⇨Zoom Preview to enlarge a selected message. Follow these same steps to deselect the Zoom feature or click the black triangle located next to the word *Preview* in the Preview pane.

> **TIP** Some people find keeping the Preview pane enabled to be pretty annoying. If you have the Preview pane enabled but it's driving you nuts, just choose View⇨Document Preview⇨Show Preview to disengage it. Each time that you select this command from the menu, Notes 6 toggles back and forth between opening and closing the Preview pane. Or, simply click the black triangle located next to the word *Preview* in the Preview pane to open or close this feature. Some people (including the author of several well-known *Lotus Notes For Dummies* books) prefer to keep the Preview pane closed all the time.

Taking Action with the Action Bar

The *Action bar* is that strip of big helpful buttons at the top of your mail. (Refer to Figure 3-1.) It contains buttons for just about every potential action that you can take with a message, such as Reply or Forward. If you see a button that you want to use, just click it.

The Action bar buttons change depending on what you're doing. In other words, the buttons you see in the Action bar while you're previewing a message are different from the ones that you see while you're reading a message.

Get Me Outta Here!

When you want to close your mail and return to the Welcome page, choose File⇨Close or press Esc. You may have to choose this command twice if you're reading a message when you decide to close your mail. The first time closes your message; the second time closes your Inbox and takes you back to the Welcome page.

Chapter 4

Making a Message

*H*ooray! You've opened your e-mail and you've read all your new messages. You're all caught up! You've called your boss back to confirm that lunch meeting, and maybe you even saw that new invitation in time to make the rescheduled 3 p.m. staff meeting. Still, it's a safe bet that at least a few messages in your Inbox e-mail need a reply, and perhaps you even want to compose a few messages of your own. It's time to get on board the Lotus Notes 6 e-mail wagon, and that means it's time to send some new messages.

This chapter's goal isn't to turn you into a Shakespeare or a Hemingway. What you say in your memos is up to you. I just want to give you some pointers so that your message gets where you want it to go.

Minding Your Good Memo Manners

The following news will probably come as no surprise: You shouldn't use e-mail for everything. Dollars to donuts, the following messages probably aren't appropriate for e-mail:

✔ Dear friends: Vicki and I are giving a little wedding for our daughter next week. Can you make it? It's BYOC, by the way (Bring Your Own Champagne).

✔ Steve: I think it'd be better if we're just friends.

✔ I'm sorry your dog died.

✔ Hey, JB: Here are a few suggestions about how to get this company turned around. First, fire all your vice presidents.

✔ Smedley, you're fired. Be out of your office in five minutes. We've already hired a replacement.

✔ Don't you think that our new manager is a jerk? I sure do. What a moron! I could do the job better than that idiot.

✔ I just found out that Roger is making $90,000.

Each of the previous points might have its place in some form of communication, but not in e-mail memos. Before you put fingers to keyboard, pause to ponder the following points:

✔ You'd never use certain words when you're at work. (Of course *Etiquette For Dummies* would suggest you shouldn't use such language, ever). And certain topics are best off being avoided altogether, right? If you wouldn't say it or discuss it over the water cooler, you shouldn't write about it in e-mail, either.

✔ At times, more formal styles of communication, even (gasp!) paper documents, are still more appropriate than e-mail.

✔ At times, talking face-to-face is preferable to e-mail.

✔ Don't use e-mail to go over your boss's head, especially if you wouldn't consider doing so under other circumstances.

✔ Resist the temptation to include the whole world in your cc: list.

✔ A message might be delivered almost instantly, but this doesn't mean that everyone is going to read it instantly.

✔ Although Notes is a secure e-mail system (a message goes only to the person who you address it to), nothing prevents that person from sending your message on to other people or from printing it.

✔ Most would never do this, but don't forget that companies consider their e-mail systems — including your Inbox — to be a corporate asset. In other words, if push comes to shove, your manager is probably (legally) allowed to read your mail.

✔ If you compose a nasty-gram or want to forward something that *you* think is funny, sleep on it before sending it.

✔ Roger only makes $70,000.

Sending an e-mail to too many people is sometimes called *spamming,* as in: "Jim really spammed his complaints around, huh? What an idiot! I wonder how soon he'll get fired?" Don't include too many people in your cc: lists — you may end up overloading your colleagues.

Composing Your New Message

So you're ready to compose an actual, honest-to-goodness, real-life memo. One of the nice things about Notes is that you can always compose a new mail message, anytime and anywhere, even if your Inbox isn't open. You might be reading a discussion database or looking at your company's phone-book database when the urge to compose a message strikes you. No matter where you are or what you're doing, if you have Lotus Notes open, a new e-mail message is just a menu choice (or mouse click) away.

When you want to write a new e-mail message, choose Create➪Mail➪Memo or just press Ctrl+M. The blank message form in Figure 4-1 appears. Your new message has four parts:

- **Action bar:** Buttons that you can use while composing your memo, such as Save as Draft and Delivery Options
- **Your name:** Whatever that may be
- **Addressees and Subject fields:** Where you enter the names of your message's recipients and a short description of its subject
- **Body:** Where you type the body of your message

Writing a new message involves just three (or four) basic steps:

1. **Figure out the people to whom you'll be sending your message.**
2. **Type the body of the message.**
3. **Mark the message with a delivery option (optional).**
4. **Save it, or send it, or (most often) do both.**

Before I get carried away explaining each of these steps in mind-numbing detail, allow me to mention that you can simply enter a recipient's name in the To: field, type something in the body, and then click the Send button (up there in the action bar) to dispatch your message.

Your name

Action bar

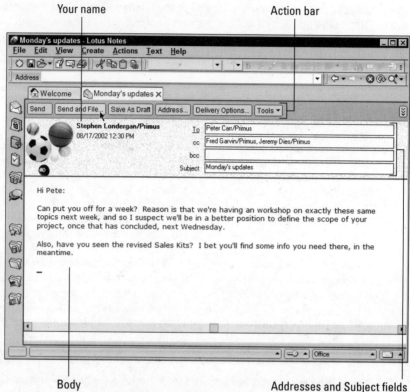

Figure 4-1:
Every e-mail
message
has four
basic parts.

Body

Addresses and Subject fields

The fine print

This is as good a place as any to tell you that what you're reading here may not be for you. Or maybe this section is dead-on, but later in the book you may notice that what I describe is not what you see on your screen. If you find a discrepancy between what you're reading and what you're seeing, maybe it's because

✔ Your company might not be set up to use Notes for e-mail. Some people use Notes for its collaboration capabilities but use a separate program to send and read e-mail messages. If this is the case for you, you probably want to stop reading this chapter

right here and instead skip ahead to Chapter 8.

✔ Your company might have you read your mail with a Web browser instead of the Notes 6 software. If that's the case, you probably *should* keep reading because that only means that some buttons might be in different places. *What* you do is the same, even if *how* you do it is a little different.

✔ You can't always believe everything you read.

Step 1: Addressing a message

Addressing a message is very easy. Just type the person's name (or names) in one or more of the address fields. As you may have noticed in Figure 4-1, you have three address fields: To:, cc:, and bcc:.

- ✔ **To:** This field is where you enter the name of the primary recipient(s) of your message. If you're sending your message to more than one person, separate each name with a comma. You can also use groups, as you'll see in Chapter 11.

- ✔ **cc:** This field is where you enter the name of anyone to whom you want to send a *courtesy copy* of your message. Again, if you have more than one name, separate each with a comma.

- ✔ **bcc:** Use this field to send a *blind courtesy copy* of the memo — that is, to send someone a copy without the rest of the recipients knowing about it. Imagine, for example, that you send a memo to a co-worker asking him or her to do a certain job. You want your manager to know that you've made the request, but you don't necessarily want the co-worker to know that your manager is aware of what's going on. Send the memo *To:* the co-worker with a *bcc:* to your manager. When your co-worker receives the message, the bcc: field won't be visible, so your secret is safe. Your co-worker won't know that you sent a copy of this same message to your boss, but your boss will. Pretty devious, huh?

Using a bcc: is a little bit like talking behind someone's back, so be judicious with your use of it.

Of course, spelling is important, so you want to be pretty careful to spell the addressee names correctly. Fear not, though; if you misspell a name, Notes 6 might be able to catch your mistake and help you correct it. You may also notice that when you type a recipient's name, Notes does its best to help you get it right. In the To:, cc:, or bcc: field, type in the first few characters of the recipient's name, wait a bit while Notes runs a search, and then Notes fills in the rest of the name (highlighted in black) of whom it guesses that you intended . If you want to accept the guess that Notes 6 offers, just press Enter to accept it.

If you're not sure how to spell a person's name, Notes provides an easy way for you to find out. Click the Address button on the Action bar, and let your fingers do the walking.

You have at least two directories full of e-mail addresses available — your very own Personal Address Book and your company's public directory. These are the two lists that Notes 6 shows you when you click the Action bar Address button, and each contains the e-mail addresses of various people. Because you can customize it, your Personal Address book can have the names of people who don't work at your company, customers, other colleagues, and family members. The public directory has the names of everyone at your company. (Find out more about your Address Book and directories in Chapter 11.)

When you click the Address button, the Select Addresses dialog box appears, as shown in Figure 4-2. Use the Choose Address Book drop-down list at the top left of this dialog box to select either your Personal Address Book or the company's public directory.

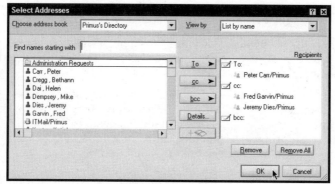

Figure 4-2:
Use the
Select
Addresses
dialog box
to get the
right name.

On the left side of the Select Addresses dialog box, you see the names of the people who are listed in your Personal Address Book or the public directory, whichever you chose. If you want to send your memo to someone on this list, select that person's name and then click the To:, cc:, or bcc: button, depending on how you want the message to be addressed. When you do, the name of the person that you select appears on the right side of the dialog box, inside the Recipients window. (If you make a mistake, click either the Remove or the Remove All button to start over.)

The simplest way to find a particular person in the list is to use the scroll bars. If lots and lots of people are listed, you can type the first letter (or first few letters) in the Find Names Starting With text field.

If you're a mouse aficionado, click and drag a name from the left window into the appropriate field in the Recipients window. Or, simply double-click on a selected name and see the name appear in the Recipients window. It's that easy.

When you've finished using the Select Addresses dialog box to choose your recipient names, click OK.

After choosing the recipients' names, be sure to type a brief description of what your memo is about in the Subject field. Keep your description short and make it interesting. What you enter here is what shows up in the View pane of your recipient's Inbox.

Step 2: Writing the body of the message

And now on to the important stuff. After you type or choose all the names of the people who will (soon) be receiving your little pearl of wisdom, you get to pen the body of the message.

Go nuts: You can enter any text you want, and you can get as fancy as you want, too. You can make the text bold or italicized, change the font, include an attachment, create a table, or even copy/paste information from someplace else. Because the body of an e-mail is what's known as *rich text*, you can make its contents pretty elaborate. Read more about jazzing up your text in Chapter 14.

Step 3: Adding a special touch to a message

Before dispatching a message, you can define Delivery Options, Security Options, and Mood Stamps. Use these Notes cues to let your recipient know just how hot your message is or what your mood is; or to request delivery confirmation, set delivery time, and more.

After you finish composing the body of your message, click the Delivery Options button up there in the Action bar, which leads, inevitably, to the Delivery Options dialog box as shown in Figure 4-3. In this dialog box, you have several choices for delivery and security and fun.

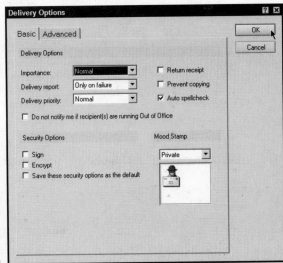

Figure 4-3: Set delivery options here.

(You may notice in your travels and in the dialog box shown in Figure 4-3 that there's an Advanced tab — the good news is that you probably won't have to mess with it.)

Setting a message Importance level

In the Delivery Options section, you can mark your message's importance level: Low, Normal, or High. You can set Notes to flag messages that you mark as High Importance; these messages show up with a red envelope icon in your recipient's Inbox. Use this feature to alert your recipient to an especially important, urgent, or otherwise time-critical message.

Adding a Mood Stamp to a message

Using the Mood Stamp list is a way to get in touch with your (electronic) inner child. A *Mood Stamp* is just a picture that shows up at the top of the body of your message so that your reader knows how you were feeling when you sent the message. Mood-stamped messages are also marked as such in the recipient's Inbox.

You have several mood stamps to choose from, including Private, Flame, and Joke. For fun, try each to see what they look like. The Joke selection (see the Groucho-esque disguise icon in the upper-left corner of the message body in Figure 4-4) is useful if you want to send a message that's just a little sarcastic, and you need to make sure that your reader realizes that yes, you were just kidding!

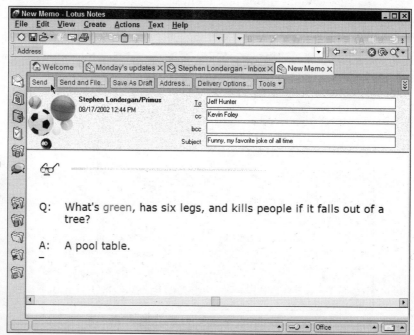

Figure 4-4:
Use a Mood Stamp to make sure your reader takes your message in the tone in which it's meant.

To choose a stamp, click the down-arrow next to the Mood Stamp drop-down list. Scroll through the list to make your choice. To preview a Mood Stamp, click its name in the drop-down list, and its icon appear under that list. Click the OK button, and the Mood Stamp appears in your new message. If you don't want any Mood Stamp in your outgoing message, just leave the default Normal set.

Requesting a message Delivery Report

Make choices from the Delivery Report option list to specify when and whether you'll be notified of the delivery status of your messages. Your four choices regarding a Delivery Report are Only on Failure, Confirm Delivery, Trace Entire Path, and None.

- **Only on Failure:** No news is good news. In other words, Notes informs you only in the event that your message can't be delivered for some reason.

- **Confirm Delivery:** This is the choice for you if you're a little less of an optimist. In this case, Notes tells you exactly when and where your message was delivered.

- **Trace Entire Path:** This choice tells you where (and at what times) your message stopped on its way to your recipient. (Trust me, you probably don't care.)

- **None:** Choose this and you throw caution to the wind, not caring to know whether your message gets delivered or not. (This is the default, by the way.)

If you choose a Delivery Report option other than None, you receive a Delivery Confirmation Report (just an e-mail message from your network to you) back as soon as the message that you sent arrives. When that will be depends entirely on the network. If your recipient is far away — at a different company, for example — it may take a few hours or even an entire day for the message to get delivered. Check out Figure 4-5 to see an example Delivery Confirmation Report.

Setting the Delivery Priority for a message

Another choice from the Delivery Options dialog box — Delivery Priority — relates to how quickly you want Notes to deliver your message:

- **Low:** Select this to send the message late at night when the network isn't so busy.

- **Normal:** Choose this to send the message as soon as possible based on the mail delivery schedules that your administrator has crafted. (This is the default.)

- **High:** Choosing this sends your message right now — step aside, coming through!

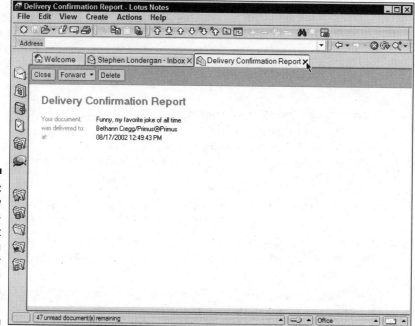

Figure 4-5:
A Delivery
Confirma-
tion Report
tells you
when your
message
was
delivered.

If you're including a huge attachment in a message, consider marking it as Low priority. The message won't be delivered until you're home fast asleep, but it may cost your company less money to send it late at night. Maybe this is a way to earn that Employee of the Month award!

Signing a message

The company president calls you and complains about a memo that you sent demanding shorter working hours and a raise for the whole department. Try as you might, you can't remember sending a memo like that. Are you losing your marbles? Memory blackout? That may be, but it's more likely that some-one sent a memo in your name. This is pretty (almost totally) unlikely, of course, but a mischievous co-worker with far too much free time could figure out how to make a message look like it came from you even when it didn't.

The way to avoid being blamed for messages that aren't really from you is to sign them. You sign messages for the same reason that you sign checks or official documents: to show that they're really from you. You don't need to sign a meet-me-for-coffee memo, but when you send a message with crucial or sensitive information, you may want Notes 6 to prove that the message really came from you.

I'm talking computers here — obviously you can't scratch your signature on the screen at the bottom of a memo. (Well, actually, you can, but I don't think your boss would appreciate it.) You sign a message by selecting the Sign check box under the Security Options section of the Delivery Options dialog box.

The signature that you use in Notes 6 is even more difficult to forge than your own John Hancock because it's a special numeric computer code added to the message when you send it and checked by the recipient's computer when the message is opened. The memo doesn't have an actual signature on it, but this type of message appears at the bottom of the screen:

```
Signed by Alan Dunkel/Primus on 07-1-02 8:30:46 AM, according
                        to Primus.
```

Encrypting a message

Sure enough, the world is crawling with busybodies, bad guys, and spies. If you use a modem, you're sending your messages over phone lines where a person up to no good could be able to somehow intercept and read them. (Again it's really, really unlikely that this will happen, but hey, you never know.) This isn't a big deal for your meet-me-for-coffee messages, but if you send a message that includes information such as confidential corporate information, employee performance appraisals, or just really, really good gossip that you don't want anyone else to read, you can encrypt it.

When you use the Notes encryption security option, you are 100 percent certain that only its intended recipient will be able to read it.

To encrypt a message, select the Encrypt check box from the Security Options section of the Delivery Options dialog box. Click OK to close the dialog box when you're finished.

When you send an encrypted message, Notes does the scrambling for you — behind the scenes. When the recipients open the message, they see the contents just as you wrote it. In other words, the reader of an encrypted message doesn't have to do anything special to decrypt an encrypted message. Only the intended recipients with the proper user IDs can read the encrypted part of the message. The only one who will see the actual jumbled-up version is the poor spy who intercepts the message in transit.

Drawing the shades

Think about it: Who can read your e-mail if it's open and visible on your screen while you're away from your desk? If you answered, "Anyone at all," you're right! If you leave a highly sensitive message visible and go for a cup of coffee, there's no telling whom you'll be letting in on the secret because the message in question is visible and readable by anyone while your screen is open. So when you need to leave your desk, close the message, and then always press F5 to disable your access to Notes. That way, the next time that you try to use Notes, you'll have to enter your password — and so will anyone else. Get it? To find out how to set a password, check out Chapter 16.

If you're sending e-mail to a person who uses a different e-mail program, or if you're sending your message through the Internet, check first with your company's Notes administrator to see whether you'll be able to encrypt it.

Requesting a Return Receipt for a message

If you use the Delivery Options dialog box to request a Return Receipt for a message, your network automatically notifies you when your recipient reads your message. This is different from requesting a Delivery Confirmation Report, which only tells you when the message arrived in the recipient's mail database. (For more, see the earlier section "Requesting a message Delivery Report.") I recommend that you request a receipt report (just enable the Return Receipt check box) to prevent the "I never saw your message" excuse and request a Delivery Confirmation Report to eliminate the "I never got your message; the network must have lost it" excuse.

If you're sending a message to someone who doesn't use Notes or if your message is going through the Internet, you might not be able to get receipt reports from them.

Preventing copying of a message

Another Notes security option at your disposal is to prevent copying. When you select the Prevent Copying check box, you can be certain that the person who receives your message won't be able to forward it to anyone else. In fact, they won't even be able to copy (Edit➪Copy) your memo to the Clipboard, in case they're intent on a little illicit pasting (Edit➪Paste). Choosing the Prevent Copying option ensures that what you send to one person doesn't get spammed all over your company.

When you're finished selecting delivery options, click OK to get back to your document. In most cases, after you make up your mind vis-à-vis these options, you then click the Send and File button.

If your head is spinning from all these delivery options, don't let it get you down. You need to use them only under special circumstances. In fact, for most messages, you'll blow right by the delivery options without opening the Delivery Options dialog box and without a second thought. What a relief!

If you find that you're always visiting the Delivery Options dialog box to sign and encrypt your messages, you can select the Save These Security Options as the Default check box. That way, any new messages that you create will have the same security settings. Of course, you can always change your mind by returning to the Delivery Options dialog box to change a default setting or to change your default security settings.

Step 4: Sending the message

After successfully choosing the addressees, entering the text of your message, and setting any delivery options, you're ready to dispatch your message. When the time comes to let 'er rip, choose Actions➪Send document or click the Send button on the Action bar. Off the memo goes, with barely a whisper.

If you change your mind and decide not to send a message (what were you thinking?), press Esc and then click the Discard button in the Send Mail dialog box. To send your message later and just save it for now (maybe you want to take a little break first), click the Save as Draft button in the Action bar. Then you can retrieve and send it later by finding it in your Drafts folder.

So exactly what happens when you send your memo? It gets handed off to your mail server — you know, the BIG computer in your office that the average Joe isn't allowed to see or touch. And you? You're right back where you were when you started composing the message in the first place. Rest assured that Notes 6 will deliver your memo to the recipients; Notes 6 even notifies you if, for some reason, it can't deliver your message.

The only possible downside to choosing the Actions➪Send command is that your memo isn't saved for you. The memo goes to the recipients all right, but you'll have no record of what you sent. This is why it's probably better to use the Actions➪Send Document and File command (or click the Send and File button in the Action bar) to dispatch your message. This choice really does two things: It saves your message and it also sends it. That way, you get a record of what you sent.

When you choose to simultaneously send and file a message, you get the Folders dialog box as shown in Figure 4-6. Click or drill down to the folder into which you want to save your outgoing message and then click OK.

Figure 4-6:
Choose a folder to save a message.

When you see a plus sign next to a folder in the Folders dialog box, just click it to expand and show its contents. Read more about expanding folders in Chapter 3. The plus sign in Figure 4-6 (next to the Planning folder) has already been expanded. (Note that the plus sign toggles to a minus sign.)

If you don't see a folder-for-filing that fits your needs — or if you forgot to create a special folder before you try to file a certain message — just click the Create New Folder button at the bottom of the Folders dialog box and give it a name.

When you're not sure about which folder to save your message in, adding it to your Inbox folder is always a safe bet. And remember that no matter where you put your message, you'll always be able to find it — either by searching (as I discuss in Chapter 13) or by looking for it in the All Documents view.

Working in Your Mail

Way back at the beginning of this chapter, I discuss how you can compose a new mail message anytime and anywhere that you have access to Lotus Notes, whether your Inbox is open or not. That's nice, but more often than not, you'll already have your Inbox open. For example, you may want to open your Inbox to do the following:

- Read the messages that have been sent to you
- Reply to messages that you've received
- Forward documents to other interested parties

I go into detail in Chapter 3 about how you read messages. Read through the following sections for the skinny on replying and forwarding messages, with a little bonus added in about forms.

See Chapter 13 for more information about searching in your mail and Chapter 5 for the scoop on managing your mail.

Replying to a message

By way of setting the stage, imagine that you open your Inbox, and therein encounter a message from a colleague, asking for your advice about something . . . a new project, perhaps. You've never been shy about sharing your opinions, so why should you be now? Plus which, being the responsive and social sort of person that you are, you want to reply to her straight away.

Here's the scoop: Either open the original message or highlight it in the View pane. Then click either the Reply or Reply to All button on the Action bar and choose one of the following options from the drop-down list that appears: Reply, Reply with History, Reply without Attachment(s), or Reply with Internet-style History.

No matter which Reply option you choose, one thing is always the same: Notes 6 starts you off with a new memo and automatically fills in the mail address of the person who sent you the original message.

Reply

Choosing Reply is the simplest — you just get a brand new message, pre-addressed to the person who sent you the message in the first place. You'll also notice that the subject for your reply has been automatically filled out, too. Isn't it nice that Notes does all that typing for you?

Reply with History

When you choose to Reply with History, Notes also includes a copy of the original memo — and any attachments inside the memo — that you're sending back. This is a nice way to make sure that the person who you're replying to will know exactly what you're talking about. All too often, you probably receive memos in which authors expound on some topic, leaving you without the faintest idea of what they're talking about or why they're talking about it. (Or consider the e-mail reply that arrives, containing just the word "No." No *what?* No *bananas?* No to your request for a raise? No way to know what they're talking about?)

To prevent this situation and to keep your technological reputation on the up-and-up, I recommend that you always choose Reply with History so that your readers know of which you speak.

Check out Figure 4-7 for a sample reply memo composed using the Reply with History choice.

Reply without Attachment(s)

You only use the Reply without Attachment(s) option when the original message — the one to which you are replying — arrives in your Inbox with an attachment or a bunch of attachments. In most cases, you probably don't need to send all those bulky attached files back to the original person in your reply, and not including them makes your message get delivered more quickly, makes for a smaller mail file for you and your recipient, and is just an all-around good idea.

The Reply without Attachment(s) option works a lot like Reply with History in that Notes automatically includes a copy of the original *memo* in the memo that you're sending back. The difference is that you only return the original memo and none of the now-unnecessary baggage contain in the attached file(s).

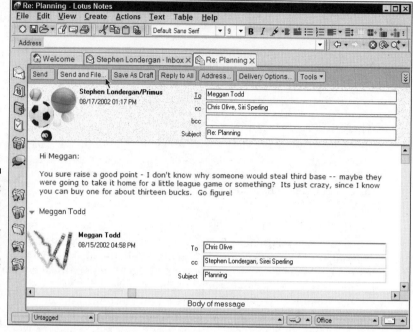

Figure 4-7:
Choose
Reply with
History
to preserve
the context
of a
conversa-
tion.

Choosing the Reply without Attachment(s) option is a really smart thing to do, especially if you or your colleagues connect to Notes with a modem. Your message will be a lot smaller, and it can be delivered a lot faster.

Reply with Internet-Style History

Choosing Reply with Internet-Style History may give you a message style that you're used to, particularly if you've used other e-mail programs. This reply choice works just like Reply with History except that the copy of the original message that's automatically included has all its text converted to Courier font, and each line begins with a bracket (>). You should just try this style of replying once or twice and see what you think; you'll find it's pretty much the same as using Reply with History, and you can use whichever you prefer.

Before I finish discussing Reply options, I want to cover using the Reply to All button. Clicking this button, which is located on the Action bar, produces a drop-down list with the same four selections as the Reply button. The only difference between Reply and Reply to All is how many names are automatically plugged in to your new reply.

Suppose that Mary sends you a message, with a carbon copy (cc:) also sent to your boss and to Lou, down in marketing. If you *Reply* to her message, Mary's name automatically pops up in your reply's To: field. Lou and your boss will be left in the dark, though, because Notes doesn't automatically include their names. If you use the *Reply to All* option, your new message is automatically addressed to Mary, Lou, and your boss. Reply to All puts all the original messages recipients in your message's address.

After clicking any of the Reply options, you are, of course, still free to alter the address fields so that you can add other names to the address list for your Reply if you feel that someone else needs to be brought in to the proverbial loop. You can also type whatever you want in the body field of your message.

Then click the Send or the Send and File button on the Action bar, and your reply behaves just like any other outgoing message.

Forward, ho!

In addition to replying to a message, you can forward a message. Perhaps you get a message asking about some company policy, but you're not the right person to ask. Just forward the misdirected document to the right person by clicking the Forward button on the Action bar or by choosing Actions⇨ Forward, and filling in the recipient's name in the To: field.

Forwarding a message is a little bit like choosing Reply because it really just tells Notes to start a brand new message for you, which automatically includes the contents of the original message.

As you can see in Figure 4-8, forwarding a message is even more like replying because you get to choose whether to forward just the message or save time and space by forwarding it without its attachments. (You can also forward a message using the Internet-style font and line styles that I discuss in the earlier section "Reply with Internet-Style History."

Forwarding mail is also a common way for your manager to get you to do things: (Someone asks your boss a question, and now all of a sudden it's *your* problem? Apparently, it *is*.) Or if you get a message (or see a document in a database) and you think that your buddy should know about it, forward it!

If you're forwarding a document to someone else so that *he* can take action on something, it's considered polite and proper (thank you, Emily Post) to include a cc: to the person who sent the document in the first place. That way, the original author knows that you're not going to reply directly.

Other kinds of mail documents

Look in the Create menu of your mail database, and you see that Notes has a few other mail forms available to you. Face it: An e-mail message is an e-mail message, but these other, extra-special forms were created with a few special purposes in mind:

✔ **To Do:** Use this form for yourself as a reminder for something that you need to do or to assign a task (via e-mail) to somebody else. To Dos that you create or receive have check marks next to them in the View pane of your Mail database. (Of course, just because you send a To Do to somebody doesn't mean said person is going to actually do it!) Check Chapter 10 to read more about To Dos.

✔ **Calendar Entry:** Use this form to schedule a meeting, which will appear on your (you guessed it) Calendar. Start with Chapter 8 to find out how to use your Calendar.

Figure 4-8:
Forward a message when you want to send along a message that you've received.

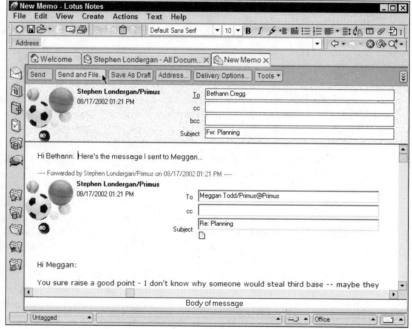

Chapter 5

Managing Your Mess(ages)

After you read your messages, then what? Do you have to do anything with them? Can you keep them or do they disappear after you read them? How can you file them so that you can easily find them later? And even though we're living in the digital age, what do you do when you want a permanent (um, paper) copy of a message?

In this chapter, I show you all about message control with Lotus Notes 6: what you can do with a message or a group of messages after you read them; how to organize them in folders; how to find them after you file them; how to keep your filing system clean and uncluttered; and how to print messages.

Digging through Your Scrap Heap of History

Actually, you don't necessarily have to do anything with your messages after you read them. They just continue to pile up in your Inbox the same way that stuff accumulates in an in-basket on your desk. (For more on reading messages, hop back to Chapter 3.) Unless you specifically decide to delete a message, Notes saves your mail, forever and ever and ever. Unless, of course, your administrator limits the size of your mail file: In that case, you have no choice but to delete and reorganize your messages!

However, just like the fate of a packrat who never throws anything away — Hey, I might need that someday! — messages can accumulate at a furious rate. Call it the Coat Hanger Syndrome: Who knows where they all come from?

Selecting multiple messages

Before you choose any command that does something to a document, you have to tell Notes which document (or documents) will be affected by the command that you're about to choose. If you want to do something to just one document, such as delete it, selecting it is easy. You either click the document in question with your mouse, or you use the up-arrow and down-arrow keys to select it in the View pane. Either way, when the selection bar is highlighting the document that you want, you're in business.

To select more than one document, highlight the first document and press the spacebar. (Watch for a little checkmark to appear to the left of the

document in the View pane.) Then you highlight the next document and press the spacebar again. Then you highlight the next document in the View pane, and press the . . . you get the idea.

To select multiple documents with the mouse, click-right where the checkmark will appear in the column immediately to the left of the message(s).

If you change your mind, you can use the same technique (with the mouse or the spacebar) to *de*select a message.

Because every message that you keep takes up disk space, you should seriously consider deleting old and unwanted messages as a regular, computer-housecleaning routine. Your hard drive will thank you. Added bonuses for being Mr. Clean include quicker-running e-mail, fewer messages to wade through when you're searching for something, and faster replication. (For more on replication, see Chapter 19.)

If you use Notes at work, your company probably has rules about how long you can keep a message before deleting it. If you think that's the case, best ask your administrator or call your help desk to make sure. You don't want to lose something important. (Like when Mom threw out all those baseball cards you'd had since third grade. . . .)

Instead of deleting a message altogether, you can also use an archive if you want to remove messages from your mail but still sort of keep them around.

 Deleting unwanted messages on a regular basis can help keep your Inbox a bit more sane. For those procrastinators out there, you can periodically find out how big your e-mail has grown (and thus whether it needs cleaning). Open your e-mail and choose File⇨Database⇨Properties. When you click the Info tab in the Database infobox, you see something remarkably like Figure 5-1. Note that this irresponsible blot on society has an e-mail database about 22MB with 385 documents!

 The most sensible course of action is to delete all messages that you won't need again as soon as you've read them. If you don't delete messages right away, you have to go back through your database every so often and delete the old messages.

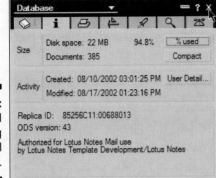

Figure 5-1:
Avoid
becoming
an e-mail
packrat.

Here's the big picture: You find a message you want to get rid off, and you delete it. Doing so doesn't *really* delete the message — it actually just gets moved from the place you deleted it (your Inbox, for example) and gets put in the Trash bin.

This is a safety net that Lotus builds in for you. Now you have a chance to change your mind if you delete a message by mistake. (Happens to the best of mousers.) Or you might change your mind about a deleted message. (So we *are* using my sales forecast after all!) You have a little while (usually 48 hours) during which you can go to the Trash bin to get it back. I know, picking through the trash isn't always the most socially acceptable thing in real life, but in Notes, this can be a real lifesaver.

Don't let too much time pass before trying to change your mind! You can't recover a mistakenly deleted message from a week ago.

To delete a message, do any of the following:

- ✔ **While the message is open onscreen**, press Delete. Doing so puts the message in the Trash bin and then automatically opens the next message in the database.

  Pressing Delete doesn't actually delete the message; it only puts the message in the Trash bin.

- ✔ **In the View pane**, select the document that you want to delete and either press Delete or click the Delete button on the Action bar. This also marks the message for deletion without actually deleting it. Although the message disappears from wherever you were when you deleted it, it hasn't been officially deleted yet — it's in the Trash bin.

- ✔ **Highlight a message** and press the spacebar or click in the far-left column. A checkmark appears next to the highlighted message, indicating that that message has been selected for torching. (I think that this is the best way to select a bunch of messages for eventual deletion.) After you check all the messages that you want to get rid of, press Delete or click the Delete button in the Action bar.

✔ **Drag the message** from the View pane and drop it in the Trash bin in the Navigation pane.

If you change your mind and decide that you don't want to delete a message after all, now is the time to act! All you need to do is

1. **Open the Trash bin by clicking it in the Navigation pane.**

2. **Select the message that you want to rescue.**

   To rescue more than one, use the spacebar to select a bunch of them or click in the column to the left of each message with your mouse until you see a checkmark by each.

3. **Choose Actions⇨Restore or click the Restore button of the Action bar.**

   Presto! The message (or messages, if you selected more than one) goes back to the view or folder from which it was originally deleted.

If you change your mind about deleting a message, go to the Trash bin to get it back. The messages that are waiting in the Trash bin are actually (and permanently) deleted according to a schedule, which is determined by your trusty administrator.

Sometimes you don't want to wait — you want to make sure that the message is really deleted, right now!

To get rid of a message for good — without waiting for the aforementioned scheduled deletion — open the Trash bin and then either choose Actions⇨ Empty Trash or click the Empty Trash button in the Action bar.

The easiest, fastest, and most direct way to delete a message is to select it and press Delete.

Organizing with Folders

Of course, you aren't going to delete *all* your messages; therefore, those that you decide to keep ought to be arranged in some sort of system. Depending on the folder that you're using, all your messages could be arranged by the date received or by the person who sent them. However, those arrangements might not be particularly useful for your day-to-day work. If you're not happy with the folders that are already in your mail, create your own. And when you get to the point that you no longer need folders that you create, you can delete them, too.

Creating a new folder

When you want to add a new folder to help manage your e-mail, follow these steps:

1. **Choose Create⇨Folder.**

   The Create Folder dialog box appears, as shown in Figure 5-2.

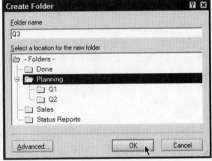

2. **Name your new folder by entering its name in the Folder Name field at the top of the Create Folder dialog box.**

3. **Click OK.**

If that seems easy, it's because, well, creating a folder *is* easy. As soon as you click OK, your new folder is visible in the Navigation pane — probably at the bottom of the list of folders.

You can also put folders inside other folders. If you want your new folder to be inside another folder, select the existing folder from the Create Folder dialog box. For example, in Figure 5-2, the new folder (Q3) will go inside the existing Planning folder.

Putting a document in a folder

To put a message (or a bunch of messages) in a folder, select the message(s) and choose Actions⇨Folder⇨Move to Folder. Select the folder name from the Move to Folder dialog box that appears and then click the Move button.

You can also drag and drop (use your mouse) to put a document into a folder: Just drag the message (or messages) from the View pane to the desired folder in the Navigation pane. You might have to drag the document to the Folder icon in the Navigation pane to expand it, and then continue dragging the document until you get to the folder that you want to put it in.

A cool e-mail filing timesaver is to set up a Rule so that incoming mail from a certain person or a particular subject is automatically added to a particular folder. Take a look at Chapter 7 if the idea of creating a Rule turns you on.

Deleting a folder

If you no longer need a certain folder that's in your mail, select the folder in the navigation pane and choose Actions➪Folder Options➪Delete Folder. Bye-bye!

A word to the wise: Check the contents of any folder first before making the commitment to delete. To open a folder, just click the folder that you want in the Navigation pane. You can also choose View➪Go To and choose the folder from the Go To dialog box that appears.

Deleting a folder doesn't delete the documents in that folder — you can always find the contents of a just-deleted folder in the All Documents folder.

Where the blazes did I put that?

Folders are a great way for you to make some sense of the piles and piles of e-mail that you receive every day, and folders will undoubtedly help you find a particular message when you need it. But what about when the boss calls and asks you to find that message that she sent you last month about one of your customers? You look in all the likely folders and don't find anything on that client, but you know that you *never* delete messages about clients.

Rest assured that if you didn't delete the message, it's still there — somewhere. Hunting down a particular message can be a chore unless you know who sent you the message. If you do, just switch to the folder that's most likely to contain the message that you're trying to find (use the All Documents folder if all else fails) and then click the little sort arrow in the Who column heading to rearrange the messages to sort and group them together by the name of the person who sent them. When you sort the folder based on the Who column, all the messages from each person are listed together, which makes it easier to find a document from a particular person. Use the arrow keys and Page Up and Page Down keys to move through the documents in the View pane.

After you sort a folder by name (sender/Who column), you can easily jump right to the messages from a particular person rather than having to scroll down through the alphabet. With the Message selector in the View pane, type the name of the person who you're looking for. Although at first it feels like you're typing into the wind, as soon as you start typing a name in the View pane, the Starts With dialog box appears, as shown in Figure 5-3. Enter the name that you're trying to find and click the Search button. Notes quickly takes you to the first message from that person.

Figure 5-3:
Quickly find messages from a particular sender.

You can also create a Full Text Index for your mail database so that you can search the contents (not just the names) of the documents very quickly. Read about this in Chapter 13.

All the News That's Fit to Print

You can print a single document, such as the one you happen to be looking at on your screen or the one currently highlighted in the View pane, or you can select a bunch of documents in a view and print them all.

If you want to print the document that's visible onscreen, choose File⇨Print, press Ctrl+P, or click the Print button on the Action bar. One way or the other, you get the Print View dialog box much like the one shown in Figure 5-4.

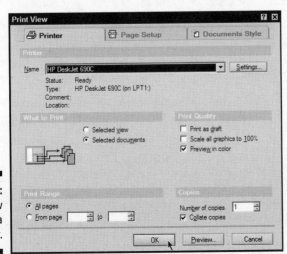

Figure 5-4:
Choose how to print a document.

Although the Print View dialog box has a seemingly endless set of options and questions, most often you'll just click OK and be done with it. You can optionally first click the Preview button to get an onscreen peek at how the document is going to look when printed.

Separating Multiple Printed Documents

To print more than one document, you also have to decide how Notes should separate one printed message from the next. Make your choices by using the selections from Documents Style tab of the Print View dialog box. Your choices for document separation are

- ✔ **Print Each Document on a New Page:** Each document starts on a new page.

- ✔ **Print Each Document as a Separate Print Job:** Each document is sent to the printer separately so that each starts at the top of a new page.

- ✔ **Print Continuously with One Blank Line between Documents:** Between each document, Notes prints a blank line to separate one from the next.

- ✔ **Print Continuously with No Blank Lines Between Documents:** Each document follows the one before it, with no separation.

If you select the Print Each Document on a New Page radio button, you may also decide how to number the pages, assuming that you *are* numbering the pages. (See Chapter 13 for more information about page numbering.) Select the Reset Page Number to 1 for Each Document, and the first page of each document you're printing will be numbered starting with the number 1. (Otherwise, the first page of each new document gets the next consecutive page number.) Check out Chapter 13 for more information about printing documents.

If you choose one of the options in the How To Print Each Document section, ain't nothin' gonna come outta that there printer until you click the Print View dialog box OK button.

Chapter 6

Making the Most of Your Messages

In This Chapter

▶ Including other information from other places in your messages

▶ Making and hiding and using sections

▶ Using custom forms

*I*n the age of power ties, power lunches, and power lifting, you won't be surprised to hear that you can also create power e-mail, too. (An admittedly corny name.) After you receive your tenth "You-bring-the-donuts-to-the-meeting" message, you might find yourself wondering, "There must be more to e-mail than this. And why is my belt so tight lately?"

Well, you can do *plenty* more with e-mail messages than just update your boss on how great you are or coordinate who's supplying the munchies. With your dazzling memos, you can be the talk of the office, a legend among your co-workers, and the pride of your hometown.

In this chapter, I walk you through the glory of using Lotus Notes 6 to craft killer messages by bulking them up with attachments and imported files. I also show you how to use sections and custom forms to become a Lotus legend in your own time.

Enclosed Please Find . . .

One fairly common reason for sending someone a message is to discuss or share some information you have — perhaps a new version of a contract or a pricing spreadsheet. For instance, say that you've been working on a Microsoft Word document for a new marketing campaign, and now it's time to show it to your co-workers to get their opinions. Or perhaps you found some interesting information on a Web page and you want to share a paragraph or two, or perhaps even a picture, with someone.

Retyping the entire report into a Notes e-mail message would be pretty counterproductive. Ick. Notes, being the high-tech marvel that it is, comes to the rescue. Read on to discover your Notes options for sharing information via e-mail.

Why, I oughta paste you

If you've spent any time copying and pasting in other programs, you're familiar with your computer's Clipboard. When you choose the Edit⇨Copy command, your computer temporarily puts whatever information you select onto the Clipboard so that you can paste it (Edit⇨Paste) into another place.

Using the Clipboard, through a little copying and pasting, is usually the simplest way to get information into an e-mail message from some place else.

Suppose that you're in the middle of preparing a Notes message and you've come to the part of it where you want to include a Microsoft Word document, such as a proposal. Here's the drill:

1. **Switch to the other program and open the document containing the selection that you want to copy and paste into your Notes message.**

2. **Select the portion that you want to copy and paste.**

3. **Choose Edit⇨Copy or press Ctrl+C to put the selected information onto the Clipboard.**

4. **Switch back to Notes.**

5. **Position the cursor (either with the cursor keys, or by clicking within the body of the message) so that it's where you want the information to appear.**

6. **Choose Edit⇨Paste or press Ctrl+V to insert whatever's on the Clipboard into your message.**

   Tah dah! Your Notes message should now contain whatever you copied and pasted.

Make sure you know where the cursor is before you complete your paste. You certainly don't want three paragraphs of your document or half of a Web page to end up in the To: field of your message.

One nice thing about pasting material into a message is that the person who gets your message doesn't have to have the original program in order to read it. So, for example, if you copy and paste a few paragraphs from Word, your message's recipient can see exactly what you pasted without having to install and run Word. Similarly, if you copy and paste information from the Web into an e-mail message, the person who reads it doesn't need to be connected to the Internet to see what you've sent.

Attaching attachments

Another way to send extra information in an e-mail message is by using an *attachment,* which can be any type of file, such as pictures, documents, Zip files, Microsoft Excel workbooks, and on so on. When you attach a file, you're attaching a copy of the file, so the original isn't affected. Using an attachment is just an easy way to send an entire file (or files, for that matter) along with an e-mail message.

See Figure 6-1 to see an e-mail message that includes a file attachment. A keen observer (pay attention!) will notice that the attachment takes the form of an icon. Also, that icon (usually) tells your recipient what program that you used to create the file that you've sent to them. For example, a Word document attachment shows up as a page with the traditional big blue W imposed on top of it.

Feel free to attach virtually any type of file to an e-mail message (or any Notes document, for that matter). You can send along word-processed documents, Excel worksheets, Zip files, pictures, PowerPoint slides, you name it.

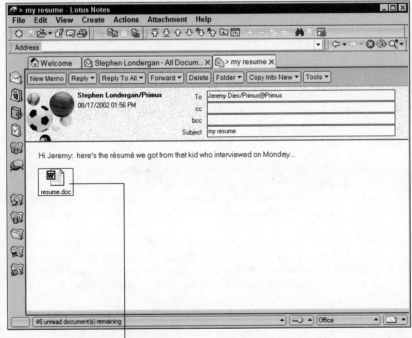

Figure 6-1:
You can attach almost any type of file to a Lotus Notes message.

A Word document attached

To attach a file, put the cursor where you want to place the attachment and then select File⇨Attach or click the File Attach button (with the paper clip icon) that's located in the Action bar. The Create Attachment(s) dialog box in Figure 6-2 appears.

Figure 6-2:
Use the
Create
Attach-
ment(s)
dialog bog
to select the
file(s) you
want sent
with your
message.

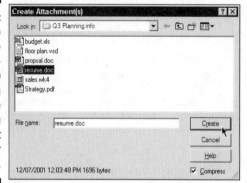

Drill down through the folder structure in this dialog box to find the file that you want to attach. Look in the File Name box to make sure that you've selected the file that you want. Then press the Enter key on your keyboard or click the Create button in the Create Attachment(s) dialog box.

You can attach more than one file at once if the files are in the same directory. Select the first file and then hold down the Ctrl key while you select the other files that you want to attach. To select several consecutive files, highlight the first one (click it) and then press the Shift key when you click on the last one; Notes selects all the files in between.

After you make your attachment selection (by pressing Enter or clicking the dialog box's Create button), Notes inserts an icon in your message wherever your cursor is to represent the file that you just attached. You can insert an attachment anywhere in the body of an e-mail message. (Actually, you can insert an attachment in any Notes document, in any rich text field.)

You can also attach files to e-mail messages and other documents by using the standard drag-and-drop method. Just find the file that you want to attach and use the mouse to drag it (from wherever you found it) into the body of the message. (You'll most likely have to play around with the size of the Notes window and/or your desktop to do this.)

Don't let your attaching prowess be your undoing, though. The more files that you attach, the bigger the e-mail message is and the more disk space that it takes up. Be kind, especially if you think that some of your recipients use a modem to get their e-mail. That file that takes 90 seconds to attach when you're at the office (and connected to the network) may take 90 minutes to download if your recipients have to dial in to get their mail.

Okay 1 Got 1t . . . Now What Do 1 Do with 1t?

Imagine getting a memo with an attachment — and nothing else. What is it? What program did it come from? What are you supposed to do with it? Sensible questions all, and ones that you should answer for the recipient when you send an attachment with your message. Don't leave the person guessing.

When you receive a message with an attachment, of course you want to be able to view it. Maybe your missive is to edit it. Perhaps the attachment is such a gem that you want to file it and save it or print out a copy for yourself. Then again, you might opt to delete it because you're such a disk-space-conscious kind of person.

You must have the program in which an attachment was created on your computer in order to be able to open it. For example, you must have Excel installed to open an Excel spreadsheet that someone sends you. If you don't have the program, however, all is not lost: You can always view it instead of actually opening it. I cover that more in the next section, "Viewing an attachment."

To open an attachment, first open the message containing it. Double-click the attachment icon, and an Attachment infobox appears, like the one in Figure 6-3. Under Attachment Actions are several options: View, Open, Edit, Save, and Remove. Click which button fits your desire. Read more about each of these options in the upcoming sections of this chapter.

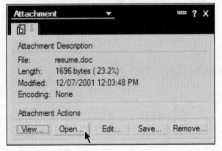

Figure 6-3: Dealing with an attachment.

Viewing an attachment

The simplest thing that you do with an attachment is view it. When you click the View button, Notes shows you as much of the file as it can through the File Viewer. Figure 6-4 shows a small Excel spreadsheet attachment that's being viewed. You can view files from most popular computer programs.

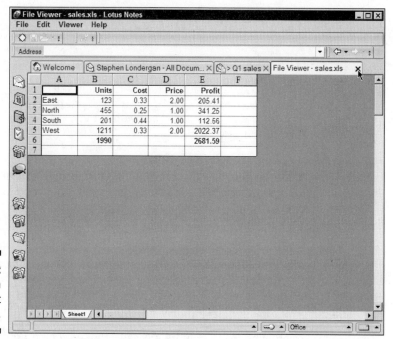

Figure 6-4:
Viewing an
attachment
is simple.

To view an attachment (as opposed to opening it), you don't need to have the computer program that was used to create the attachment.

Choose File⇨Close or click the X in the window's task button to close the File Viewer and return to the document that you were reading in the first place. (Careful which X you click: Don't close the Notes window by mistake!)

Opening an attachment

If you choose Open rather than View from the Attachment infobox, Notes starts the program that was used to create the attachment and automatically opens the file in that program.

In Notes 6, you *open* an attachment, whereas in previous versions, you *launched* it. Easier to remember, wouldn't you agree?

To open an attached file, you must have that file's program installed on your hard drive. If you don't have the program, you have to rely on the File Viewer to see what's in the file. To avoid this potential problem, skip down to the upcoming section "Importing Files."

Editing an attachment

Use the Edit button when you want to change the contents of the attachment and then have those changes stored right in your message. When you click the Edit button of the Attachments infobox, you're whisked away to whatever program was used to create the attachment you plan to edit. The cool part is that when you use that other program to save your work, the file is saved right into Notes. Needless to say, you have to have the program that was used to create the file if you want to edit it.

If someone sends you a file that you intend to edit and return (or if you intend to edit the file and then send it to someone else), be careful: You should *not* edit the attachment in the message that you received. Rather, use the Forward button to start a new mail message and then double-click that attachment to open it to do your editing.

Saving an attachment

You may want to save an attachment for many reasons, including the following:

- ✔ You want to use the file.
- ✔ You don't have the software required to open the file right away.
- ✔ You want to put the file on a disk or a CD to take to another computer.

When you click the Save button from the Attachment infobox, you get the Save Attachment dialog box, as shown in Figure 6-5. Use this dialog box to tell Notes where on your hard drive that you want to save the file and what you want to name it.

A jargon update for you wily Notes veterans: In Notes 6, you *Save* an attachment, as opposed to Notes R5, when you would *Detach* an attachment.

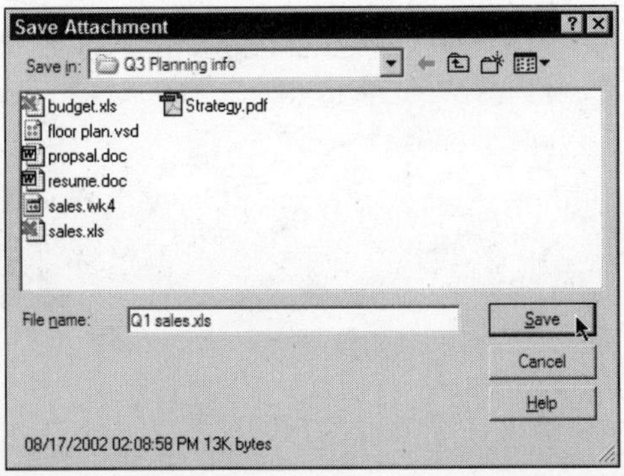

Figure 6-5:
Save an attachment where you want it.

Notes (Windows, actually) relies on a file's *extension* (those three characters after the period, such as .doc or .xls) to know what kind of file it is, so don't change the file's extension.

Note that when you save an attachment, a copy of the file is saved to a disk or your hard drive but the attachment also lives on, remaining attached to the memo in your e-mail.

Printing an attachment

If possible, don't print from the Viewer. Instead, print files from the application that was used to create it by opening the file and then printing the document as you normally would in that application. Printing files from the Lotus Notes Viewer may give you unexpected results, but if you insist, choose File➪Print to do so.

Removing an attachment

Sometimes you receive a message from someone that includes an attachment that you don't need. You can remove the attachment to save space without deleting the message itself. This is a new feature in Notes 6. To do so, just click the Remove button in the Attachment info box.

Removing attachments that you don't need is the best way to speed up your mail, make your e-mail file smaller, and expedite replication. It also makes it a lot faster and easier for the recipient, who may be working through a slow-downloading modem, to open your message!

Importing Files

Another way to include content to a message is to import a file. If you want the recipients of your message to be able see the contents of a file right when they open your message, import a file instead of attaching a file. *Importing* converts a file that was created in another program into a format that's readable in a Notes document.

Files that you import have to be some sort of data file, with real words or numbers or graphics that people can look at. You can't, for example, import executable files (files ending with the .exe extension) because they're program files, not data files.

To import a file, place the cursor where you want it to appear in your message and then choose File⇨Import. The Import dialog box appears, as shown in Figure 6-6.

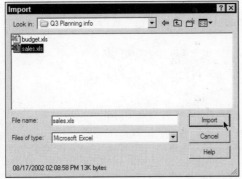

Figure 6-6:
Importing a
file makes
viewing
easy.

Drill through the Look In box to find the file that you want to import. Then, in the Files of Type list box, select a file type (in Figure 6-6, I select Microsoft Excel, which bear an .xls extension). Click the file (highlight it) that you want to import, click the Import button, and as quickly as your hard drive can spin, you have the contents of that file in your Notes message.

Deciding Whether to Paste or Attach or Import

Feeling a bit confused? Don't know whether to add message information by using the Clipboard (pasting) or by attaching or by importing? Use the following list to help clear up your confusion.

✔ **Pasting (using the Clipboard)**

- When you want to put only part of a file in a Notes document.

- When the recipient doesn't have the software necessary to open the file.

- When the recipient of your message doesn't use Notes.

✔ **Attaching**

- When the file can't be imported, such as an executable (.exe) file.

- When you want the recipient to have an actual copy of the file to keep for his very own.

✔ **Importing**

- When you aren't sure whether the recipients have the software necessary to open the file you want them to see, and you can't use the Clipboard.

- When you need to include a file that's too large for the Clipboard, and you know that your message's recipient doesn't use Notes.

Find out more about importing and exporting files in Chapter 17.

Creating Sections

Nothing's worse than receiving (or sending, for that matter) an e-mail that's too long. In this age of information overload, how many times have you been forced to wade through pages and pages of text, only to find that about half of it is irrelevant?

None of that in Notes! By using a *section*, you make your messages easier to read. Sections enable you to make parts of your document *collapsible;* that is, your readers don't have to read or view a particular part if they don't want to.

Don't underestimate the power of readability. If you routinely send messages that are too long or too boring or have ugly fonts and colors, people won't read them. Some companies even offer classes in how to create interesting and readable e-mail.

To create a section, select the paragraph(s) that you want to be able to hide and then choose Create⇨Section. Faster than a New York minute, the paragraph disappears, and you see only the first line of the paragraph, as shown in Figure 6-7.

Notice the little triangle to the left of the first line of each paragraph? That triangle (also known as a twisty) is the reader's cue that more is here than meets the eye. When you click the triangle, the section expands to display all the text; when you click it again, the section collapses and hides the words again.

Consider adding a title to your hidden section to make your document even more readable. Just type a heading before the section that you want to hide and then highlight both before choosing Create⇨Section.

That's it! Easy to make and use, sections are invaluable for keeping messages readable and concise. Use the Section command whenever you want to make your documents more reader friendly. And remember that you can create a section in any Notes document, not just in your e-mail!

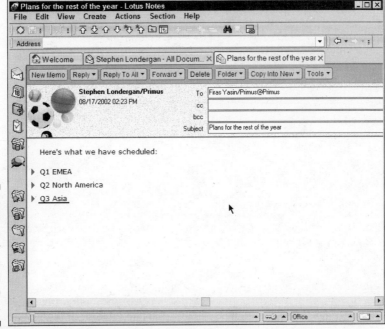

Mail Is More Than Just Messages

Most of the time when you use your e-mail database, you use the Create menu to write a message. In some organizations, however, perhaps someone behind the scenes created special forms for everyone to use. For instance, suppose that you need to order some staples. Or perhaps you need to reserve the conference room for your Monday morning poker game. Some genius may have already created a Staple Order Form or a Conference Room Reservation Form. Your company may also have forms for special announcements, special requests, status reports, or information sheets.

Choose Create➪Other, and Notes presents you with a list of the custom forms that you can use for special occasions. The forms may even be addressed so that you don't have to run around trying to find out who's in charge of ordering staples or reserving conference rooms or scheduling vacations.

Chapter 7

Mastering Your Mail

. . . .

In This Chapter

▶ Sending mail to people who don't use Notes

▶ Customizing your Inbox view

▶ Making Notes follow your rules

▶ Going on vacation

▶ Creating reusable stationery

▶ Using some special delivery options

. . . .

*L*ook at you! How you've grown! Why, it seems like it was only yesterday that you just discovered how to create a message and use the Trash, and now here you are! In this chapter, I present some pretty advanced mail options, including how to customize your Inbox view, set rules for Notes to follow, create an Out of Office message, and craft stationery. You might never need to use any of these Lotus Notes 6 features, but if you have the time to read about them, I have the time to explain them.

You Know, Not Everyone Uses Notes

As much as IBM hates to hear it, not every person who uses e-mail uses Notes, so the chances are pretty strong that you'll need to exchange e-mail with someone who uses a different e-mail program. Maybe it's someone in a different part or division of your company, or perhaps it's someone (like a customer) who works at a different company altogether.

Suppose that you want to send a message to your buddy who uses a different mail system. Addressing the message is easy: If he tells that you his e-mail address is `jim.murphy@principlesoftware.com`, you just enter exactly that in any of the address fields (To, cc, bcc) of your message.

Take a look at Chapter 11 to learn a cool way to *not* have to remember e-mail addresses.

To be able to send e-mail to someone on the Internet, your company has to have its mail system connected to the Internet. In this day and age that's a pretty safe bet, but check with your administrator if you're not sure.

Of course, one of the things that you take for granted with Notes e-mail is that it's pretty; you may already know that you can use different fonts and colors and even include pictures, tables, and such in the body of a message.

But here's the rub: When you send a message to someone who doesn't use Notes — especially someone with one of those .com e-mail addresses — there's a pretty good chance that your pretty fonts and colors and pictures and tables will be lost in the translation. Rest assured, though, that the person will get your message okay and be able to read it. The message just won't be all *purty*.

You can, however, get most of the formatting work that you do in Notes to carry through so that the person who receives your pretty message does see the fonts and colors. It's a little work, though, so you have to make this decision: whether or not to bother. If you're happy just sending the text of the message and you don't tend to use different fonts and colors anyway, you can stop right here. If, on the other hand, you want your e-mail to include fonts and colors, you need to know about. . . .

HTML mail

Perhaps you already know that HyperText Markup Language (HTML) has become the vernacular of the Internet. That is, HTML is a kind of programming language that people use to create Web pages. They use HTML so that they can be certain that their Web pages will look the same regardless of the type of computer, operating system, or Web browser being used.

The point — and there is a point to all this — is that you can use HTML to encode your e-mail messages, too. That way, the person on the other end gets to see your message's pretty fonts and colors, any pictures that you include in the body of the message, and so on. Before I show you how to turn on the capability to encode your mail with HTML, I must mention one small issue: Not all mail programs can understand HTML mail. Fortunately, most do.

Now you have to decide how you want your mail sent through the Internet. You set this choice from the Internet tab on the User Preferences dialog box (choose File⇨Preferences⇨User Preferences). You can read more about this dialog box in the upcoming section "Choosing your Internet mail format."

You can choose from the following:

- ✔ **HTML Only:** Your message is automatically coded in HTML. You're assuming that your recipient uses an e-mail program that understands HTML, and your message arrives with special fonts and colors intact.

- ✔ **Plain Text Only:** Your message is sent in plain American Standard Cord for Information Interchange (ASCII) text. You're assuming that your recipient can use any e-mail program to read e-mail and that your message arrives without any special fonts or colors or embedded pictures.

- ✔ **HTML and Plain Text:** Your message is sent in two formats. You're not sure whether your recipient can read HTML-based mail, so Notes prepares and sends the person two versions of your message: one with a pretty, HTML-ized version and the other with just the plain text version. That way, if the recipient uses a mail program that can handle the HTML, your pretty message appears. But if the recipient's mail program can't handle HTML, your message can still be read.

- ✔ **Prompt When Sending:** Lets you decide for each message you send which format to use.

If you choose the HTML and Plain Text method of sending mail, your recipients will get two versions of the message, but fortunately they never see two messages in their inbox. Their mail program sorts out which to use, and they'll see only that one.

Choosing your Internet mail format

To tell Notes how you prefer to have Internet mail encoded, choose File➪ Preferences➪User Preferences, and then click the Internet tab under Mail. As you can see in Figure 7-1, you can choose one of four settings in the Internet Mail Format field: HTML Only, Plain Text Only, HTML and Plain Text, and Prompt when Sending. You can read in detail about these choices in the preceding section.

If you choose one of the first three selections in the Internet Mail Format field, you tell Notes that you want all your outgoing Internet-based mail to be prepared that way. If, on the other hand, you choose the last option — Prompt When Sending — you tell Notes that you would prefer to be asked how the message should be formatted each and every time that you send an Internet message.

Click OK in the User Preferences dialog box when you're finished with this selection.

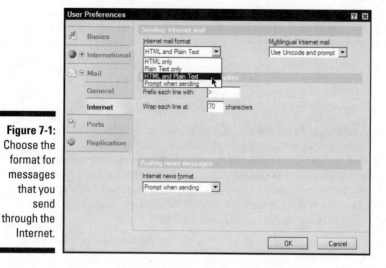

Figure 7-1:
Choose the
format for
messages
that you
send
through the
Internet.

Choosing the encoding message for an individual message

If you use the User Preferences dialog box to set the Internet Mail Format field to Prompt When Sending, prepare yourself for the Internet Mail Format dialog box that's shown in Figure 7-2.

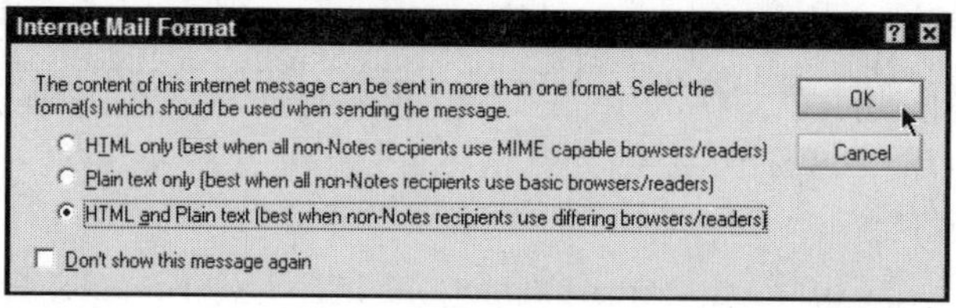

Figure 7-2:
Choose a
format for
an individual
message.

This dialog box appears when you click the Send button for a new message. As you can see in the figure, you can select one of the three options that will be used as the encoding method *for that message only*. Select one of the three radio buttons that appears here: HTML Only, Plain Text Only, or HTML and Plain Text. In other words, you'll be asked again — and you get to choose again — each time that you send a message . . . unless, of course, you select the Don't Show This Message Again check box.

Customizing Your Inbox

Your Inbox default settings are supposed to be easy to use, so you may not feel the need to change them at all. If, however, you're one of those people who just has to have things your own way, read on to see how you can make the appearance of your Notes Inbox meet your own particular (and, no doubt, quite discriminating) tastes.

Sorting the columns

You can sort the messages in your Inbox (or any folder for that matter) very easily. Any time that you see a column heading with an arrow next to it, you can click the column heading to sort (or re-sort) the messages based on that column. For example, you can easily have messages re-ordered based on the name of the person who sent the message, the message's subject, or its size.

Choosing the columns in a View

A new feature in Notes 6 is the ability to easily reorder the columns and select which (and how) appear in a view. In the old days (before Notes 6, in other words), your mail always presented the person's name in the first column, always had the message's date in the second column, and so on. Well, no more! If you absolutely have to have a folder displayed with, say, the dates in the first column, that's easy to do. Or you can choose exactly which message columns appear in a folder. You might decide, for example, that you want to save a little space and not have Notes show you each message's size.

To choose which columns appear in your Inbox (or any other folder, for that matter), open the folder in question and then choose View➪Customize This View.

As you can see in Figure 7-3, you use the Customize View dialog box to select each column in the folder and then make decisions about whether it appears, how wide the column is, and so on.

To hide a column (like the Size column shown in the upcoming Figure 7-4), select the column name in the Columns to Display list and then clear the check box in the Visible column to deselect it.

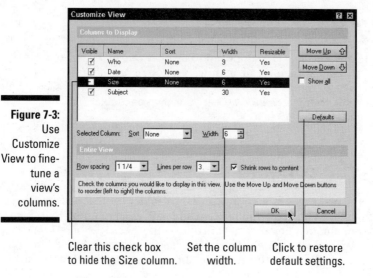

Figure 7-3:
Use
Customize
View to fine-
tune a
view's
columns.

Clear this check box   Set the column   Click to restore
to hide the Size column.   width.   default settings.

In the Customize View dialog box, you can also

✔ Set a column's width as well as decide how many rows are used to separate one document from the next.

✔ Use the Move Up and Move Down buttons if you want to make a particular column appear before the others. In fact, those buttons should be called Move Left and Move Right, since that's what you're doing.

✔ Decide how much space separates each row (a message, in your Inbox) from one another with the Row Spacing list box.

✔ Control how much space each row (message, in your Inbox) will take up with the Lines Per Row list box. Use this field if you have messages with long subjects that are getting cut off. Also, use the Shrink Rows to Content check box if you only want Notes to use the Lines per Row setting when it needs to. Not all messages will take up, say, three rows, for example.

Click OK when you're finished.

You should feel a little adventurous: Even if you make a disastrous choice and, say, hide all of the columns by mistake, you can always return to this dialog box and put things back the way they were (by clicking the Defaults button).

Just click and drag the whole column (grab it by the column heading) to its new location if you don't want to use the aforementioned dialog box.

Special colors for certain people

Another new feature on Notes 6 enables you to have messages from certain people highlighted in a special color. For example, you may want to color-code all messages from your boss a lovely pinkish hue, or perhaps mail from your CEO should always be green. That way, you know which messages in your Inbox carry special significance, or should be replied to before others. Although color doesn't appear too well in this book's black-and-white figures, trust me: Figure 7-4 shows all the messages from Bethann Cregg in a special color, and the messages from Bernd Wagner in a different color.

To decide which people get this special treatment, open your Inbox and then choose Actions➪Tools➪Preferences. Click the Colors tab (as shown in Figure 7-5) in the Preferences dialog box that appears. Enter their names in the Sender Names fields on the left side of this tab, and then use the drop-down color lists on the right to determine which colors will be used for messages from each. When you've made your choices, click OK.

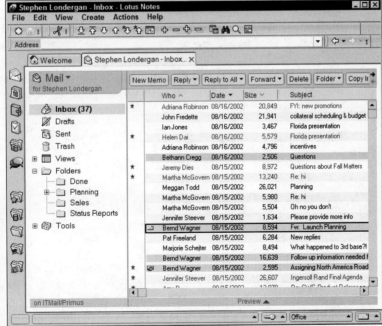

Figure 7-4: Highlight messages from special people in special colors.

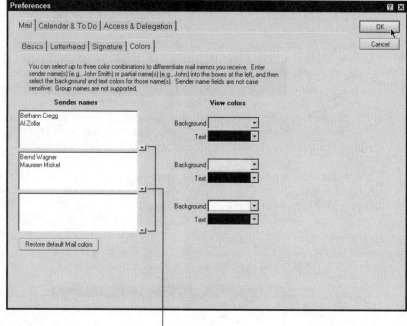

Figure 7-5:
Match
special
people with
their special
colors.

Click to choose names from a directory.

Click the little triangles next to each of the three fields to choose names from the directory (instead of typing the name and risking a spelling error).

Just click the Restore Default Mail Colors button to undo some less-than-perfect color combination choices.

Showing only certain documents

Finally, you have two menu choices that you can also use to limit what appears in your Inbox.

Why bother? Simple. The more messages that you send, the more that you receive. And even if you are pretty conscientious about using folders to file messages, you'll probably still end up with an Inbox that's fairly full. And the fuller your Inbox is, the harder it is to find one certain message or print just a few.

One way to separate at least some of the wheat from the chaff is to use View⇨Show⇨Unread Only, which does exactly what it sounds like it does. Specifically, it changes the folder that you're in so that only the documents that you haven't read yet show up. Use the exact same menu choice to switch back to the original all-encompassing, you-can-see-everything view.

Another way to limit what's in your Inbox (or any other folder) is to select the documents in question and then choose View⇨Show⇨Selected Only. This is useful whenever you want to do something to a bunch of documents that you've selected, such as print, forward, delete, or copy them. You could do that anyway without changing the Inbox to display only selected documents, or course, but sometimes changing the folder to only show you the documents that you've selected makes things easier.

A new feature in Notes 6 that's quite handy in certain situations is a new menu that you can use to select a bunch of documents and then copy them for inclusion in a table. Anyone who has ever tried to create a message that summarizes a Notes database will love this new feature.

First, select the documents in question and then choose Edit⇨Copy Selected as Table. Although nothing immediately seems to happen, what you've actually done is put a snapshot of those selected documents on your computer's Clipboard. When you then paste (Edit⇨Paste) them somewhere, you get what you see in Figure 7-6: a table describing each of the documents as well as a DocLink (discussed in Chapter 16) to the document in question. Cool!

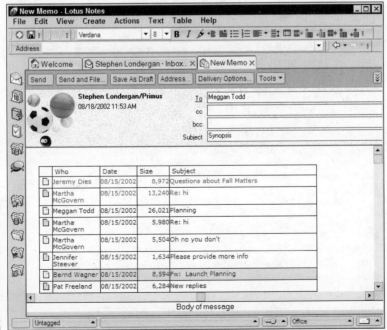

Figure 7-6: Copy and paste a summary of documents from a view into a table.

Following My Rules

Momma told you that you should always follow the rules, right? On the other hand, Katharine Hepburn was once quoted as saying, "If you obey all the rules, you miss all the fun." Be that as it may, *rules,* as far as Notes is concerned, are a way to have Notes help manage your mail.

For the sake of argument, suppose that you get a regular sales update e-mail every Thursday. And for reasons known only to yourself, you always save these sales updates in a folder called (you guessed it) *Sales Updates*.

Or perhaps you use e-mail to communicate with customers, and consequently want to have Notes help you select and manage the message from them.

By using a rule, you can make it all happen automagically. A *rule* tells Notes what to do with certain incoming messages. For example, you could have a rule that always puts messages with a certain word in the subject field in a certain folder, or a rule that moves e-mail from a certain person directly into the Trash folder, or perhaps a rule that instantly changes the importance of any message that you receive from your boss to High. In Figure 7-7, you can see the Rules view in a mail database. As you can see in the figure, you can have more than one rule. See your rules by clicking the word Rules in the Navigation pane.

Click to create a new rule.

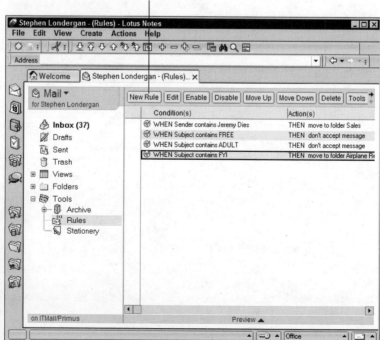

Figure 7-7:
Use Rules
to help
manage
your mail,
automati-
cally.

Creating a rule

To create a new rule, first click the Rules folder in the Navigation pane of your mail. Then click the Action bar's New Rule button (refer to Figure 7-7). Figure 7-8 shows the (rather large) New Rule dialog box that appears.

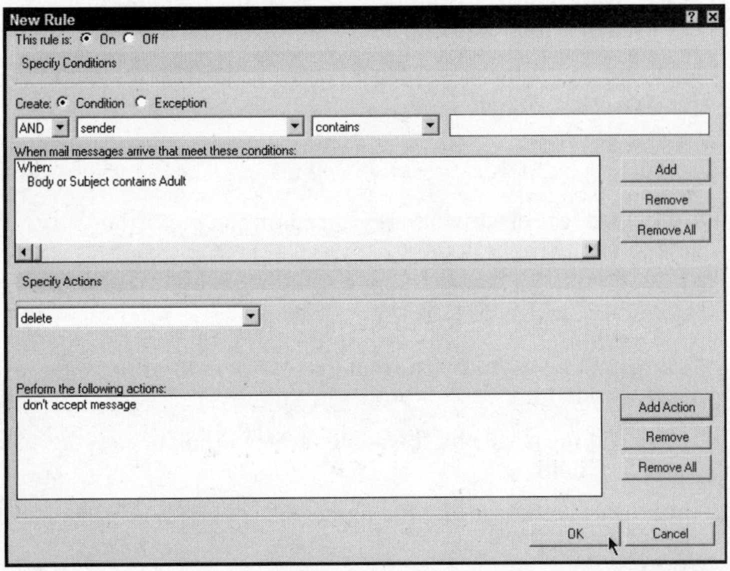

Figure 7-8:
Create a
new rule
here.

As you can see from Figure 7-8, the New Rule dialog box is divided into three sections. This Rule Is determines whether the rule is enabled, Specify Conditions decides on which messages the rule will act, and Specify Actions determines what the rule will do with the messages it chooses.

Any new rule you create is enabled, by default. You might, however, have a rule that you want to temporarily disable; for example, perhaps you don't want incoming mail messages dispatched to that folder, for the time being. At the very top of the dialog box, use the This Rule Is radio buttons to decide whether the rule is being enforced. Select the On radio button in the field (the default), and the rule does whatever you told it to do. On the other hand, if you select the Off radio button, your rule is suspended until you activate it again.

Creating a rule's condition

The fields in the Specify Conditions section of the New Rule dialog box determine the messages to which your rule will apply. The basic idea is to use these fields to set up a criterion and then to use the Add button to save the condition. Some rules may have only one condition, such as *Subject contains Adult*. Others may be more complicated, with more than one condition. For example, you could have a rule that looked for incoming message with the words *Sales Updates* in the subject line that were sent by a guy named *Rob Fichtel.*

When you define the second drop-down field in the Specify Conditions section of the dialog box, you can choose from 13 different places to look:

- ✔ **sender:** Choose messages by the name of the person who sent the message. You could, for example, create a rule that automatically looks for messages from your boss.

- ✔ **subject:** Select messages based on what's in the subject of the message, such as *Sales Update.*

- ✔ **body:** Find messages with a certain word or phrase anywhere in the body of the message.

- ✔ **importance:** Select messages based on the importance that the sender chose for it (High/Medium/Low).

- ✔ **delivery priority:** Select messages based on the delivery priority that the author assigned to the message.

- ✔ **to:** Select messages by the name of the person or persons in the message's To field.

- ✔ **cc:** Select messages by the name of the person or persons in the message's cc field.

- ✔ **bcc:** Select messages by the name of the person or persons in the message's bcc field.

- ✔ **to or cc:** Select messages by the name of the person or persons in the message's To or cc field.

- ✔ **body or subject:** Enter a criteria that Notes will look for in both the subject and body of messages.

- ✔ **Internet domain:** Specify messages from a particular company, such as `ibm.com` or `yourcustomerscompany.com`.

- ✔ **size:** Specify messages of a particular size.

- ✔ **all documents:** Apply your rule to all new messages.

After you tell Notes where to look, you use the third drop-down field in the Specify Conditions section of the dialog box to tell Notes what kind of comparison that you're interested in:

- ✔ **contains:** The term that you enter in the third field can occur anywhere in the field that you select in the first field.

- ✔ **does not contain:** Whatever you chose in the first field can't include what you enter in the third field.

✔ **is:** Whatever you chose in the first field must be exactly equal to what you enter in the third field.

✔ **is not:** Whatever you chose in the first field can't be what you enter in the third field.

Finally, use the third field in the Specify Conditions section to tell Notes what you're looking for. Just type the search term — a person's name, the word that you want to find in the message body, the Internet domain name, and so on — in the third field.

After you define the three parts of the condition, click the Add button to save the condition. If you change your mind after saving a condition, you can use the Remove and Remove All buttons to edit any mistakes. You have to select the condition in the When Mail Messages Arrive that Meet These Conditions field and click the Remove button to remove it.

Sometimes you might want a rule with more than one condition. Maybe the rule is intended to find messages that are from a certain customer and that also have the words *new order* in their subject line. A rule can have as many conditions as you want; just keep using that Add button if you need more than one.

When you specify multiple conditions for a rule, you might want to tell Notes to act only if *every* criterion is met. Other times, you may want Notes to act if *any* of the specified criteria is met. For example, in Figure 7-8, Notes is set up to delete every message whose body or subject contains the word *Adult*. The word *Adult* doesn't have to appear in both places to activate the rule. If you prefer, you can set up Notes so that the word *Adult* must appear in the body *and* subject in order to activate the rule. You control this feature by selecting AND or OR in the first drop-down field. This drop-down field appears only after you've clicked Add to add at least one condition to your rule.

Defining a rule's action

After you tell Notes on which messages a rule will act, use the Specify Actions section of the dialog box to determine what Notes will do with those messages. This is the part of the dialog box where you tell Notes that you want these certain messages to be moved to a certain folder, deleted, and so on.

This section of the dialog box has two fields. The first — a drop-down list — tells Notes what you want to do to these messages. The second field tells Notes where to put them.

In the first field, you can choose from six things with a message that meets the condition(s) that you established at the top of the New Rule dialog box:

✔ **move to folder:** Tell Notes to move the matching messages to a certain folder, the name of which you enter in the second field or use the Select button to choose, both of which appear when you select this option.

- ✔ **copy to folder:** Tell Notes to move the matching messages to a certain folder, the name of which you enter in the second field or use the Select button to choose, both of which appear when you select this option. This differs from moving to a folder in that the message remains in your Inbox.

- ✔ **send copy to:** Automatically forward the message to someone else.

- ✔ **set expire date:** Mark the date on which the message will expire.

- ✔ **change importance to:** Mark the message's importance as High, Medium, or Low — regardless of how the sender set the message's importance.

- ✔ **delete:** Remove the message.

After you use this drop-down list to decide what's going to happen to the messages, use the field to its right to enter the name of the folder, or the name of the person the message will be forwarded to, and so on. The field to the right appears or doesn't depending on what you've selected in the drop-down list.

After you define the rule's condition and action, click the OK button at the bottom of the New Rule dialog box to save it. Your new rule will appear in the Rules view in your mail.

Like with conditions, a rule may have more than one action. For example, you may set up a rule that looks for messages from a certain customer and then automatically forwards that message to your assistant after also filing the message in a special folder.

Managing rules

The Rules view in your mail lists, in order, all the rules that you define (refer to Figure 7-7 for an example). You could have a few rules that both select the same message — maybe one does something with mail from stevo@beld.net, and the other does something to all messages from the Internet domain beld. net. Use the Action bar Move Up and Move Down buttons to determine which rule gets first crack at incoming mail. In other words, if there's one rule that should always get the first shot at a new, incoming message, you would select it and then click the Move Up button in the Action bar to make it first.

To change a rule, click the Action bar Edit button to access the Edit Rule dialog box. From here, you can change any or all conditions that you set earlier. If you need to delete the rule's condition or action, access the Delete Rule dialog box by clicking the Delete button in the Action bar.

A new rule applies to messages that arrive *after* you create the rule; it won't do anything to the mail that you already have.

I Need a Vacation

You work hard and you certainly deserve a break. A week of fun and sun? Heading to Jamaica or the Bahamas? Great! Be sure to change the message on your office answering machine so that callers know that you're away from the office. You have to keep up your reputation for responsiveness, after all.

And while you're at it, set up your e-mail so that Notes automatically replies to any mail that you get while you're on the beach.

Okay, not everyone gets to go on vacation. You can still fantasize, can't you? You can use this feature whenever you're away from your e-mail — even if it's just a (boring) two-day business trip during which you won't be able to read (and, more important, reply to) your mail.

1. **Open your mail.**

2. **Click the Tools button on the Action bar.**

3. **From the drop-down menu that appears, select Out of Office.**

   Up pops the Out of Office dialog box, as displayed in Figure 7-9, with which you can tell Notes how you want to handle your mail while you're away.

4. **In the Leaving and Returning fields of the Dates tab, enter the dates when you'll be gone.**

   Notes automatically replies to any mail that you receive during this period. You can also select the Book Busytime for These Dates check box so that anyone who checks your calendar will also know that you're unavailable.

5. **Fill out the fields on the Out of Office Message, Special Message, and Exceptions tabs.**

   (See the rest of this section for all that this step entails.)

6. **Click the OK button.**

Entering your profile involves answering three questions on the other three tabs of the Out of Office dialog box:

- What reply should automatically be sent, in your absence, to most people?

- Which reply will automatically be sent, in your absence, to some special people?

- Which people shouldn't get one of these automatic replies at all?

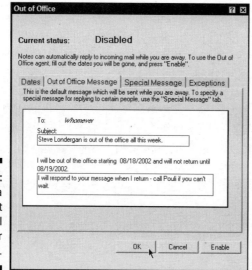

Figure 7-9:
Notes can automatically reply to mail you receive while you're away.

On the Out of Office Message tab, type the subject and body of the message that you want Notes to automatically send to the majority of the messages that you receive. Figure 7-10 shows a sample response, but feel free to say anything you want.

It's a good idea to edit the message field to include the dates when you'll be gone so that your colleagues have some idea of when they might get a real answer from you.

Figure 7-10:
Create a reply that Notes will send in your absence.

You might decide to send a different, special reply to certain people. Maybe you want a unique message for your boss or your co-workers? Enter the names of these special people on the Special Message tab of the out of Office dialog box.

To choose people and group names on the Special Message tab, click the arrow next to the To field. The Names dialog box appears with your Personal Address book, from which you can choose these special recipients.

Some messages might not deserve any response; use the Exceptions tab to tell Notes who doesn't get an automatic reply while you're away. As you can see in Figure 7-11, you can tell Notes to pretty much ignore messages from the Internet, or from a certain person, or addressed to certain groups, or containing a certain word or phrase in their subject.

Figure 7-11:
Not *every*
message
you receive
has to
prompt an
automatic
reply.

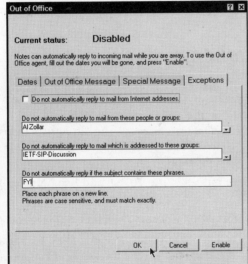

If you subscribe to any Internet-based mailing lists, be sure to include those names on the Exceptions tab. If you don't, every message that you receive from the mailing list triggers one of your automatic responses, which might very well end up being sent to the whole list, over and over again.

When you finish entering your profile, click the Enable/Disable button on the Action bar. Select the name of your home Domino server from the Server Name dialog box.

Don't forget to turn off your automatic replies after you return from your little vacation. When you're back at the office and ready to start replying to e-mail yourself, return to the Out of Office dialog box and click the Disable button so that Notes stops sending messages for you.

Reusing the Same Memo

If you find yourself regularly sending essentially the same memo to essentially the same people containing essentially the same information, you may want to consider using *stationery*. Then, next week, when the time comes to send your regular message again, you won't need to create a new message from scratch. Instead, you edit the stationery, which has the names, subject, and so on already filled in. And the week after that, you do the same thing. And the week after that, and the week after that. . . .

Creating stationery

Creating stationery is really just a matter of starting a new message, filling out the address fields (To, cc, bcc) and the Subject field, typing the part of the message that's going to be the same each time that you send it, and then saving the document in a special way. Here are the nitty-gritty steps:

1. **Start by creating a new message.**

2. **Enter the appropriate names in the To, cc, and bcc fields and a topic in the Subject field.**

   Don't worry if this information will vary from time to time. You can change these fields each time that you use this stationery to send a message.

3. **In the Body field of the stationery, type the parts of the message that you want to send each week.**

4. **When you're finished, choose File➪Tools➪Save as Stationery.**

5. **Enter a name for your stationery document in the text field of the Save as Stationery dialog box and then click OK.**

Don't get confused by the message that you use to create stationery. Despite all appearances to the contrary, you're not entering the text of a real message. Rather, you're entering the parts of the message that you'll be sending on a regular basis *later*. In fact, you probably won't even bother saving the message itself.

Using stationery

When the time comes to send an e-mail based on your stationery, open your mail and click the Action bar Tool button. From the drop-down menu that appears, click the New Memo - Using Stationery button. The Select Stationery dialog box appears, shown in Figure 7-12.

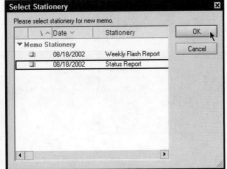

Figure 7-12: Select stationery that you create.

Choose from your creations in the Select Stationery dialog box to select the stationery that you want to use. Then add whatever you want to the To, cc, bcc, and Subject fields as well as to the body of the message. When you send the message, Notes saves a *new* document in your mail database and leaves the stationery document just the way it was when you started — so you can use it again next time.

You can also see and manage the stationery that you create (if you've created any) by using the Stationery folder in your mail.

Special Options for a Message

In Chapter 4, I discuss such delivery options as importance, Mood Stamps, delivery reports, and delivery priority. You can find even more advanced options on the Advanced tab of the Delivery Options dialog box (see Figure 7-13). When composing a message, access this box by clicking the Delivery Options button in the Action bar, and then clicking its Advanced tab.

If you need a response by a particular date, use the Stamp Message with a 'Please Reply by' Date field to warn your recipient. The date that you enter in this field appears at the top of your e-mail, and the message that you send is also placed in the recipient's To Do view.

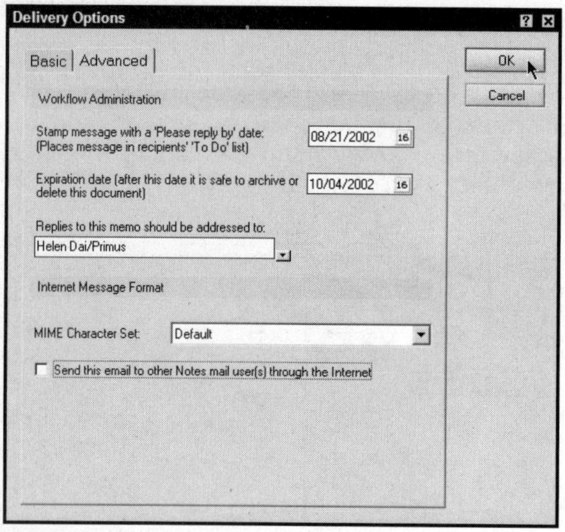

Figure 7-13:
Set
advanced
delivery
options for a
message.

As Figure 7-13 also shows, you can do a favor for the people to whom you're sending your message by indicating that your message has an expiration date. Doing so helps the readers determine which messages to delete if they're cleaning up their mail database or mail archive.

When you use your mail database to create a reply to a message, Notes automatically puts the name of the person who sent you the e-mail in the first place in the To field. If you're sending a message but want replies to come back to someone other than you, use the Replies to This Memo Should Be Addressed To field to enter the name of the person who should receive replies to your message.

Part III
When It's Not a Mail Thing

The 5th Wave — By Rich Tennant

"IT'S ANOTHER DEEP SPACE PROBE FROM EARTH, SEEKING CONTACT FROM EXTRATERRESTRIALS. I WISH THEY'D JUST INCLUDE AN E-MAIL ADDRESS."

In this part . . .

Important as it is, e-mail is only one part of the miracle that is Lotus Notes 6. The other work that you do in Notes involves using Notes databases. If you've already read Part II, you already know a fair amount about how databases work in Notes (really!) because your e-mail is a database itself. The purpose of Part III is to help you peer into the heart of the rest of Lotus Notes 6 and discover what makes it tick.

In these next chapters, I guide you through the maze of features that Notes has that don't necessarily have anything to do with e-mail. *Caution:* Reading this part can cause you to use Notes more efficiently, tinker with various parts of a database, and gain the skills that have propelled many *Lotus Notes For Dummies* readers on to fame and fortune.

Chapter 8

Your Calendar

In This Chapter

▶ Viewing your Calendar

▶ Keeping track of your appointments and meetings

▶ Group calendars

▶ Creating appointments, anniversaries, all-day events, and reminders

A handy Calendar that's always available to you is built right into Lotus Notes 6. You can use this to keep track of your daily comings and goings, as well as coordinate meetings with other people, remember those oh-so-very-important anniversaries, and set helpful reminders. Even if you're accustomed to keeping track of your meetings and appointments in one of those leather-bound, take-it-with-you calendar books, here are some really cool reasons why you should use Notes for all your scheduling needs:

✔ Keeping track of your Calendar in Notes means that all your information is on the computer. An added bonus is that you can view your Calendar by the day, week, fortnight, or month.

✔ If you use a Personal Digital Assistant (PDA) such as a Palm handheld device or an IBM WorkPad, you can carry your Calendar with you in your shirt or blouse pocket. Or your pants pocket, or strapped to your belt. Look, the point isn't where you carry it: Your Notes Calendar can be portable.

✔ If your organization uses shared calendars, you can easily use Notes to see other people's calendars to check their free time — and let them view your Calendar, also.

✔ You can use a feature of Notes called *delegation* to let your assistant schedule meetings for you. (If you're lucky enough to have an assistant, that is; otherwise, you're on your own.)

✔ You can print your Calendar in a variety of ways.

✔ You don't have to buy any fancy leather covers for your Notes Calendar or worry about a monogram.

Using Your Calendar

You'll most likely use your Calendar in three ways:

- ✓ **Daily tasks:** You'll read it (or perhaps print it) to see where you're supposed to be.
- ✓ **Reminders:** You'll put appointments and reminders on it for yourself — like a note to remember to go to the dentist or a reminder about which programs you want to record on your TiVo.
- ✓ **Meeting scheduling:** You'll send and respond to meeting invitations from your friends and colleagues.

But before you can reach out and touch your Calendar, you have to open it.

Opening your Calendar

Just like there are many ways to skin a cat (such a pretty thought), you have a few ways to open your Calendar. The following list below presents them, in no particular order:

- ✓ Click the Calendar bookmark (see it in the left margin).
- ✓ Click that big Calendar button on the Welcome page.
- ✓ If you're in your Inbox or To Do list, click the title of the Navigation pane, as you can see in Figure 8-1, and choose Switch to Calendar from the drop-down menu that appears.

Exactly what you see upon opening your Calendar — regardless of how you choose to open it — depends on how you left your Calendar when you were last in it. In other words, if you were using one of the Week views the last time that you closed your Calendar, you shouldn't be surprised to see that same Week view the next time that you open your Calendar.

You always get the same Calendar view *next* time that you had the *last* time.

Looking at your Calendar

After you have your Calendar open, you'll find that you can view it in lots of different ways and that you can do lots of things with it. Before you rush off, though, take a minute to look at the big picture — or at least one week's worth — as shown in Figure 8-2.

As you can see in Figure 8-2, when you open your Calendar, the screen gets a little busy, so you have a decision to make.

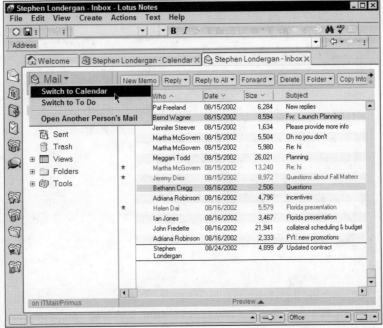

The more days that you view in your Calendar, the less you'll be able to see about each item in your Calendar. On the other hand, if you choose one of the smaller views (say, two days), you'll be able to see all the information about the actual Calendar items for those two days, but you'll lose your sense of what's planned for later in the week. Fortunately, you can easily switch from one view to the other, so try them all on for size and see which fits you best.

Changing your Calendar contents

In the upper-left corner of the Calendar window is a small calendar that shows the entire month of the view that you have open on the right side of the window. In this calendar, you can navigate from day to day within the active month or you can move from one month to the next. For example, in Figure 8-2, this little calendar shows August 2002. To switch the Calendar's display to any month in the future, just click the little right-facing arrow next to the month's name as many times as it takes to get to the month that you want. You can, of course, click the left-facing arrow to navigate to a previous month.

The right part of the screen, where the details for the day, week, or month in question are shown, changes to match what you click in the small calendar.

Another item worth noting in the little calendar is that one of the dates has a little block around it — August 26, in Figure 8-2. This is a cue to tell you which date is being displayed. You can click any other day in the little calendar to change the detail view to show that particular day.

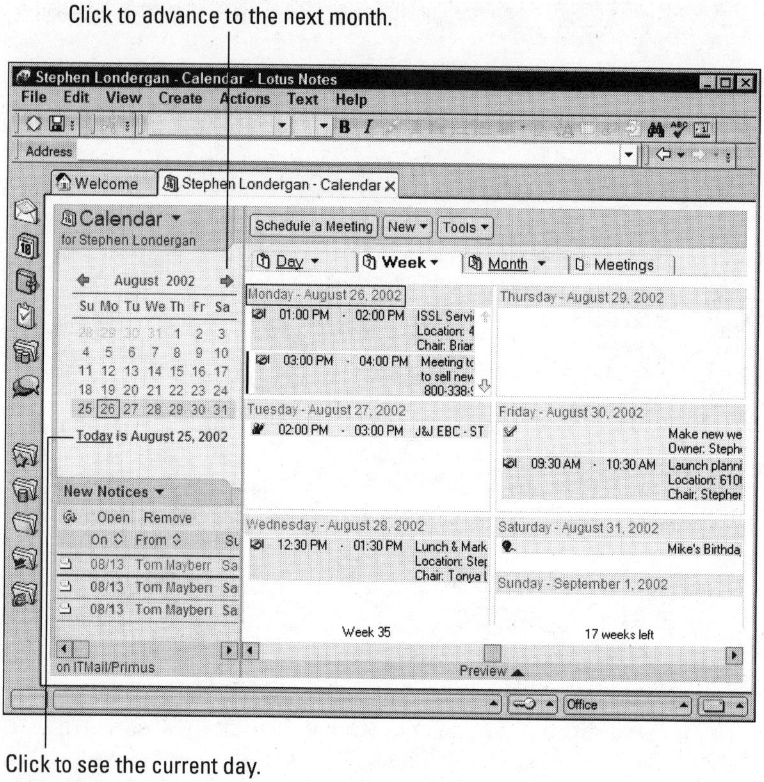

Click to advance to the next month.

Figure 8-2:
View your
Calendar by
the week.

Click to see the current day.

At the bottom of the little calendar, you can always see what the current date is. Click the Today link to switch the calendar to the current day.

Showing To Dos and Meeting Notices

Immediately under the month calendar in Figure 8-2 is your New Notices list. This is displayed (automatically) so that you can see which meeting invitations have arrived for you, which of your colleagues have replied to the invitations that you've sent, and so on.

Although I'm getting a little bit ahead of myself (I discuss in Chapter 9 how to reply to and send invitations), note that the New Notices heading has buttons at the top of the pane that you can use to open and/or remove Calendar items.

To display your To Dos instead of meeting notices, click the little triangle next to the words *New Notices* (as shown in Figure 8-3) and then choose To Do from the drop-down list that appears.

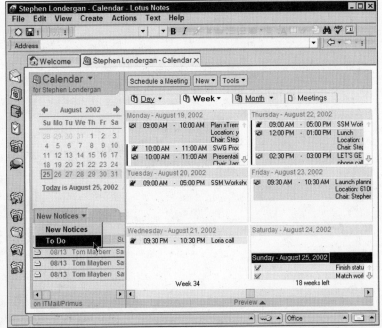

Figure 8-3:
Display
your To Dos
from the
Calendar.

The devil's in the details

The real action — and the really important information in your Calendar — is displayed in the right part of the screen. This is where you find the blow-by-blow details of all the meetings, appointments, and so on that you've booked. In Figure 8-4, you can see a daily view of Calendar information.

Calendar views

Use the four tabs at the top of the Calendar detail window to select how your Calendar appears. As you can see in Figure 8-4, these tabs are Day, Week, Month, and Meetings. You can also see in Figure 8-4 that each tab also has a *twisty* (a little triangle that you can click to uncover more options). For example, click the twisty on the Week tab, and you get a drop-down menu from which you can pick from One Week, One Work Week, Two Weeks, or Two Work Weeks views. In Figure 8-5, you can see how the Calendar looks after you click the Week twisty.

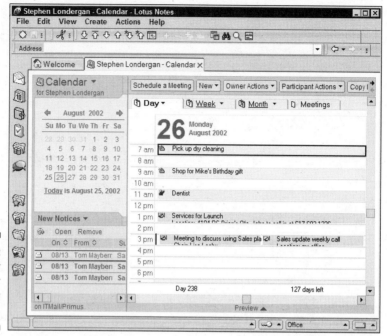

Figure 8-4:
Take your
Calendar
one day
at a time.

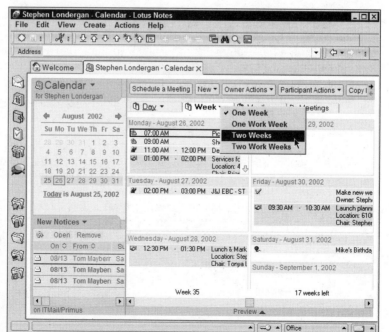

Figure 8-5:
Change
how your
Calendar
displays.

You have a few different options to choose from when deciding how your Calendar is displayed. Luckily, you can easily switch from one view to the other, so it's worth a little clicking and experimenting on your own to decide which view you prefer and which best suits you. Here are the ways that you can display your Calendar:

- **Day tab**
  - **One Day**
  - **Two Days**
- **Week tab**
  - **One Week**
  - **One Work Week:** Omits Saturdays and Sundays
  - **Two Weeks**
  - **Two Work Weeks:** Omits Saturdays and Sundays
- **Month tab**
  - **One Month**
  - **One Work Month:** Omits Saturdays and Sundays
- **Meetings tab**

You'll probably find that the Month views are hard to use — too much information and too little screen space.

That last tab — Meetings — is a special view of your Calendar that's laid out much the same way as your Inbox. This view is particularly useful if you schedule meetings with other people and need a quick snapshot of who has accepted or declined your invitations. (Read more about meetings and invitations to them in Chapter 9.)

When you're consulting your Calendar to see where you're supposed to be — as opposed to consulting your Calendar to see when you're free — here's a trick you can use to make it more readable. Choose View⇨Show⇨Summary menu; see the results of this in Figure 8-6. As you can see, this view is a little more readable because the items are listed one after the other with no white space. You can also see all the information about each Calendar item, such as the name of the person who sent each invitation as well as that meeting's location.

Compare Figure 8-5 with Figure 8-6 to see the difference. Figure 8-6 has the Summarize option turned on, and Figure 8-5 doesn't. Just choose View⇨Show⇨Summary menu again when you want to switch back to the standard, non-summarized view.

Summarizing your Calendar shows you when you're booked and where you're supposed to be, but this view doesn't show you when you're free.

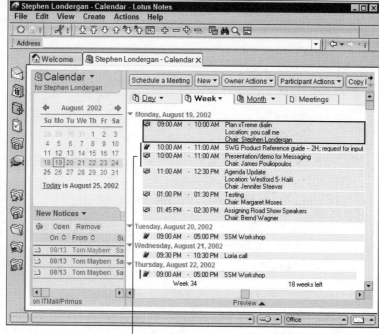

Figure 8-6:
One week's worth of your calendar, summarized.

This vertical line indicates a double-booking.

You can turn on the Summarize feature for a weekly or monthly view.

The most important part of your Calendar is the individual items that appear in the detail window: Each represents something that you've booked yourself to do at a certain time. For example, you can see in Figure 8-6 that I have a Testing meeting with my friend Margaret at 1 p.m., an *Agenda Update* meeting at 11 a.m., and so on.

Each Calendar item has more information that the view can show. When push comes to shove, remember that Calendar items are just documents — so the surest way to see all the information about a particular item is to open it, just as you would any other document. Either double-click the Calendar entry or select the item that you're interested in and then press Enter.

Here's a trick: Just put your mouse on an item without clicking anything (this is called *hovering*). As you can see in Figure 8-7, hovering over any Calendar item gets you a little pop-up box that shows all the item's details.

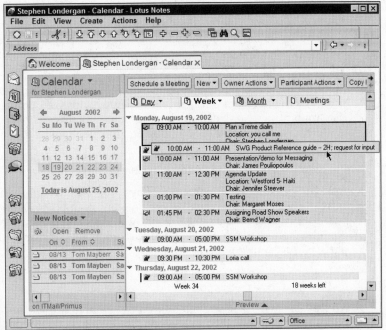

Avoiding double-bookings

It's a sad and inevitable fact that we're all busy. Not too busy to reply to e-mail messages, of course, but so busy that you may find yourself double-booked for more than one Calendar event at the same time. Notes certainly can't solve the eternal "How can I be in two places at once" problem, but it can alert you when you get double-booked with two items on your Calendar scheduled for the same time. Such a crisis is indicated on your schedule by a black vertical line, as you can see by referring to the 10 a.m. time slot in Figure 8-6; I'm overbooked because I'm scheduled for two meetings then.

Keep reading in this chapter (and also in Chapter 9) to discover how to use the tricks that Notes has up its sleeve to minimize double-bookings. For example, you can check your own free time — or someone else's — before booking a meeting. In the meantime, watch out for those side-by-side meetings.

Discovering Calendar Events

Your Notes Calendar includes more than just meetings. You'll find up to six kinds of things in your Calendar:

- **To Dos:** These are your tasks, which appear by default in your Calendar. (If you don't want them to show up, choose Actions➪Tools➪Preferences, click the To Do tab, and enable the Do Not Display To Do Entries in the Calendar check box.)

- **Appointments:** These are places where you need to go or meetings that you have to attend but to which you don't need to invite other people, such as a dentist's appointment or a meeting with your parole officer. Use Appointments to keep track of personal scheduled items and also to alert your colleagues to not book you for meetings at those times.

- **Meetings:** These are just like Appointments but with other people from the office. (I cover these in detail in Chapter 9.)

- **Anniversaries:** These include birthdays, holidays, wedding anniversaries, and so on. Anniversaries are one-day affairs that repeat from one year to the next. You can enter your own Anniversaries (such as your birthday), and you might also be able to enter Anniversaries that are particular to your company (holidays, payday schedules, and so on).

- Listing an Anniversary in your Calendar does *not* prevent people from inviting you to a meeting on that day.

- **All Day Events:** These are affairs that can span multiple days, such as an out-of-town meeting. If you list an All Day Event on your Calendar, people won't be able to invite you to a Meeting.

- **Reminders:** Think of these as sort of like a To Do. A Reminder entry is something that you want to remember to do at a particular time on a particular day.

Adding stuff to your Calendar

To add a new item to your Calendar, you can either click the New button in the Calendar tool bar or you can choose Create➪Calendar Entry. What you do next depends on the type of entry that you're creating.

Instead of using the Create menu, just double-click a particular time on your Calendar. Notes starts a new Calendar entry for you, automatically filling in the start time with the time that you click. (Choose View➪Show➪Time Slots to have the Calendar show the times when you're free.)

Adding an Appointment

To record an Appointment on your Calendar, open your Calendar, click the New button on the Action bar, and then choose Appointment from the drop-down menu that appears. See Figure 8-8 for a sample appointment.

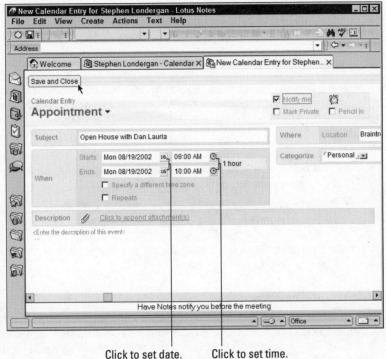

Figure 8-8:
Create
a new
Appoint-
ment here.

Click to set date.   Click to set time.

To schedule an Appointment, fill in the following:

- ✔ **Subject field:** Type some words here describing the Appointment.

- ✔ **When fields:** Use the fields in the When area (the Starts and Ends dates and times for the Appointment) to enter when the Appointment begins and will finish.

   You can click the little calendar and clock buttons here to set the date and time, respectively, if you prefer.

- ✔ **Specify a Different Time Zone:** Select this check box if your appointment is in a different time zone. (Maybe you work in Boston, but the appointment you're entering will be in California.)

- ✔ **Repeats:** Use this check box to automatically add several appointments with the same Subject and times. (I cover this later in this chapter.)

- ✔ **Where field:** Enter the place of your Appointment in the Location text box. You want to remember where you're supposed to be, right?

- ✔ **Description field:** You may enter any text — or nothing at all — in this area at the bottom of the form. You can also attach a file to the Appointment document that you're creating by clicking the paper clip icon.

- ✔ **Notify Me check box:** Select this if you want Notes to warn you of the Appointment so that you don't forget to go. (How could you forget to go to the dentist, anyway?) If you do choose to be notified, you see a special dialog box to choose the type of warning you'll get and when you'll get it.

- ✔ **Mark Private check box:** Select this to prevent people from seeing what you're doing at the time of the Appointment. Other people are able to tell that you're busy, but the details of your activity aren't available to them.

- ✔ **Pencil In check box:** Select this check box if you want your colleagues to still be able to invite you to meetings during the time that you have scheduled for an Appointment.

- ✔ **Categorize field:** Optionally, you can type (or choose) a category for the appointment in this field.

Click the Save and Close button on the Action bar when you finish setting the options on the Appointment form.

Adding an Anniversary

To record an Anniversary in your Calendar, click the New button in the Calendar Action bar and then choose Anniversary from the drop-down menu that appears. Watch for a new blank form, which looks an awful lot like what you see in Figure 8-9. Notice that an Anniversary form automatically has the Repeats check box selected. Without even asking, Notes assumes that you want the Anniversary to be automatically entered in your Calendar for the next ten years. (Of course, you can clear the Repeats check box to change that.)

Fill out the following to schedule a new Anniversary:

- ✔ **Subject field:** Type some words here describing the Anniversary. As with all Calendar items, what you enter in this field is what appears for the item in your Calendar.

- ✔ **When fields:** Use the Starts date field to type (or select) when the Anniversary begins. (No, this isn't when you got married; it's the starting date of when the item will appear on your Calendar.)

- ✔ **Where field:** If your new Anniversary has a location associated with it, enter that in the Location text box.

- ✔ **Description field:** You can enter any text — or nothing — in this area at the bottom of the form. You can also attach a file to the Appointment document that you're creating by clicking the paper clip icon.

- ✔ **Notify Me check box:** Select this check box if you want Notes to warn you of the Anniversary so that you don't forget. (***Hint:*** Think flowers.) If you do choose to be notified, you see a special dialog box to choose the type of warning you'll get and when you'll get it.

✔ **Mark Private check box:** Select this to prevent people from seeing the Anniversary.

✔ **Pencil In check box:** Select this check box if you want your colleagues to still be able to invite you to meetings during the time that you have scheduled for an Anniversary.

✔ **Categorize:** Optionally, you can type (or choose) a category for the anniversary in this field.

Click the Save and Close button on the Action bar when you're done.

Adding a Reminder

To add a Reminder to your Calendar, click the New button on the Calendar Action bar and then choose Reminder from the drop-down menu that appears. See a sample new Reminder form in Figure 8-10.

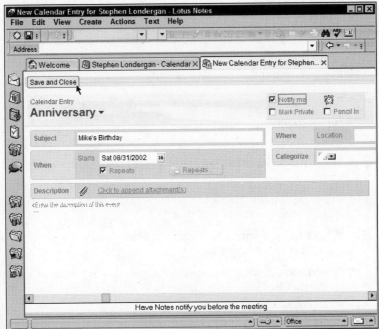

Figure 8-9:
Create
a new
Anniversary
here.

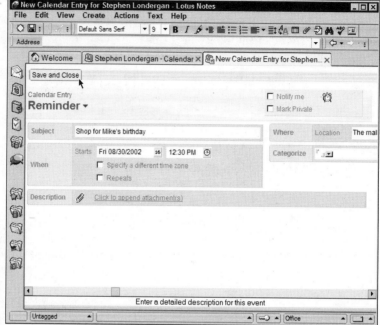

Figure 8-10:
Create
a new
Reminder
here.

To add a new Reminder, do the following:

- ✔ **Subject field:** Type some words here describing the Reminder.
- ✔ **When fields:** Use the fields in the When area (the Starts date and time text boxes) to determine when the Reminder appears on your Calendar.
- ✔ **Specify a Different Time Zone:** Select this check box if your appointment is in a different time zone.
- ✔ **Repeats:** Use this check box to automatically add several appointments with the same Subject and times.
- ✔ **Where field:** If your new Reminder has a location associated with it, enter that in the Location field.
- ✔ **Description field:** You may enter any text — or nothing — in this area of the form. Click the paper clip icon to attach a file, if you want.
- ✔ **Notify Me check box:** Select this check box if you want Notes to warn you of the Reminder. Sort of a reminder to you that you have a Reminder, huh?
- ✔ **Mark Private check box:** Select this to prevent people from seeing what you're doing at the time of the Appointment. Other people are able to tell that you're busy, but the details of your activity aren't available to them.
- ✔ **Categorize field:** Optionally, type (or choose) a category for the reminder in this field.

Click the Save and Close button on the Action bar when you finish.

Adding a new All Day Event

To record an event on your calendar, open your Calendar, click the New button on the Action bar, and then choose All Day Event from the drop-down menu that appears. See Figure 8-11 for a sample All Day Event form.

To schedule the event, fill out the following:

- ✔ **Subject field:** Type some words describing the event.

- ✔ **When fields:** Use the fields in the When area — the Starts and Ends dates — to enter when the event begins and will finish. You can click the calendar to set the date if you prefer.

- ✔ **Repeats:** Use this check box to automatically add several appointments with the same Subject and times.

- ✔ **Where field:** To help you remember where you're supposed to be, enter your destination in the Location field.

- ✔ **Description field:** Enter any text — or nothing — in this area at the bottom of the form. You can also attach a file to the document that you're creating by clicking the paper clip icon.

- ✔ **Notify Me check box:** Select this check box if you want Notes to warn you of the event.

- ✔ **Mark Private check box:** Selecting this check box prevents people from seeing what you're doing at the time of the event. Other people can tell that you're busy, but the details of your activity aren't available to them.

- ✔ **Pencil In check box:** Select this check box if you want your colleagues to still be able to invite you to meetings during the time that you have scheduled for an All Day Event.

- ✔ **Categorize field:** Optionally, you can type (or choose) a category for the event in this field.

Click the Save and Close button on the Action bar when you finish setting the options on the All Day Event form.

An *event* is just a day-long affair, and it can last more than one day. Therefore, using the All Day Event form is a lot like using the Appointment or Meeting form to schedule yourself for a meeting or an appointment that lasts the whole day.

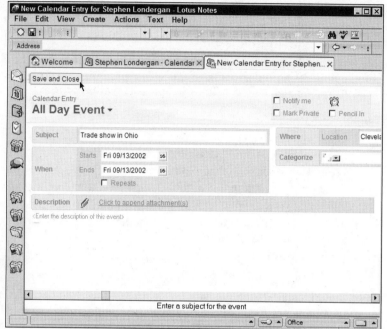

Figure 8-11:
Create a
new All Day
Event here.

Editing a Calendar item

To make any kind of change at all to a Calendar item — perhaps you want to change the start date of an Appointment or change the time when a Reminder should appear on your Calendar — select the item in question and then press Ctrl+E. Make the necessary changes, and then click the Save and Close button on the Action bar when you finish.

Managing Group Calendars

Group Calendars are a quick and easy way to see an overview of several people's calendars all lumped together. You can use a Group Calendar to manage an entire department's appointments or any time that you need to see more than one person's calendar at the same time. Or, on the other hand, you might never use Group Calendars at all. (I don't.)

Creating a Group Calendar

Before you can view a Group Calendar, you first have to create a Group Calendar, as follows:

1. **Open your Calendar.**

2. **Click the Calendar heading (upper-left corner).**

3. **From the drop-down menu that appears, choose View & Create Group Calendars, as shown in Figure 8-12.**

4. **Click the New Group Calendar button on the Action bar and then enter a name for the new Group Calendar in the Title field in the New Group Calendar dialog box.**

5. **In the Members field, type the names of the people whose calendars will be included.**

   You can either click the drop-down arrow at the bottom of the field to choose the names from the Public Directory, or you can type their names in the Members field.

6. **Click OK to create the new Group Calendar.**

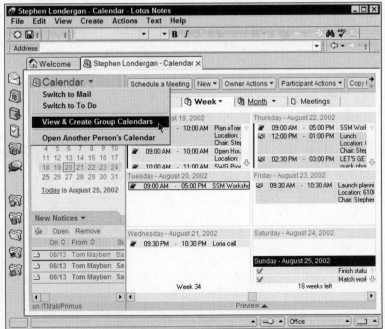

Figure 8-12:
Create a
Group
Calendar
here.

Using a Group Calendar

Use the following steps to view a Group Calendar that you've already created:

1. **Open your Calendar.**

2. **Click the Calendar heading in the Navigation pane.**

3. **From the drop-down menu that appears, choose View & Create Group Calendars (refer to Figure 8-12).**

4. **Choose the Group Calendar that you want to see.**

Figure 8-13 shows a sample Group Calendar.

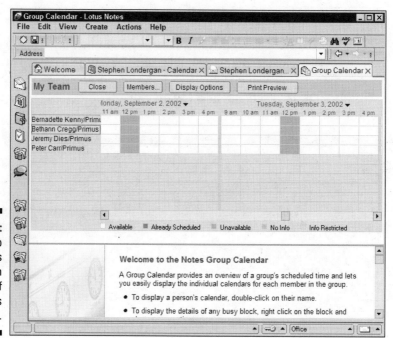

Figure 8-13: Group calendars provide an overview of a group's activities.

Printing Your Calendar

Printing your Calendar isn't all that much different from printing any other view in any other Notes database. The basic idea is that you open up the Calendar view that you want and then either press Ctrl+P or choose File⇨ Print. Then trust in your handy printer to do the rest.

One thing that is different, though, is that Notes comes ready-made with a series of print styles that are handy if you want to print your Calendar in such a way that it automatically fits inside and matches the format of a regular, book calendar, such as Day-Timers, Day Runners, and the like.

To print your Calendar, choose File⇨Print, and then click the Calendar Style tab, as shown in Figure 8-14.

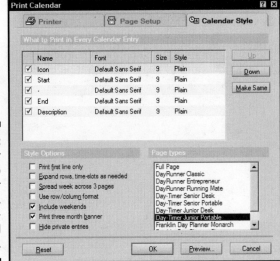

Figure 8-14:
Print your
Calendar to
fit into your
regular,
leather-
bound
schedule.

Just select the page layout that you want from the Page Types list and then click OK to start seein' those pages.

Click the Preview button to see what you're gonna get before you waste any paper.

Chapter 9

Managing Your Calendar

*T*he most interesting and compelling part of the Lotus Notes 6 Calendar is its ability to help you initiate, schedule, and manage meetings and appointments with other people. For example, when you set up a Calendar item that involves other people, you can have Notes automatically examine each invitee's Calendar to find the best time when all parties are available. That feature alone is worth the price of admission.

You also have a whole bunch of things that you can do when you get invited to a meeting, such as accept or decline the invitation or even suggest a better time for the meeting.

The bottom line? Working with other people and coordinating schedules is a whole lot easier with Notes than without. In this chapter, I make sure that you discover what you need to know to schedule meetings with aplomb. Or a plum, if you prefer. But not a quince.

Makin' a Meetin'

If you've already read through Chapter 8, you already know all about the various types of Calendar items that you can create, with one exception: a Meeting. As you can see in Figure 9-1, a Meeting looks just like an Appointment except that it has some additional information — the names of all the people who have been invited to attend, as well as information about their availability. That's different from an Appointment, which would only have your name in it.

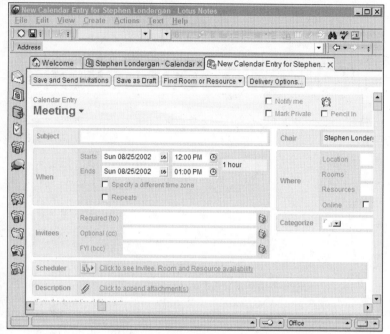

Figure 9-1:
Your basic
Notes
Meeting
form.

Create an Appointment if the event is just for you. Use a Meeting when you need to invite other people from your organization.

You'll find yourself using a Meeting in a few different ways. Sometimes it's your party — you're the person scheduling the new meeting and inviting other people. Sometimes, though, you'll be on the other end of an invite. That is, in your Inbox, you receive a Meeting invitation that was sent to you by someone else. When you receive one of these invites, you have to decide whether you want to go to the meeting, or not, or what.

Creating a Meeting

To create a new Meeting, first open your Calendar and then click the Schedule a Meeting button on the Action bar. (For all things Calendar, read through Chapter 8.) A blank Meeting form appears. In Figure 9-2, you can see a Meeting form that I've created.

Most of the fields on a Meeting form are the same as those on an Appointment form. You need to fill in the basics, such as a subject, when, duration, and location. (To discover how to fill out an Appointment, read Chapter 8.) Here I focus on the Invitees, the Scheduler, and rooms/resources because those are the fields that matter and the ones that differentiate a Meeting from an Appointment.

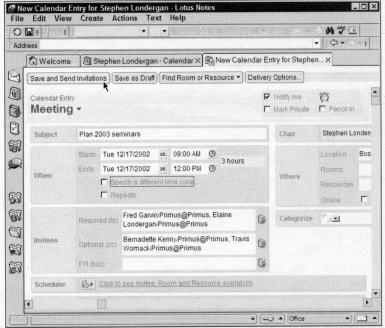

Figure 9-2:
Creating
a new
meeting.

Inviting the Invitees

In the simplest case, you simply enter the names of the people whom you want to come to your meeting. Just fill in the fields of the Invitees section (bottom-left side) as well as the date, time, and location sections of the new Meeting form. (Refer to Figure 9-2.) As you can see in that figure, you can invite three types of people: Required, Optional, and FYI.

✔ **Required:** Anyone whose name you list in this field is considered by Notes to be a mandatory participant of your meeting. This is especially important when you ask Notes to find the best times for a meeting. For more on determining schedule availability, skip down to the upcoming section "Using the Scheduler."

✔ **Optional:** As far as Notes is concerned, these folks are really just like Required people. Notes consults their schedules if you ask Notes to find the best times for your meeting. If a person is listed as an Optional invitee in a Meeting invitation, his attendance isn't necessarily mandatory. It's a lot like cc-ing folks on an e-mail message: They get the message, but they're not considered primary players.

✔ **FYI:** Use this field if you want to send a Meeting *notice* — different than an *invitation* — to someone. Suppose that you need to schedule a meeting with your team members. You could enter each team member's name in the Required field but put your boss's name in the FYI field. That way your colleagues each receive an invitation to the meeting, but your manager just gets a meeting notice instead. That way your boss knows that you're having the meeting and that you sent the invitations but also that she isn't expected to attend.

The people in the Required and Optional fields won't see the names of anyone whom you list in the FYI field of a Meeting invitation.

Click the buttons that look like a little phone book to the right of the Required, Optional, and FYI fields to select names from the Public Directory.

The simplest way to create a new Meeting invitation is the following:

1. **In the Subject field, enter a subject.**

2. **In the When fields, choose a start and end date and time for the meeting.**

3. **In the Where fields, set the location.**

   Skip down to the upcoming section "Reserving rooms and resources" for the lowdown on booking rooms.

4. **In the Invitees fields, enter the names of the people whom you want to invite.**

5. **Click the Save and Send Invitations button on the Action bar.**

All your Invitees receive a message in their Inbox asking them to come to your meeting. Figure 9-3 shows such an invitation. This one is from Jeremy, and he has invited Stephen and Mike to attend his Marketing Discussion meeting, Thursday at 12:15 p.m.

The only problem with this approach — although it's certainly direct — is that it typically starts a volley of e-mail messages back and forth between you and your guests. You know, the "I can't make it at 9:30, but how about 10, instead?" variety. Depending on the number of people whom you invite to any particular meeting, you may actually spend quite a bit of time after sending the invite trying to coordinate them as they all get back to you with these "Yes, I can" or "No, I can't" responses.

You can easily skirt this dilemma. Rather than using the simple process that I list above, ask the Notes Scheduler to first review each invitee's Calendar to find a common time when everyone is available. Armed with this information, you can set a meeting time convenient for (hopefully) everyone. Your invite arrives in your guests' Inboxes already pre-loaded with a date and time that you know (heh, heh) when they're free. Any of your guests can still decline, of course, but you reduce the chance of that happening pretty dramatically because you avoid most schedule conflicts up front. I show you how in the next section.

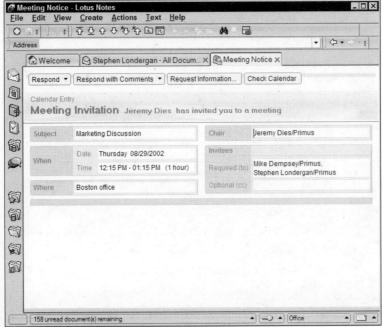

Figure 9-3:
Invitees get
automatic
Meeting
Invitations.

Using the Scheduler

To have Notes suggest an optimal time for a meeting based on when your Required and Optional meeting participants are available, hold off clicking that Save and Send Invitations button just yet. Rather, fill out your Meeting form as usual and then click the Click to See Invitee, Room, and Resource Availability button, which you can find in the Scheduler section (bottom) of the Meeting form. (Refer to Figure 9-2.)

Figure 9-4 shows a sample Meeting invitation with the Scheduler opened.

When you use the Scheduler to have Notes find meeting times for you, you have two ways to look: by best times or by schedule details. In Figure 9-4, you can see that I selected the Summary radio button (under the Show heading, left side) to secure that view. This view is probably the easiest to use because you can see at a glance a blow-by-blow set of time suggestions during which all the people you're inviting are available.

To use one of the times that Notes suggests, just select a time convenient to everyone from the Suggested Times for Selected Day drop-down list and then click the Use Selected Time button below it. Notes will then adjust the times of your Meeting invitation. You can see the fields in the When section at the top of the Meeting form change accordingly when you click an entry in this list.

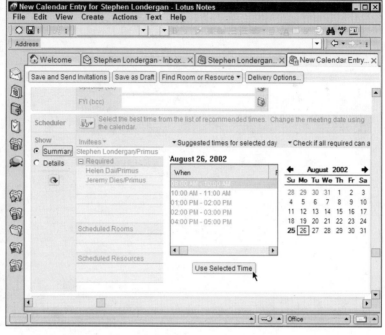

Figure 9-4:
Use the
Scheduler
to find out
when your
guests are
available
to meet.

You can also click any of the dates in the small month calendar (bottom-right of the form) to examine a different day and to see when your pals are available on that day.

Check out the little arrow next to the Suggested Times for Selected Day list heading. Click this arrow to display more schedule availability choices. From the drop-down list that appears (as shown in Figure 9-5), you can choose to search for compatible free time during a particular day, week, or month. This is especially useful if the people you're inviting don't have any availability on the original date you chose.

If you have trouble finding a time that works for *all* your Invitees, click the Check if All Required Can Attend option and then use the ensuing drop-down list to pick a time for a smaller group of people, as you can see in Figure 9-6. This is helpful when you're trying to schedule a meeting with a larger number — greater than 20 — people.

Another more visual way to find times when your Invitees are available is to view them by schedule details. Select the Details radio button (under the Show heading) to see a table that shows the times when each of your guests are available. You can see such a view in Figure 9-7. One advantage of this scheduling table is that you can see, per person, the free-time availability over the course of two weeks.

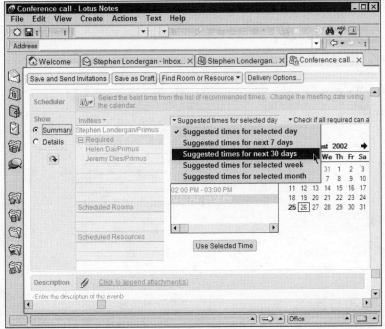

Figure 9-5:
Have Notes
propose a
time from a
given day,
week, or
month.

The Check if All Required Can Attend option

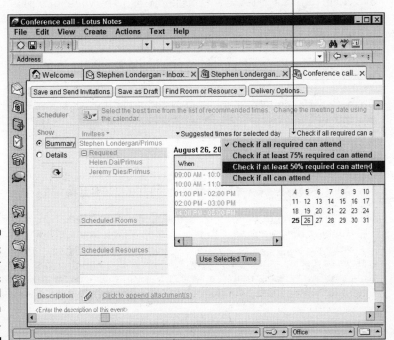

Figure 9-6:
Check your
options
if not all
invitees can
attend.

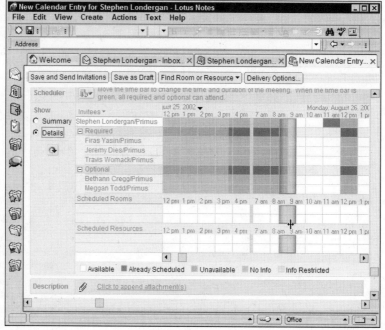

Figure 9-7:
View individual schedule details to find free time.

Drag the big, transparent vertical bar until you find a time when everyone is available. (It turns green when this happens.) The white blocks in the table represent the times that are open and available, and the colored blocks represent the times when the given participant is otherwise occupied. If all the invitees aren't available, the vertical bar turns red to let you know that your entire posse cannot attend. (A key at the bottom of the screen reminds you of what status each color indicates.)

No matter which method you choose to find a time when you can all meet, you must click the Save and Send Invitations button on the Action bar when you're finished.

Reserving rooms and resources

Your company might have also set up the Notes calendaring system to include the ability to reserve rooms and resources. If not, this section is not for you.

A room is just what it sounds like it is — usually a shared conference room, which ends up being treated a lot like a person. In other words, Notes maintains a schedule for the room so that you can reserve it for a meeting. You reserve a room by entering the name of the room in the Rooms field of the Where section of a Meeting form.

Reserving a resource works the same way. A *resource* is usually a piece of equipment, such as an overhead projector, that you can reserve and book for your meeting. A resource's availability is also maintained and considered by Notes when you select the all-powerful Click to See the Invitee, Room, and Resource Availability button.

It's up to your administrator to do all the requisite behind-the-scenes work to make Rooms and Resources scheduling work, so it's worth asking someone to make sure this has been set up for you.

Online meetings

A companion product to Lotus Notes is Sametime. This next-big-thing, totally cool product is used, in IBM-speak, for real-time collaboration. You use Lotus Sametime instant messaging (also sometimes called *chat*) and online meetings right from your desktop to let other people see what's on your screen. Imagine giving a PowerPoint presentation without having to leave your office!

If your company is set up to use Sametime, select the This Is an Online Meeting check box on the Meeting form (in the Where section) to enter information about the meeting. You can see this setting in Figure 9-8. These fields are used to connect your Notes-based invitation to the Sametime meeting server, which you and your colleagues will use at meeting time to share your screen and use the Sametime electronic whiteboard together.

The Online meeting fields are

Type: Determines whether the meeting has one presenter or many. Options can include a Moderated Presentation/Demo or Broadcast Meeting.

Place: The name of the Sametime server on which the online meeting will be held.

Online Meeting Attachments: Used to attach (if appropriate) any materials (PowerPoint slides, for example) to use during an online meeting.

Sametime is a separate product, and your company might not have it. (Your company has to pay extra for it, in other words — it's not built into Notes.) Ask your administrator whether you can have online meetings.

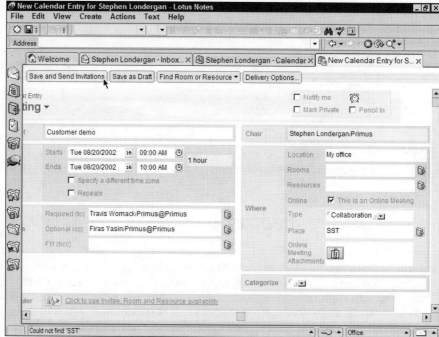

Figure 9-8:
Schedule
an online
meeting
with
Sametime.

Replying to an Invitation

What happens when you're on the other end of meeting invite . . . when you're the invitee, not the inviter?

It all starts with the Invitation delivered to your Inbox, as shown in Figure 9-9.

The Invitation Action bar presents you with a series of buttons: Respond, Respond with Comments, Request Information, and Check Calendar.

Regardless of which button you click — and rest assured that I explain all of them in this section — the basic question is, "Will you, or will you not, come to the meeting?"

Accepting an Invitation

Accepting an Invitation means that you intend to go to the meeting. When you either click the Respond button on the Action bar and then choose Accept or choose Actions⇨Respond⇨Accept, three things happen:

✔ First, a message gets sent to the meeting's chair (the person who invited you, in other words). That way, she knows that you'll be there, with bells on.

✔ Second, the Invitation is converted into a Calendar item that's posted on your Calendar at the appropriate time and on the appropriate date.

✔ Third, your Calendar now knows that you're now busy at that time on that date, so any subsequent meeting invitations won't try to book you then. Now, if anyone uses the Scheduler when inviting you, they'll see that you're busy.

An alternate way to accept an invitation is to either click the Respond with Comments button on the Action bar and then choose Accept or to choose Actions⇨Respond with Comments⇨Accept. The only difference in this method is that you get to type something in the message that's sent to the meeting's chair — something along the lines of "Thanks for inviting me" or "See you then." You can say whatever you want; just remember to click the Send button when you're finished.

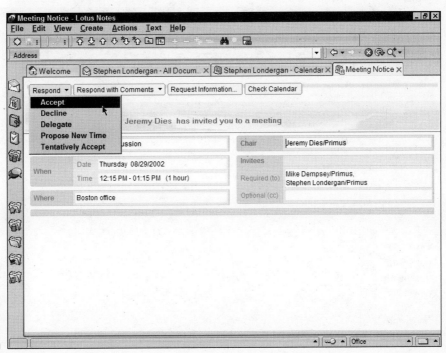

Figure 9-9:
A basic
meeting
Invitation.

Declining an Invitation

If you can't make the meeting, you can always decline an Invitation. Just either click the Respond button on the Action bar and then choose Decline or choose Actions⇨Respond⇨Decline. This sends a message to the meeting's chair, who will then know that you ain't coming.

An alternate way to decline an invitation is to either click the Respond with Comments button on the Action bar and then choose Decline or to choose Actions⇨Respond with Comments⇨Decline. Then you get to type something in the message that's sent to the meeting's chair — something along the lines of "Sorry I can't make it" or "I'll be at the ball game that day." Click the Send button when you're finished.

Figure 9-10 shows a sample message declining an Invitation.

When you decline an invitation, the meeting is NOT posted to your Calendar.

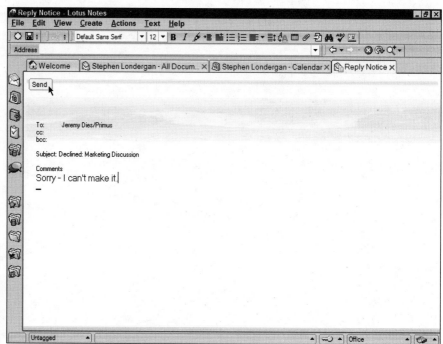

Figure 9-10:
Decline an Invitation with a message.

Sending a meeting Delegate

If you can't make a meeting but want to suggest that someone else attend in your stead, either click the Respond button on the Action bar and then choose Delegate or choose Actions⇨Respond⇨Delegate. This forwards the invite to the person whom you nominate as your replacement and also sends a message to the meeting's chair so that he won't be surprised when someone else appears at the meeting in your place. Your delegate, of course, gets to make his or her own decision about accepting or declining the invitation.

You can include a few words on the Delegation message that's sent to the meeting chair by clicking the Respond with Comments button on the Action bar and then choosing Delegate or by choosing Actions⇨Respond with Comments⇨Delegate. Then you get to type something in the message that's sent to the meeting's chair — something along the lines of "Sorry I can't make it, but I hope Sally can" or "I'll be at the ball game that day, maybe Joe can come instead?" Click the Send button when you're finished.

Proposing a new time

If you really, really want to go to a meeting but you're already booked at the time that's been proposed in the Invitation, consider proposing a new time for the meeting. Either click the Respond button on the Action bar and then choose Propose New Time or choose Actions⇨Respond⇨Propose New Time. This lets you suggest an alternate time and date that's more suited to your availability and also sends a message including the same to the chair. (As you can read in the earlier section "Using the Scheduler," you wouldn't be going through this if the chair used the Find Best Times for Meeting feature.)

If you want to say something in the message that's sent to the meeting chair, click the Respond with Comments button on the Action bar and choose Propose New Time or choose Actions⇨Respond with Comments⇨Propose New Time.

Tentatively accepting an Invitation

Tentatively accepting an Invitation is the same as accepting an Invitation except that your free time won't mark you as unavailable. In other words, any subsequent free time search still shows you as available during the times of a Meeting that you tentatively accept. Respond with any of the following: click the Respond button on the Action bar and then choose Tentatively Accept;

choose Actions⇨Respond⇨Tentatively Accept; click the Respond with Comments button on the Action bar and then choose Tentatively Accept; or choose Actions⇨Respond with Comments⇨Tentatively Accept.

Sometimes you may want to take a quick look at your Calendar before deciding on an Invitation. That's what the Check Calendar button on the Action bar is for. As you can see in Figure 9-11, clicking this button opens a new pop-up Check Calendar window with your Calendar in it. Take a look there to see whether you're available, and then click the Done button to close the window to pick up where you left off.

Request Information

You may occasionally receive invites to meetings that catch you by surprise — you have no idea why the meeting is happening, or why you are invited, or who else is coming. That's where using the Request Information button (located on the Action bar) comes in. Click this to start off a brand-new (and empty) e-mail message, addressed to the person who sent you the invitation in the first place. (The idea being that you can ask this person why the meeting is happening, or why you are invited, or who else is coming.)

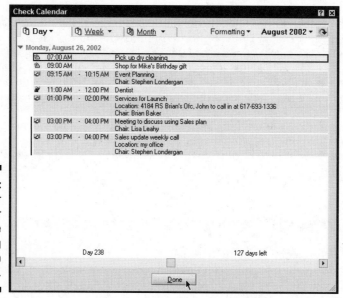

Figure 9-11:
Check your
Calendar
before
deciding
on an
invitation.

Your free time

One of the lynchpins of the Notes Calendar system is the fact that Notes knows, to the extent possible, when you're busy. Your free time, which is what Notes consults when someone invites you and checks your schedule from the Click to See Invitee, Room and Resource Availability button, is based on a number of factors.

First, your free time is based on the times when you've indicated that you're generally available. You set these times by choosing Actions⇨Tools⇨Preferences⇨Calendar⇨Free Time. Or, if you're in your Calendar view already, simply click the Tools button in the Action bar, and then choose Preferences⇨Free Time. (Read more about this in Chapter 16.) Use the Free Time tab of the Preferences dialog box to determine when you're usually available; for example, if you never

work on Fridays, you would indicate this by clearing the Friday check mark on this tab.

Second, your free time is based on the appointments and meetings that you've already accepted and booked.

Third, your free time is based on the names that you enter (or don't enter) in the Allow Only These People to View My Free Time Information or Allow Only These People to View My Free Time Details fields on the Preferences dialog box. Leaving these blank (the default) means that anyone in your organization can query your Calendar to see when you're available. If, on the other hand, you want only certain people to have this insight into your availability, you can enter their names in the fields in the Preferences dialog box.

Before the Meeting

Finally, you have a couple of options in advance of a meeting. For example, you might need to change your mind and decline a meeting that you've already accepted, or perhaps you'd like to send a message to your meeting's participants to confirm the meeting itself.

What you get to do with a meeting that's on your Calendar depends upon whether you sent out the invitations in the first place: that is, if you are the meeting's chair.

To access any of the following options, just select the meeting and use the Action bar's Owner Actions bar to select the item that you want from the menu.

When you're the chair of a meeting and have sent out your invites, you have action options available to you in relation to that meeting. When you open a scheduled meeting invite, select the Owner Actions button in the Action Bar. As chair, you will see the following options:

- ✔ **Reschedule:** You still want to hold the meeting but at a different time. Choosing Reschedule starts an entirely new round of invitations, which your invitees have to re-accept or decline.

- ✔ **Cancel:** No more meeting? Canceling a meeting sends a notice to your Invitees and removes the meeting from their calendars.

- ✔ **Confirm:** This is just a short e-mail message to your invitees, reminding each that the party is ON.

- ✔ **View Invitee Status:** This is a good way to see exactly whom you invited and, more important, whether each has accepted, declined, or not yet responded to your invitation.

- ✔ **Send Memo to All Invitees:** Similar to confirming a meeting, this starts you off with a new e-mail message that's automatically addressed to all your Invitees.

- ✔ **Send Memo to Invitees Who Have Not Responded:** This starts a new message but only to the people who haven't responded to your invitation.

- ✔ **Send Memo to Invitees Who Have Responded:** This starts a new message for the people who've either agreed or declined to attend.

When you're a participant in the meeting — meaning that you didn't send out the original invite but agreed to attend — you can select one of the following options in the meeting invite by selecting the meeting in question and using the Participant Actions button in the Action bar:

- ✔ **Decline:** This lets you change your mind, informs the meeting's chair that you won't be attending, and removes the meeting from your Calendar.

- ✔ **Delegate:** Select this to change your mind, inform the meeting's chair that you want someone else to come in your place, and remove the meeting from your Calendar.

- ✔ **Propose New Time:** Select this to suggest a different time to the meeting's chair.

Chapter 10

Tracking Your To Dos

*N*o more keeping that ever-increasing To Do list in your head, and you can forget all those little yellow sticky notes that you've got pasted all over the place, too. Lotus Notes 6 has a built-in way for you to track and manage your To Dos — and even a way to delegate a task to someone else.

Read through this chapter to discover how you can use the Notes 6 To Dos to make yourself more efficient. Notes can help you organize and prioritize your time by letting you know which of your To Dos needs your immediate attention.

 Certainly the easiest and most direct way to see what you've supposed to be doing instead of reading this book all day (now get back to work!) is to click the To Do button in the Bookmark bar. (See this icon in the left margin.) Clicking this brings up the All To Do's view, as shown in Figure 10-1. The encircled numerals (1, 2, and 3) represent the priority assigned to each.

 The Bookmark bar is always onscreen when you use Notes.

You can also click the To Do List button on the Welcome page. Or switch to your To Dos when you have your Inbox or Calendar open by clicking the database title, as you can see in Figure 10-2.

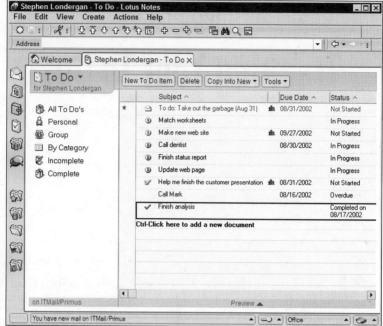

Figure 10-1:
Use To Dos
to keep
track of
things that
you need
to do.

Figure 10-2:
Here's an
easy way to
switch to
your To Dos.

Viewing Your To Dos

Refer to Figure 10-1 to see the All To Do's view of To Do. This view has five column's worth of information about each To Do. Although each To Do item has several other fields, these are the most important parts of each To Do:

- ✔ **Subject:** This column holds a sentence or two that describes the thing that needs doin'.

  The next column doesn't have a tile, but it tells you whether the task is assigned to someone else. The little thumbnail icon, which is supposed to be three people standing together, appears next to any To Do item that's not assigned to the person who created it.

- ✔ **Due Date:** This lists the date by which the To Do is supposed to be complete.

- ✔ **Status:** This details whether the particular item is *Current* (you should be working on it now); *In Progress* (you or someone else is working on it); *Not Started* (you don't need to work on it yet); *Complete* (it's finished); or *Overdue* (you were supposed to have already completed it, so what are you waiting for?)

- ✔ **Assigned To:** The name of the person who is on the hook to get the thing done. No name in this column means that the To Do is assigned to you. (Get to work!)

- ✔ **Category:** Use this column to collect and organize To Dos by project name or customer or anything else.

Eagle-eyed readers will also notice that you can sort the To Dos in the All To Do's view by clicking any of these column headings.

Click the Personal view of To Do, and up pops what you see in Figure 10-3. This view arranges the To Dos based on their respective priorities: High, Medium, Low, No Priority, or Completed.

What's the difference between the All To Do's view and the Personal view? It comes down to whom the To Do has been assigned. As you can read later in this chapter in section "Assigning a task to someone else," you can create a To Do but assign it to someone else. Gotta like that. To Dos such as this — that you assign to others — appear in the All To Do's view but not in your Personal view.

The All To Do's view displays all the tasks that you create, regardless of to whom the To Do was assigned. The Personal view, on the other hand, only displays the To Dos that are assigned to you.

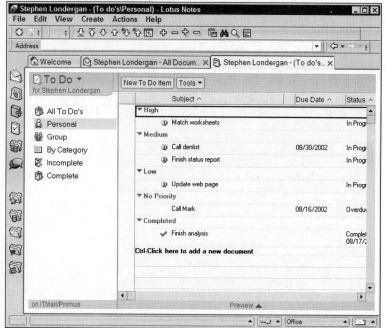

Figure 10-3:
View your
Personal
To Dos.

Besides the All To Do's and Personal views of your To Dos, the four other
views in your To Dos are

- ✔ **Group:** Shows your To Dos organized by Group.

- ✔ **By Category:** Lists To Dos organized by the Category field.

- ✔ **Incomplete:** Shows the To Dos that are, well, incomplete.

- ✔ **Complete:** Shows the To Dos that are done, done, done. (What a sense of
  accomplishment this view brings.)

To see more information about a To Do than appears in any of these views,
select the To Do in question and press Enter or double-click it to open it. As
you can see in Figure 10-4, the To Do Item form itself has more fields than
appear in the views.

- ✔ **Subject:** This field holds a short phrase or sentence or two that
  describes the thing that needs doin'.

- ✔ **When:** This section of the form holds the fields that you use to tell Notes
  when the task needs to be completed and also when the work should
  begin.

- ✔ **Priority:** This is the relative importance (High, Medium, Low, or None)
  by which the To Do is classified.

✔ **Category:** This shows how the task is classified — such as by project or customer name or what have you.

✔ **Status:** This field details whether the State of the To Do is Complete, Overdue, Current, or Not Started. (It's set automatically by Notes.)

✔ **Assign To:** In this area, you can see who's on the hook (usually you, unfortunately) to get the To Do done.

   • **Myself:** This radio button is selected if it's you.

   • **Others:** This radio button is selected if it's someone else. For more on this feature, skip down to the upcoming section "Assigning a task to someone else."

✔ **Notify Me:** Selecting this check box tell Notes to sound an alarm in advance of the To Do's completion date.

✔ **Mark Private:** Use this check box to set whether other people who can see your Calendar can see the To Do.

To Dos appear in your Calendar.

✔ **Description:** This entire area at the bottom of the form can contain a longer, more expansive description of the task at hand, which can include file attachments, pictures, and so on. (Alert readers will recognize the Description field as a rich text field, meaning that you can write and edit and insert documents and other files here.)

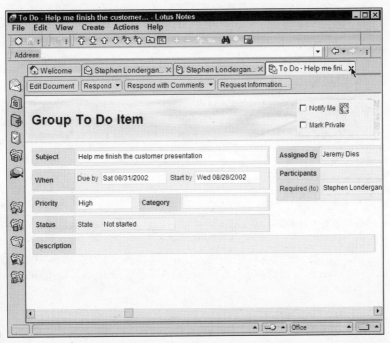

Figure 10-4:
A sample
To Do.

Close a To Do and return to the To Do view by either clicking the Save and Close button or by pressing Esc.

Creating a New To Do

To add a new To Do, either click the New To Do Item button on the Action bar or choose Create➪To Do. Figure 10-5 shows a sample To Do form.

Click the Save and Close button on the Action bar when you're finished filling out the fields of the new To Do Item form. You can always press Esc if you change your mind and want to abandon the new To Do. You can also press Ctrl+E to edit it later on.

Click to save   Click to mark   Click to create
and close.   complete.   a new To Do.

Figure 10-5:
Create a
new To Do.

When You're Finished: Marking a To Do as Complete

One of the reasons to use To Dos in Notes in the first place is that Notes can help you organize and prioritize your time by letting you know which of your To Dos needs your immediate attention. Of course, that's 100 percent dependent upon Notes knowing the start dates, due dates, and status of your workload. To read more about how to set these parameters, skip back to the earlier section "Viewing Your To Dos."

The most important thing that you have to do to keep your To Do list accurate and up to date is to be responsible about updating the completion status of your To Dos. In other words, you need to tell Notes when you complete a To Do.

To mark a To Do as done, compete, finito, over . . . select the To Do item and then click the Mark Complete button on the Action bar or choose Actions⇨ Mark Complete.

Working with Other People

One of the coolest things about To Dos in Notes is that they can help you work with others. Imagine a team of people who work together on some common project or goal. As a member of this team, you could use Notes to assign, delegate, and accept To Do assignments between the team members, using the same forms and views that you use to track, organize, and manage your own To Dos.

Of course, a big part of the success of such an endeavor has to do with the people on the team and their level of cooperation. In other words, just because you use the Assign To radio button in a To Do form doesn't mean the person is actually going to do the work!

Using To Dos with other people is quite similar to using Calendars with other people. (For the lowdown on the Calendar, read through Chapter 8.) In other words, how you assign a To Do or decline and delegate assignments is a lot like how you invite folks to, assign a delegate to, or decline meeting invitations.

Assigning a task to someone else

To assign the To Do to someone else in a new To Do form, select the Others radio button in the Assign To section of the form, as shown in Figure 10-6.

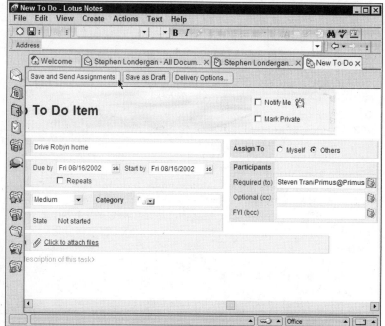

Figure 10-6:
Assign a
To Do to
someone.

You can enter any number of names in the three fields of the Participants area that appears: Required, Optional, and FYI. Most important, anyone whose name is in the Required field will see this To Do (assuming they agree to do whatever you are asking them) in their To Do list. The new To Do will be sorted and categorized, as I discuss earlier in the section "Viewing Your To Dos." All those who you list in the Optional field also receive this To Do item, but they'll know that they aren't, well, on the hook to complete it. The people who you list in the FYI field receive a copy of the To Do but aren't asked to accept it.

Imagine that you're working with the members of your company's art department to make a new product brochure, and you need to collectively decide on a new picture to use on the cover of the brochure. You might use a new To Do item to help the process. You could, for example, create a new To Do item and assign it to the person in the art department (Stu) who has to review the photo. You could list Stu's assistant (Jimmy) as an optional assignee just in case Stu is on one of his frequent vacations or out sick. You could also list your boss (Louise) in the FYI field so that you keep her apprised of what's going on.

When you finish filling out a To Do that you intend to assign to someone else, click the Save and Send Assignments button on the Action bar.

You'll see when your minion has agreed to do your bidding by selecting the To Do in question, right in your To Do list, as you can see in Figure 10-7 — Jeremy has agreed to go fetch the java.

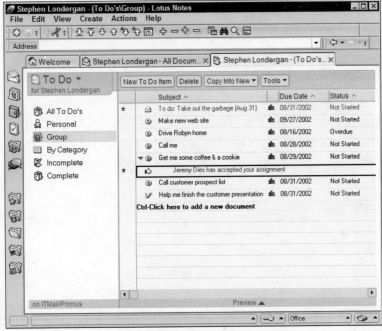

Figure 10-7:
Check
whether
your
assignee
accepts the
To Do.

When a To Do gets assigned to you

When you're on the wrong end of an assignment . . . that is, someone assigned a To Do to you . . . these assignments show up in your Inbox just like any other e-mail. They look like the one in Figure 10-8.

You have five options for dealing with a To Do assigned to you. Use the Action bar Respond button to

- ✔ **Accept:** Adds the To Do to your list and also confirms with the assignor that you're willing to do whatever needs doin'.

- ✔ **Decline:** Nope, no way, you're not gonna do it. When you choose this, the assigned item isn't added to your To Do list; also, Notes tells the assignor that you're not playing ball.

- ✔ **Delegate:** Lets you sidestep the To Do by suggesting the name of someone else who would be a better alternative.

- ✔ **Propose New Date:** Provisionally accepts the To Do but only if the assignor agrees to your new Due Date.

- ✔ **Completed:** Sends a message to the assignor indicating that you have finished the To Do. (How did you get *so* efficient, by the way?)

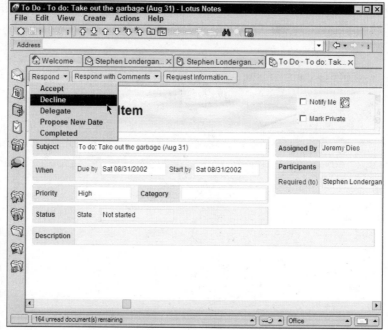

Figure 10-8:
To Dos
assigned to
you arrive in
your Inbox.

You can alternately use the Action bar Respond with Comments button to send an e-mail message along with your decision to accept or decline the To Do.

Setting To Do Preferences

You can customize the way that To Dos work in a couple of ways. To set your To Dos to match your own inimitable sense of purpose and taste, first open the Mail. Then choose Tools⇨Preferences and click the Calendar & To Do tab on the Preferences dialog box that appears.

As you can see in Figure 10-9, you have two settings to choose. Select the Do Not Display To Do Entries in the Calendar check box if you want your To Dos to appear only in the To Do view and not on your Calendar, interspersed amongst your meetings and appointments.

Mark the Allow Notes to Update To Do Status and Dates for Incomplete Entries check box to have Notes automatically help you by marking things that were due when they're not complete.

Finally, you can use the Colors tab of the Preferences dialog box to select the background and text color for To Dos. The colors that you choose here determine the way that the To Dos appear in your Calendar and Inbox. See all your choices in Figure 10-10.

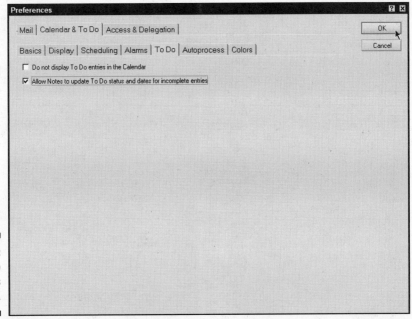

Figure 10-9:
Set To Do preferences here.

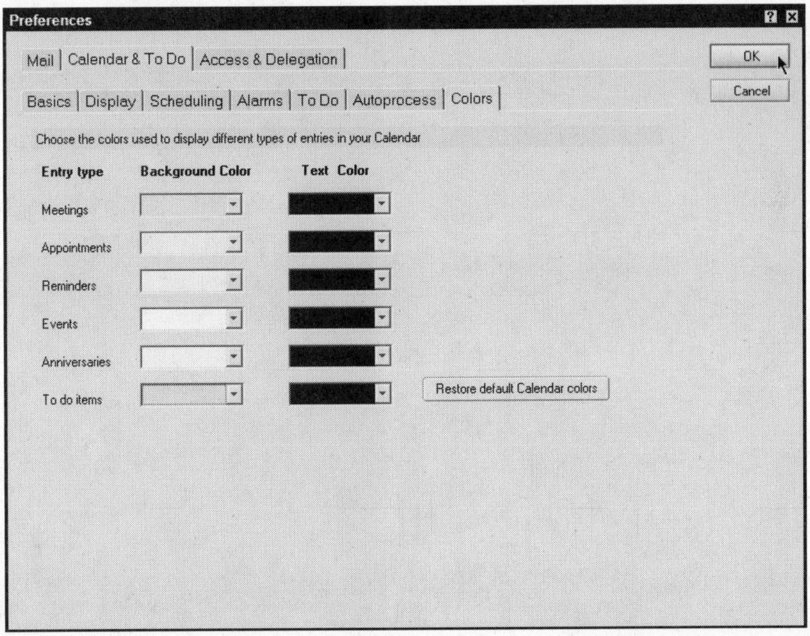

Figure 10-10:
Choose the color for your To Dos.

Click OK when you're finished with the Preferences dialog box.

Chapter 11

Your Personal Address Book

*Y*ou probably have customers (or perhaps, friends, family members) whose e-mail addresses you need to remember. Maybe you need to create your very own, just-for-you mailing list. You've come to the right place because in this chapter, I show you how to use the Lotus Notes 6 Personal Address Book to do all this and more.

Making It Personal

Your company probably maintains a big list of all the employees at your company. Called the *Public Directory* or *Public Address Book*, this is the tool that you use when you create a new message and address it by clicking the Address button in the Bookmark bar. (For more on the Bookmark bar, see Chapter 2.)

Usually these directories are compendiums with a lot of information about each employee, such as first and last name, e-mail address, and perhaps even phone number, manager's name, office location, and so on. (It depends on the size of your organization, of course, but it could easily be a list of several hundred thousand people.)

The Public Directory certainly is a convenient tool; all the information that's in it is available to everyone at your organization, and that's a good thing . . . most times. Actually, I can think of two situations when keeping contact information in the Public Directory isn't necessarily a good thing.

First, suppose that you have a customer, or a friend, or perhaps a family member with whom you need to swap messages. It'd be easier if you could tell Notes what this person's e-mail address is so that you don't have to remember the intricacies of that person's e-mail address. You know, is it `.com` or `.net`, or is it `stephen_londergan` or `stephen.londergan`? You *could* ask your network administrator to put this person's particulars in the Public Directory, but if this person is your friend and your friend only, chances are that your administrator is going to balk at adding your personal entry to the Public Directory.

Second, maybe you regularly send mail to a group of people. This group could be members of your department, or three friends from college, or any other collection of names. Again, you could ask to have a mailing list created for these people and added to the Public Directory, but that would only make sense if everyone at your company needs to send mail to that particular collection of people. Of course, sometimes that is the case — and then it's perfectly reasonable to ask your administrator to create a mailing list that everyone at the company can use. But sometimes it isn't — sometimes you need a mailing list that's yours and yours alone.

You can control both of these situations by using your very own Personal Address Book. Because this address book is yours and yours alone, you can put anything in it that you want. Add all those e-mail addresses that you collected at your last reunion or perhaps the names and addresses of your top ten customers. You can also use your Personal Address Book to create your own mailing lists (Groups).

The only difference between the Public Address Book and your Personal Address Book is their respective scopes. Information in the Public Address book is available to everyone at your company, and information in your Personal Address Book is only for you.

Using Your Personal Address Book

Your Personal Address Book is really just a file that Notes automatically creates for you. In other words, whether you realize it or not — and whether you've ever used it before, or not — you've already got one.

Opening your Personal Address Book

The easiest way to open your Personal Address Book is to click the third icon in the Bookmark bar. (See this icon in the left margin.) You can also click the Contacts button if you're at the Welcome page.

In Figure 11-1, you see an open Personal Address Book — it's essentially just a sorted list of the people (Contacts) that you add. Of course, if you haven't added any people, don't be surprised to see that your Personal Address Book is empty!

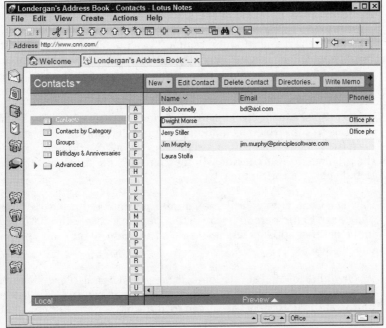

When you first open your Personal Address Book, you see the Contacts view, as shown in Figure 11-1.

As you can see in the figure, it's organized a little bit like your e-mail with a list of folders on the left side, such as Contacts, Contacts by Category, and Groups.

The center part of the screen is the list of the names of the people in your Personal Address Book. The horizontal list of letter buttons (A–Z) in between the folders and Contact names is a very convenient way to jump from person to person. For example, if you want to get to the first person whose name begins with the letter *L*, you would just click the (you guessed it) the L button.

As you can also see in Figure 11-1, each of the columns can be used to sort your Personal Address Book's contents in the same way you can sort your mail messages. Just click the column heading, such as Name or Business, and Notes automatically re-orders the Contacts based on that column.

Finally, note the buttons (New, Edit Contact, Delete Contact, and so on) in the Action bar that you use to manage your Personal Address Book contents.

Each person whose name you have in your Personal Address Book is known, in Notes parlance, as a *Contact*.

Reading a Contact document

To read all the details about a Contact, you open it the same way that you open an e-mail message or any other document in any other Notes database. Select the Contact (person) in question, and then either press Enter or double-click that entry to open the person's Contact document.

As you can see in Figure 11-2, Contact documents use a series of tables and sections to show the information about the person. For example, you could click the Personal tab to see Jeremy's home information, or you could click the Advanced Tab to decide whether Jeremy's Personal or Business information displays in the Summary view.

Having a Contact in your Personal Address Book helps makes it easy to send a message to the person because that person's name automatically shows up in the list that appears when you click the Address button to prepare a new e-mail address.

When you're looking at the Contacts view, you can also use the Preview pane to see more details about a Contact, as shown in Figure 11-3. Click the Preview button at the bottom of the screen to show or hide the Preview, just as you would in your Inbox.

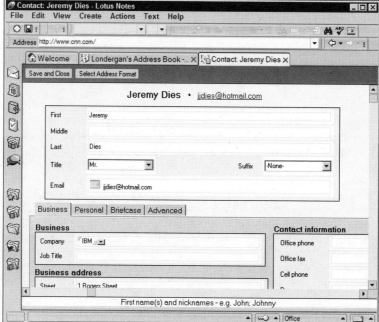

Figure 11-2:
Add descriptive info for your Contacts in your Personal Address Book.

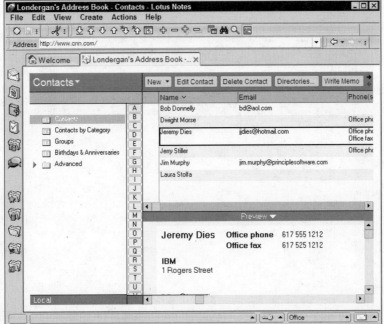

Figure 11-3:
Preview a
Contact for
details.

Adding a Contact

You have a couple of different ways to get information about a person into your Personal Address Book. Depending on how hard you feel like working today, take the high road or the low road.

Creating a new Contact the hard way

The most direct way to add a new Contact is to open your Personal Address Book, click the New button on the Action bar, and then select Contact from the drop-down menu that appears.

After a new Contact form opens (see a partially filled out form in Figure 11-4), it's just a matter of entering as much (or as little) information as you want about the person. Depending on the kind of information that you intend to enter, you'll probably end up clicking the form's tabs and sections (such as the Personal tab, for example, or the Briefcase tab).

Of special interest is the Briefcase tab, which contains a special field where you can enter things such as attachments (maybe you have the person's resume) or even a photograph.

Click to save and close.

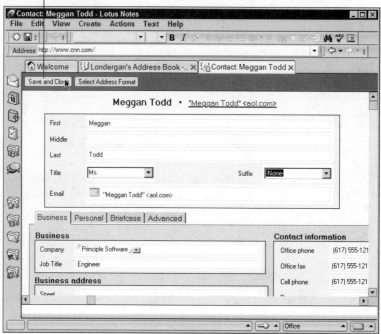

Use the Edit Contact Labels button (above the phone numbers) to use a special form that makes it a little easier to enter phone numbers. You can also use this form to change what the numbers are called so that if a person has an extra phone number, you might change the second field to read *Downstairs phone* instead of *Office fax*.

When you finish entering information about your Contact, click the Save and Close button (check it out in Figure 11-4) on the Action bar.

To edit an existing Contact (perhaps you just found out a Contact's cell phone number or got an updated e-mail address), just select the person's name in the Contacts view. Click the Edit Contact button on the Action bar and then complete your update(s) to make the changes that you need. When you're finished editing information about your Contact, click the Save and Close button on the Action bar.

Creating a new Contact the easy way

The most common reason for adding a Contact to your Personal Address Book is to make it easy to remember his or her e-mail address. Consequently, those good folks at IBM (creator of Notes) have made this *very* easy to do.

Suppose that a new customer sends you a message, and you want to add that person's e-mail address to your Personal Address Book so that you don't have to remember it or repeatedly go find it and retype it.

You may have not noticed it before, but every message that you receive has a button especially prepared just for this purpose.

1. **To add a contact the easy way, first open or select a message from the sender whose name you want to add to your Personal Address Book.**

2. **Choose Actions⇨Tools⇨Add Sender to Address Book.**

This neat little trick saves you the trouble of having to open your Personal Address Book, manually type in the person's name, and so on. And of course, after you add this Contact to your Personal Address Book, the new Contact name automatically appears in the Address list for a new message. Cool!

You can also add a new Contact via Quick Notes; just click the blue arrow at the right of the Notes Welcome page, and then click the Contact button. This is a new feature in Notes 6.

Discovering All about Groups

Groups, also sometimes called *mailing lists,* are just an easy way to address a message to a bunch of people without having to type each individual person's name. This is a great tool to use for easily addressing messages that you send to committees at work or a personal list of friends.

Use the Groups folder in your Personal Address Book to see the groups that you've already created.

Just like adding a new Contact, you have a couple of ways to add a new Group to your Personal Address Book: hard or smart.

Adding a Group the hard way

To create a new Group, open your Personal Address Book, click the New button on the Action bar, and then select Group from the drop-down menu that appears.

Even though the New Group form has a lot of fields, you're only concerned with two, and these two are found on the Basics tab (see Figure 11-5): Group Name, and Members.

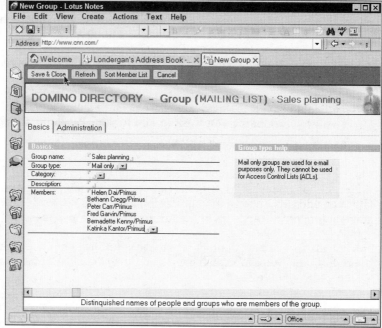

File Edit View Create Actions Text Help

Figure 11-5:
Add a new
Group
to your
Personal
Address
Book.

You can call a Group anything you want, so enter the name by which you'll address messages in the Group Name field.

Next, enter the names of the people who will be members of the Group in the Members field.

TIP

If you don't want to type in each Group member name, use the little arrow next to the Members field to choose the Group members from the directory.

When you're done entering information for your new Group, click the Save & Close button on the Action bar.

To edit a Group (to add or remove members or to change the group's name), just select the Group name in the Groups view. Click the Edit Group button on the Action bar and make the changes that you need. Then click the Save & Close button on the Action bar when you're finished editing the Group.

Creating a Group the smart way

You might decide to add a Group to your Personal Address Book because you find yourself regularly exchanging messages with a group of people. If you already have a message that's been addressed to these individuals, check out this easy way to create a new group that automatically includes the right people.

1. **First, open the message that was sent to the group of people that you want to make into your new Group.**

2. **Choose Actions⇨Add Recipients⇨To New Group in Address Book.**

   The Add recipients to New Group dialog box appears (see Figure 11-6), in which you can create the new group without even having to open your Personal Address Book.

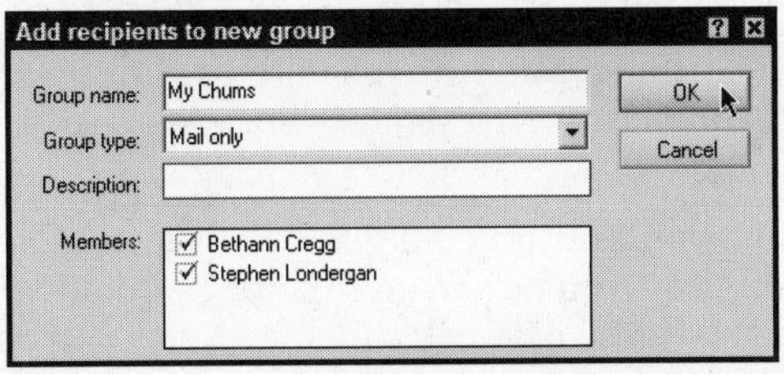

Figure 11-6:
It's easy to create a new Group right from an e-mail message.

Add recipients to new group	? ✗
Group name: My Chums	OK
Group type: Mail only ▾	Cancel
Description:	
Members: ☑ Bethann Cregg	
☑ Stephen Londergan	

3. **Click the OK button in the Add Recipients to New Group dialog box after entering the group's name and (optionally) a description.**

Another way to create a new Group is based on the Contact documents that you already have in your Personal Address Book. Open your Personal Address Book, select the names that you want from the Contacts view (either with the mouse or by selecting each and pressing the spacebar to check it off) and then choose Copy Into New Group from the Tools menu of the Action bar.

Uncovering Other Cool Address Book Toys

You may have noticed other things in your Personal Address Book besides just Contacts and Groups (refer to Figure 11-3). Although you may never have to use these other parts, here's a brief description of each.

In addition to Contacts and Groups, your Personal Address Book also has forms and views for:

- **Birthdays & Anniversaries,** which shows your Contacts, sorted by birthdays (assuming that you've entered one per Contact). You can also sort Contacts by an anniversary date, such as the date when you got a first order from a customer or the hire date of a co-worker.

- **Accounts,** which are used if you connect Notes to other systems, such as a directory service. (Ask your network administrator if you think you need to set up one of these.)

- **Certificates,** which are used to establish identity. This is also one to talk to your network administrator about.

- **Connections,** which are used to define how your computer talks to the server — especially if you use Notes away from the network or with a modem. Take a look at Chapter 19 to read about Connections.

- **International MIME Settings,** which are used to help Notes translate characters. This is *definitely* one to talk to your network administrator about.

- **Locations,** which help you use and configure Notes for use in more than one place. You'd use this if you have a laptop, for example, when sometimes you're connected to the network and sometimes you're not. Take a look at Chapter 20 to read about Locations.

Setting Preferences

 Finally, your Personal Address Book gives you the opportunity to make a couple of decisions about the way that you prefer it to work. Figure 11-7 shows your Personal Address Book Preferences form. Activate this form by clicking the Tools button (see this in the left margin) on the Action bar and then choosing Preferences.

As you can see in Figure 11-7, the form enables you to set make five preferences:

- **Address Book Owner,** which should have your name in it. Don't change this field!

- **Sort All New Groups by Default,** which tells Notes whether a new group's member list should be automatically alphabetized.

- **Allow Detailed LDAP Queries of This Address Book,** which tells Notes whether this address book is searchable. (Leave this field alone unless instructed to do otherwise.)

✔ **Newly Created Contacts Should Have Names Formatted As,** which tells Notes whether Contacts appear surname first or the other way around. Choose one of the two radio buttons here. Choosing one of these radio buttons determines how subsequent entries appear. To update your previously existing Contacts, click the Update All Entries button.

✔ **Default Address Format for All Contacts,** which tells Notes how you want new Contact documents to be displayed. Set your preference from the preset format choices given here.

Click the Save and Close button on the Action bar when you're done setting your Personal Address Book preferences.

Unless you have a really, really good reason to do so, you probably shouldn't mess with your Personal Address Book preferences.

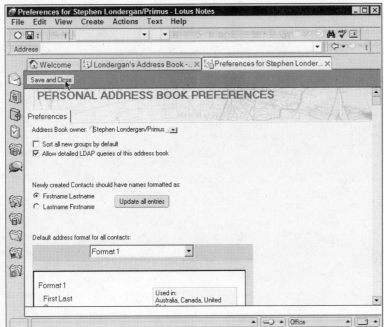

Figure 11-7:
Set
Personal
Address
Book
preferences
here.

Chapter 12

It's Databasic

In This Chapter

▶ Understanding basic database terminology

▶ Finding and opening Notes databases

▶ Using Notes servers

▶ Getting some database Help

A *lot* of fancy language and $10 words (or €10 words, if you prefer) start flying around when people discuss Lotus Notes. Perhaps you've heard all about *collaborative workspaces* and *working together* and *building more effective teams* and all that. Anyone up for a quick round of Buzzword Bingo?

But where the rubber hits the road, Lotus Notes 6 is just a program that uses files called *databases*. Because most of these special databases are kept on Lotus Domino servers, more than one person can use them at a time. And because more than one person can use a database to add documents and read information and all that, some people get all excited and feel the need to start tossing around all that €10 language.

Part of the excitement is because Notes databases are different from more traditional databases such as DB2 from IBM, and other database products such as Microsoft Access. I could fill a whole book on the technical differences between traditional, relational databases and Notes, but you certainly wouldn't want to read it.

All you need to know is that those other databases (like DB2) are really good at tracking and managing data, which is typically organized in rows and columns and tables. Notes is much, much better at tracking, managing, and sharing information, such as an e-mail message or an expense report or contract written in Microsoft Word.

In this chapter, I look under the hood of the average database and make sure that you can recognize what you see there. I also show you how to find and start databases. You need to know how to do this because in a word processing program, you simply open a document and start reading. But before you open a document in Notes, however, you must open the database in which that document is contained.

Est-ce que vous parlez Database?

Non? No doubt that you're much more comfortable in a country when you speak the language. Because the same is true when you enter the world of databases, I start this chapter by getting some of the basic vocabulary out of the way. Here's a list of the types of words that you routinely hear from people who are fluent in the database language:

- **Database:** A *database* is a collection of information. Most of the Notes databases that you'll use aren't on your computer but are rather housed on a Domino server somewhere.

- **Document:** A *document* is what's in a Notes database. Notes documents are created and saved by people, at least one of whom looks just like you. In a database, you can read and sometimes edit other people's documents.

- **Form:** A *form* is the part of a database that you use to view, compose, and edit documents. Filling in a form creates a document, for example.

- **Folder:** A *folder* is sort of like a table that lists the documents in a database. Any given folder displays documents in a database but not necessarily all of them. One database can have many folders, so you might have one folder that shows just your customers in California and another that lists your customers by shoe size. Yet another folder might display documents that have nothing to do with your customers, such as a list of companies that are hot sales prospects. Depending on the database that you use, you might or might not be able to create your own folders in it.

- **Field:** A *field* is a place where you grow herbs, like cilantro. Some fields are also used to grow vegetables, such as Swiss chard and lettuces. For example, in the book *Peter Rabbit*, one of the characters is a small bunny who. . . . Okay, wait. In Lotus Notes, a field is a place where you enter data, such as the place where you enter the name of the person to whom you're sending a message. When you're composing or editing a document, each field is marked by little L-shaped brackets or by a box in which you enter data or make choices. Notes boasts lots of different kinds of fields. Consult the following list if anyone ever asks you what those fields are:

  - Authors
  - Check box
  - Combo box
  - Date/Time
  - Dialog list
  - Formula
  - List box

- Names

- Number

- Password

- Radio button

- Readers

- Rich text

- Text

✔ **Data:** The *data* is whatever information that you or someone else enters into a field when composing or editing a document in a database.

So, putting it all together, you could open the Company Personnel *database,* compose a new *document* by using the Personnel Information *form,* type **Ted Farrell** in the Full Name *field,* and then enter some other *data* and save the whole thing in the *database* as a new document that will be listed in the All Employees by Name *view.* Then you can go out and plant some lettuce.

I spend a lot of time in this chapter going through the ins and outs of using a Lotus Notes database. The good news is that without realizing it, you probably already know most of this stuff — especially if you read the earlier chapters on how you use e-mail (Chapters 3 through 7). Your e-mail is a database, after all — did you know that? The only difference between the databases that I discuss in this chapter and your e-mail is the level of access that people have.

Finding a New Notes Database

Your boss — communicating with you through e-mail, of course — tells you to start using a particular Notes database to respond to customer inquiries. Although you've heard other people in the department talking about this thing, you've never used it before. What do you do?

First, get the specifics. No one can expect you to know about the existence of every database in use in your organization or where each one is located. (Some companies have thousands of databases.) And you certainly wouldn't expect to find the database in question on your own computer's hard drive; databases are usually placed on a server somewhere so everyone can use them. After all, databases aren't *yours;* they're *ours.*

After you open a new database for the first time, consider creating a bookmark for it so that you don't have to go looking for it the next time (as you can read in Chapter 2).

Before you try to find any database, ask your boss or a colleague for both the database's name *and* its host server's name. Knowing its filename may be helpful, too. Often several databases have similar names — Customer Tracking, Customer Data, Customer Leads, and so on. Knowing the filename guarantees that you're accessing the correct database.

Notes databases usually have the extension `.nsf`.

Whenever you need to open a database that you haven't used before, just follow these steps:

1. Choose File⇨Database⇨Open or press Ctrl+O.

The Open Database dialog box appears, as shown in Figure 12-1.

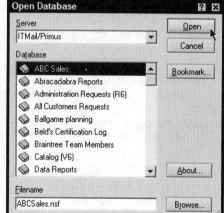

Figure 12-1:
Look for
Notes
databases
here.

2. Look in the Server list box.

In Figure 12-1, this list box reads `ITMail/Primus`.

The Local server is the one you want if the database you're seeking is on your own hard drive.

3. If you're looking for a database that isn't on your hard drive, click the down-arrow to the right of the server name in the Server list box.

You now see the names of one, a few, or lots of Domino servers, depending on how your network administrator has set up your company's databases. If you don't see the name of the server that you're after, use the scroll bar to move down the Server list.

If you're looking for a database on your own computer but are having trouble locating it, click the Browse button to search the various nooks, crannies, and directories on your hard drive to find it.

4. **Select the server that you want by clicking its name.**

   When you click the name of a server in the Server list box, a list of the databases on that server appears in the Database list box. The Database list changes according to the server that you choose. If you still aren't sure which database you want (sometimes several databases bear similar titles), check the filename in the Filename text field at the bottom of the dialog box.

5. **In the Database list box, select the database you want by double-clicking its name or by highlighting it and then clicking the Open button.**

   Verify the filename in the Filename text box if you aren't sure which database you want.

If your company has lots of Domino servers, all the server and corresponding database names might not appear in the Open Database dialog box. If you're trying to find a server that's doesn't seem to be in the list, try typing the server's name in the Server list box and then clicking the Open button. If that doesn't work, contact your network administrator.

Sometimes, for all sorts of reasons, database designers flip a switch in a database so that the database won't appear in the Database list. In this case, you have no way of seeing the name on your computer, so you have to ask a living, breathing person for the filename. The horror! Then you can type that filename in the Filename text box to open that database.

I hear you knocking, but . . . (certification problems)

As you may imagine, your network administrator has all kinds of tricks to determine which people get to use which servers. If you ever double-click a server name in the Open Database dialog box and get an error message that reads either `Your ID has not been certified to access the server` or `You are not authorized to use the server`, it probably means that your administrator has to do something to allow you to use that server. You can't do anything to correct this problem, so send your administrator an e-mail message asking for access. Be sure to copy your boss on this message so that your administrator knows that you're not kidding around here.

To be able to use a server, both your user ID and the server's user ID must have a common certificate, which is actually quite a complicated little piece of technology that Notes uses to make sure that you really are who you say you are. (Not that you'd ever lie, of course.) Fortunately (or maybe unfortunately), there's almost nothing you can do to resolve certificate and access problems; you almost always have to ask someone else to fix it for you. For more information about certificates, see Chapter 16.

The server names that you see in the Open Database dialog box are based on the whim of your administrator. The names may be functional (and grownup), such as Marketing or Sales. Or they might be more imaginative, such as Sleepy, Bashful, Doc, or Grumpy (bet you can't name all seven). When push comes to shove, though, you should ask someone which server you're supposed to use. Searching for a particular database can make you feel as though you're looking for hay in a needle stack.

Fumbling in folders

Just like you have folders on your hard drive to help you organize your files and folders in your e-mail to help manage messages, your administrator might set up folders on the server to help organize the databases. If your server has folders, they appear at the bottom of the list of Database titles of the Open Database dialog box; see the directories named ids, iNotes, mail, Marketing, and so forth in Figure 12-2. An additional hint that something is a folder rather than a database is that its icon is a folder.

Figure 12-2:
Databases
can be
organized in
folders on
the server.

To see a list of the databases in a particular folder, double-click its name. You can use the item on the list that looks like an up-arrow with two periods to return to the parent folder on the server; this up-arrow is visible only if a folder is expanded.

Should you bookmark or open a database?

As you can read in the earlier section "Finding a New Notes Database," you have two choices after you locate the server and database that you want to access. You can

- ✔ Open the database right away
- ✔ Bookmark the database so that you can open it easily later

If you want to open the database now, click Open. Or you can double-click its title, which has the same effect. Notes does three things:

- ✔ First, it adds that database to the list of bookmarked databases in your Databases folder so you can open it in the future without having to go through these File⇨Database⇨Open steps again.
- ✔ Second, it closes the Open Database dialog box.
- ✔ Third, it opens the database that you chose.

 If, instead, you want to bookmark the database and open it later, click the Bookmark button in the Open Database dialog box. When you do, the Add Bookmark dialog box appears, as shown in Figure 12-3. Use this dialog box to determine where the icon for the new database appears. (See this icon in the left margin.) Bookmarks are covered, incidentally, in rather nauseating detail, in Chapter 2.

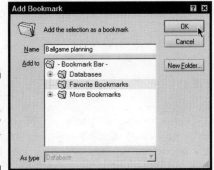

Figure 12-3: Bookmark a new database for later use.

When you make a bookmark for a database, the following happens:

- ✔ By default, the new database is listed in the Databases folder. To designate a different folder, choose a folder from the Add To list box of the Add Bookmark dialog box.

> ✔ If you want to create a new folder for your new icon, click the New Folder button of the Add Bookmark dialog box. Then type a name for your new folder in the Name text box of the Open Database dialog box that appears. Click OK and the database is added to the workspace and to your new folder.

Notice what *didn't* happen? The database did not open. It's not supposed to. Why not? Because you're in the Open Database dialog box, which gives you a chance to open or bookmark more databases. The Bookmark button is useful if you need to collect a few databases and you want to get them all in the same trip to the Open Database dialog box. Opening each database individually and then returning to the Open Database dialog box to open another one can be quite time consuming and cuts into the things for which you were really hired — having meetings and doing power lunches. (Or is it *doing* meetings and *having* power lunches?)

After you've bookmark all the databases that you need, click the Cancel button. Yes, Cancel. Despite what you might be thinking, Cancel will not undo all your hard work — it just closes the Add Bookmark dialog box.

Whichever method you choose, either opening the database or bookmarking it for later use, you won't have to go searching for it in the Open Database dialog box the next time that you want to get into this database. Just double-click the database's icon from your desktop or Bookmark folder.

You'll find that using a new Notes database can be a little bit like visiting a Web page for the first time — you might not decide until you get there whether you want a bookmark for it. Of course, you can use any of the techniques that I discuss in Chapter 2 for creating a bookmark if you find a database that you like (or at least need to have easy access to).

All about About . . .

The list of databases on a server can be long, confusing, and not always helpful. For example, if you open the company's sales database and you see listed such names as Sales Regions, Sales Forecasts, and Sales Accounts, it may be difficult to know which one to choose. The database's so-called *About document* (more specifically called *About This Database*) sometimes gives you a clue as to what the database contains and what it's used for.

To access this help file, click the About button in the Open Database dialog box. If the database's owner wrote an About document for that database, you can read it to glean whether this database is the one that you want. If no About document exists, you get a message reading `Special database object cannot be located`. Oh, well. It never hurts to try.

The Database Door Creaks Open

So exactly what *is* inside a database? That depends.

When you open a database for the first time, you see what the database's owner decided that first-time users should see. It might be the About document; it could be a graphic navigator or site map with buttons that you can click to go to important areas in the database; or you might just see a folder that lists some of the important documents in the database.

Most often the first thing that you see is the About document, written by the database's owner. Of course, some database designers are more conscientious than others; thus, some About documents are more instructive than others. In fact, a lazy database designer might not create an About document at all, so don't be surprised if you occasionally see a blank screen when you open a new database. If that happens, just press the Esc key on your keyboard to dismiss the blank About document, and chances are that you will be in the database.

After carefully reading and dismissing the About document screen, you usually will see one of the folders in the database. This folder is probably just one of several in the database, but it's the one that the database's owner decided you should see first.

A database usually has several folders, and most don't contain all the documents in a database. (That's kind of the point to folders, really — to organize and segregate the documents in a database.) Fortunately, most databases have a Navigation pane (like your e-mail does) to help you see what's available and move from one folder to another. You can also use the View ➪ Go to View menu to see a list of what folders are available.

And, in the just-so-you-know department, there may even be folders in a database that you don't see and don't know about. Don't be paranoid; no one is out to get you! It's just that a database owner can make very specific decisions about who gets to see what in a given database, and the database's owner may have decided that there are folders that you don't need to care about.

Usually, each time that you open a database (after the first time, that is), you see the folder that you were using the last time that you were there. Notes is pretty good about remembering what you were doing the last time you were there, even if you aren't.

> ### Out of sight, out of mind: Finding the About document later
>
> After you use a database for a few months, you'll probably forget all about the About document. After all, you saw it only once — the first day that you used the database. Because the About document could have lots of useful information, remember to refer to it in the future, especially if you dismissed it quickly the first time that you saw it. Don't worry, the About document is always close at hand. Just choose Help⇨About This Database, and bingo! — there it is.

Opening a Database on the Internet or an Intranet

Sometimes, depending on how the database owner set it up, you might be told to open a database with your Web browser instead of Notes. Ironically, doing so might even be easier than opening a database in Notes.

To open a database via the Internet, just crank up your favorite browser, type the URL for the database, and you're in business.

Unlike Notes, your browser might sort of forget what you were doing the last time that you visited this database, so you start at the initial screen every time and navigate from there.

If this is how you access a Notes database, that first screen is either a list of views or a map of the database, or it's an opening page with places to click to dig further into the database, create documents, or get more information before you move on.

When You Need Help

Sometimes you try to do something and get caught halfway through the procedure, unsure of the next step. Or maybe you're trying to figure out how to do something new. Help is just a few clicks away because you can always use the Help feature of any Notes database you're cruising. Also, the Notes Help feature is itself a giant database.

No matter what the task, look to any of these places for a helping hand:

- The built-in Help feature in Notes.

  Notes has a Help system that you can use in two ways: You can ask for help about the particular activity you're stuck with, or you can peruse the entire Notes Help database.

- The Using document, which is in every database. (Read about this in the upcoming section "Turning to a database's Using document."

Using context-sensitive help

Good news: Like most software these days, context-sensitive help is always just a keystroke away in Notes. Whenever you get stuck, you can always press F1 (or the Help key on a Mac), and Notes will do its best to show you a help screen that's related to whatever you're doing at the time. As always, you press Esc to close the Help document.

Press F1 anytime, anywhere, for help with what you are currently doing.

Bad news: The context-sensitive help in Notes doesn't give you database-specific help. That's because the Help that comes with the program deals only with how to use the Notes program, not any particular database. The programmers at IBM who make Lotus Notes are smart, but they have no way of knowing what kind of databases will be created by the thousands of worldwide database owners and managers out there in the world. When you have a question about the particulars of an application you're using, you have to get to the database's own Help screen. I cover getting database-specific help in the upcoming section under "Turning to a database's Using document."

Figure 12-4 shows the basic Help screen that you see when you press F1 in the Open Database dialog box. The point here (and I do have a point) is that the Help screen you'll see when you press F1 depends on what you're doing, at the time.

Reading the Help database

Got a few minutes before your next meeting? All the screens that you see when you press F1 come from a Notes database called (appropriately enough) *Notes Help*. You can rifle through the documents in the Help database just like you read any other database. They have lots of information that you may never even think to ask about with the F1 key.

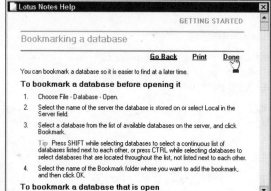

Bookmarking a database

Go Back   Print   Done

You can bookmark a database so it is easier to find at a later time.

To bookmark a database before opening it

1.   Choose File - Database - Open.

2.   Select the name of the server the database is stored on or select Local in the Server field.

3.   Select a database from the list of available databases on the server, and click Bookmark.

   Tip   Press SHIFT while selecting databases to select a continuous list of databases listed next to each other, or press CTRL while selecting databases to select databases that are located throughout the list, not listed next to each other.

4.   Select the name of the Bookmark folder where you want to add the bookmark, and then click OK.

To bookmark a database that is open

Figure 12-4:
Press F1
anytime,
anywhere to
get help.

To use Notes help, use the menu and choose Help.

Turning to a database's Using document

Every database has a *Using document,* which is similar to the About document that I describe earlier in the section "All about About . . ." Like the About document, the Using document (if there is one) is created by the person who created the database and is supposed to help you figure out how to use the database. To see a database's Using document, you have to open the database in question and then choose Help ⇨Using This Database.

Some people (but not the good ones) are lazy, so don't be surprised if you occasionally see a message that reads No help is available for this database when you try to see a database's Using document. If this happens to you, call the database's owner, directly, on the phone, with your questions. When these folks get sick of answering the same questions over and over again, they might decide after all to create an overdue Using document. My caveat: The world would be a better place if all Notes databases had help documents.

Chapter 13

Using Databases

When you open any Lotus Notes 6 database, you get your first glimpse of the contents of the database itself. Depending on what the owner of the database decides that you should see when you first open a database, you might wonder, "Where do I go from here?" In this chapter, I give you an idea of what you may see and do after you open a Notes database. I cover folders, views, forms, documents, and searches.

What exactly you see when you open a database varies from one database to the next, so don't be surprised if what you see looks different from what the figures in this chapter look like. Each database is designed differently, so read this whole chapter before you start to think that I've really lost my marbles.

I Was Just Thinking of View

Every database has at least one view, and most databases have several. Views are created by an esteemed colleague of yours, who shall, from here on out, be known as the *database designer*. The bad news is that a particular view's workings are entirely at the discretion of this person. That means that I can't predict exactly what kind of views you'll see and use in your Notes travels. The good news, on the other hand, is that their basic operation — how you select documents, how you print documents, and so on — is pretty much the same from view to view (and database to database).

A view usually does four things:

- ✔ **Summarizes** the documents in the database
- ✔ **Sorts** the documents in the database
- ✔ **Helps** you find documents in the database
- ✔ **Selects** at least some of the documents in the database to display

In Figure 13-1, you can see a view of a very simple database that lists customer requests. This view shows (or *selects*) requests for the North region only; surveys from customers in the East, West, and South aren't included in this particular view. This view sorts the documents by customer name and then lists the customer's city. By the way, it's a pretty safe bet that each of the documents shown in this view has more information than this particular view shows; the designer of the view decided that this selected information best summarized each document.

Views and folders are *almost* the same thing, so don't sweat the terminology. The subtle but important difference is how Notes decides which documents are displayed in which view. A view's contents are determined and decided upon by the database designer — in other words, you can't do anything to make a particular document appear (or not appear) in a particular view. Conversely, you *can* create and determine the contents of a folder.

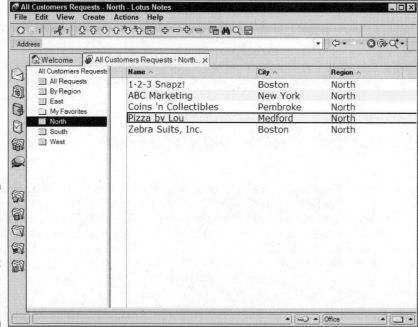

Figure 13-1:
Views summarize, sort, and select documents in a database.

Because what you see when you open a database varies from one database to the next, don't be surprised when what you see looks different from the figures in this chapter. Each database is designed differently.

What's in a view, anyway?

Each line (row) in a view represents an individual document, and each column represents information contained in that particular document. Depending on how the view works and how many documents are in the database that you're looking at, it's fairly common that more documents are in the view than can be displayed on the screen at one time.

You can navigate amongst the documents by pressing the arrow keys, by using the mouse to click on a document that you're interested in, or by using the scroll bars.

Database designers often make it possible for users to change the width of a column. Just click and drag the right-hand border of a column head to the left to narrow the column or to the right to widen it.

When the stars come out

In many databases, Notes knows which documents you've read and which ones you haven't. This distinction is particularly helpful in a discussion database, in which you don't want to waste time on the documents that you've already read. You can usually tell that a document is new (or at least unread by you) because it's a different color from the documents that you have read. *Note:* A document that you haven't read before *always* has a little star next to it in the leftmost column of the view.

Unread documents are usually red, but don't be totally surprised if they're some other color. The database designer gets to decide what color they are.

Response documents are documents composed by users to, you guessed it, respond to another document in a database. Most databases, like the one shown in Figure 13-2, display response documents indented under the document that they're responding to.

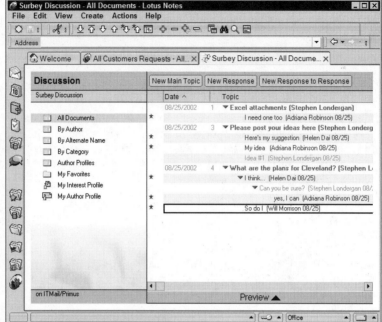

Figure 13-2:
Response
documents
help you
figure out
who is
saying what
to whom.

A Sort of Category

Views are great for sorting documents. With the help of the sort feature, you can list documents in a given database in whatever order you choose: by the customer type, by the sales rep's name, or by sales region, for example. Some views (and folders) not only sort documents but also categorize them.

When a view *sorts* its documents, it lists them in alphabetical or numerical order according to what they have in a particular field. It also shows what each document has in that field even if it's the same as what the document above it has. On the other hand, when a view *categorize*s its documents, it still sorts the documents but lists a particular field value only once, followed by all the documents that have the same value in that field.

Confused? It's easier to see than it is to read. Take a look at Figure 13-3, in which you can see all the Request forms that have been entered in the database, sorted by their region. This view shows you that this view has two surveys from the East, three from the North, and so on.

This arrow means you can re-sort.

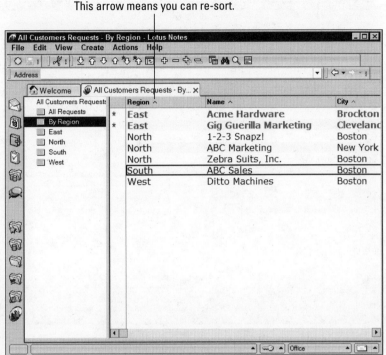

Figure 13-3:
Documents
sorted by
region.

Put on your glasses or squint, and then look carefully at the Region heading of the first column in Figure 13-3. See the little arrowhead? When you see one or two arrowheads, you can re-sort the view based on the contents of that column. For example, if the column is arranged in ascending alphabetical order, clicking anywhere in that column heading changes the sort order from ascending (A–Z) to descending (Z–A).

Now take a look at Figure 13-4, which is essentially the same view. You can see all the surveys that have been entered in the database, categorized (instead of sorted) by their region. Categories just simplify what's in a view, making it easier to read.

One of the reasons that views have categories is to make the view a little neater and easier to look at. You can further organize a view by collapsing and expanding categories.

In Figure 13-5, the South category is completely expanded, and the East, North, and West categories are collapsed. The documents in a collapsed category are still there, of course, and they appear like magic when you expand a category.

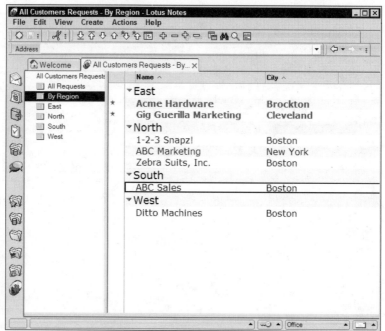

Figure 13-4:
Documents
categorized
by region.

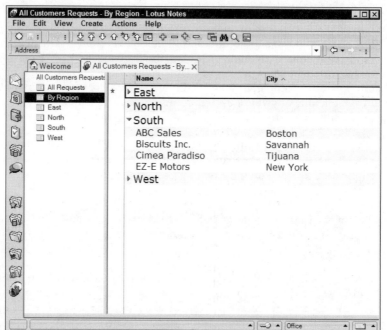

Figure 13-5:
You can
expand and
collapse
categories.

Here are the ways to expand or collapse a single category. (It depends on what you want to expand or collapse.)

✔ **Menu:** Select the category in question and then choose View➪Expand/Collapse. From the drop-down menu that appears, choose Expand All, Collapse All, Expand Selected Level, Expand Selected & Children, or Collapse Selected Level. (If you have visions of little flat children running around your neighborhood, you missed the point about Expand Selected & Children: It just means to expand the current category and any subcategories that it might have.)

Keyboard: It's even easier to press + (the plus key) to expand a selected section or - (the minus key) to collapse a selected section.

✔ **Buttons:** Click the toolbar Expand or Collapse buttons (shown here in the margin).

✔ **Twisty:** Click once directly on the green triangle (a *twisty*) located to the left of the category name. Refer to Figure 13-5.

✔ **Double-click it:** Best yet, rather than trying to remember all that, either double-click the category row that you want to expand or collapse, or highlight the category and then press Enter.

To expand or collapse the whole view:

✔ **Menu:** Choose View➪Expand All or View➪Collapse All.

✔ **Buttons:** Click the toolbar Expand All or Collapse All buttons (shown here in the margin).

✔ **Keyboard:** Press Shift++ (that's Shift and the plus sign) to expand the whole view or Shift+- (Shift and the minus sign) to collapse the whole view.

Sometimes you'll find categories inside categories; maybe you'll encounter a view that categorizes documents by country and then subcategorizes them within each country by state. Subcategories work the same way as major categories — you can expand them and collapse them, too.

Using Folders as Holders

No doubt about it, views are great, and you won't hear me criticizing them. But they do have a disadvantage: You can't decide what should be in a view because that's up to your database designer. Imagine that you want to store a bunch of documents of your own choosing together in one place in a database. Perhaps you want to put together all the surveys that need your immediate attention or group documents on a vague subject. You could bookmark them all, of course, but if a database has folders in it, they may be easier to use.

The answer to this penetrating question is . . . folders. Like views, *folders* can display some of the contents of a database. In Figure 13-6, you can see a discussion database with a folder called *My Favorites*. For those who like a challenge, can you tell how to distinguish between views and folders? (***Hint:*** You see a folder icon next to the names of folders and a little rectangle with what is supposed to look like words next to a view.)

Keep in mind the following things you can do with folders:

- ✔ **Storing documents in folders**

  - You put documents in a folder by clicking and dragging a document from a view or a folder into a folder.

  - You might also find a button somewhere onscreen that enables you to assign the selected document(s) to a folder.

  - Putting a document in a folder doesn't create a new copy of the document; it just lists the document in a new place.

- ✔ **Removing documents from folders**

  - You can remove one or more selected documents from a folder by choosing Actions⇨Remove from Folder.

    Removing a document using the preceding method doesn't delete it from the database. It simply removes it from the folder.

  - You might also have a button somewhere with which you can remove a document from a folder, depending on how your database designer set up the database.

  - Don't press the Delete key to delete a document from a folder. Pressing Delete removes it from the database permanently.

- ✔ **Views in folders**

  - Folders, like views, have columns. Each column shows the contents of various fields in the documents.

  - If you add a document to a folder and that document doesn't contain any of the fields listed in the folder's columns, there won't be any data to display in the column, so you won't see the document listed there. The document is represented by a blank line.

Odds are that you sometimes want to see the documents in a database listed in a different way. In other words, if you want to switch to a different view or folder, click its name. Give Notes a second or two, and the new choice opens.

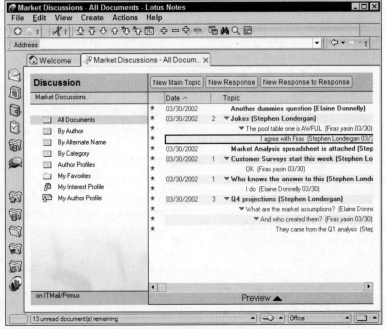

Figure 13-6:
In some databases, you can use folders to organize documents.

So, What Can You Do with Documents?

Among the things you can do with documents in a view are

✔ Select them

✔ Read them

✔ Forward them

✔ Add them to a folder

✔ Print them

✔ Delete them

In this section, I give you tips on how to do all these things.

Selecting documents

You can do all kinds of things with documents — print them, delete them, forward them as e-mails — but first you need to select them.

Select a document one at a time

In a word-processing program, if you want to make a word bold, you first select the word and then use some command to make the word bold. This concept applies also to selecting documents in a view. If a view has a few documents and you want to do something to one of them — print it, delete it, or open it — you have to select it first.

By now, you've probably noticed that a box surrounds a single document in a view or a folder. That box is called the *selection bar,* and you use it to highlight an individual document. The document in that box is thereby *selected,* and Notes knows that you want to do something to it.

But what if I want more than one?

Funny you should ask. Suppose that you want to print five documents in a view. Sure, you use the selection bar to select them, but how do you tell Notes that you want more than one? The easiest way to select multiple documents is to select the first document in question and then press the spacebar. When you do so, the document gets a check mark off in the far-left column of the view, as shown in Figure 13-7. (You can use your mouse to select the items of choice by clicking in the far-left column as well.) If you see no check marks, the highlighted document is selected; if you do see check marks, the documents with check marks are selected. Careful observers will also note that you get a running tally of how many documents you have selected in the bottom-left of the view.

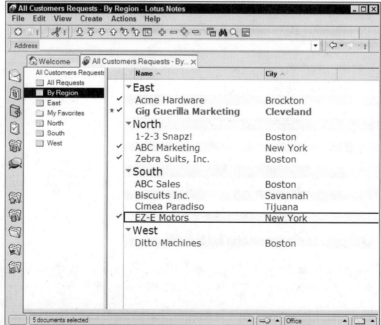

Figure 13-7:
You can select more than one document at a time.

If you need to select a few documents, highlight each one and press the spacebar. If the documents that you want are one after the other, it's a little easier to hold down Shift while you press the up- or down-arrow keys to move the selection bar over the documents. Notes checks them off as the highlight bar passes over them.

Better yet, if you use a mouse, you can select a bunch of documents all at once by clicking and dragging them over to the left column where you saw the check marks appear.

Finally, you can deselect a document that you mistakenly select (oops!) by using any of the methods that you used to select it in the first place. In other words, if you have already checked off the document, selecting it again unchecks it.

You can select all the documents in a folder or view by choosing Edit⇨ Select All.

Reading documents

It's very easy to read a document in a database. Reading a document in a database is the same as reading a message in your Inbox. Use these steps to open and close a document:

1. **Select (click) the document that you want to read.**

2. **Press Enter to open it.**

3. **If needed, use the scroll bars to read the document if it's bigger than the screen.**

4. **To close the document and return to the view or folder that you started out in, press Esc or choose File⇨Close.**

One of the reasons, of course, that you open a document is to make changes. I discuss editing in the upcoming section "Wait — can I create?"

You can also double-click a document to open it and read it.

Previewing documents

Another way to read a document is through a document's preview window.

To turn on the document preview, choose View⇨Document Preview⇨Show Preview. As you can see in Figure 13-8, doing so makes some of the view's contents go away in favor of the added Preview pane, in which you can see the top of the selected document.

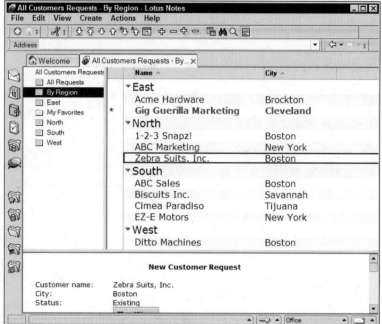

Figure 13-8:
You can
preview
documents
in any
database.

Whether you choose to use the Preview pane or not is entirely up to you. You really can't do much with it open other than read the document displayed there.

To change your mind and get rid of the document preview, just choose View⇨Document Preview⇨Show Preview again. Each time that you select this command, Notes toggles opening and closing the Preview pane.

Some people prefer to keep the Preview pane closed all the time to save screen real estate.

Forwarding a bunch of documents

Every now and then, you want someone else to see a document of interest. You can call them and tell them to open the Sales Database on the Marketing Server, use the Hot Prospects View, and check out the doc with the title *This Guy Has a Million Dollars to Spend*. But why not save the call and a lot of time and just send the document to that person? Highlight one document or select several documents and then choose Actions⇨Forward. Enter the name of everyone who should see the documents and then send the memo. The selected documents become the body of the memo.

Adding documents to a folder

In the earlier section "Using Folders as Holders," I describe the process for adding documents to a folder. Be sure that the documents that you add to a folder are visible in that folder. If the documents don't contain fields listed in the columns, the documents won't appear to be listed in the folder. You'll only see a blank line acting as a placeholder for the document that has no fields to display in the columns. Double-clicking the blank line opens the document.

Printing from a view

When you have a view or a folder (as opposed to a document) open and you choose File⇨Print, you get Print View dialog box, as shown in Figure 13-9.

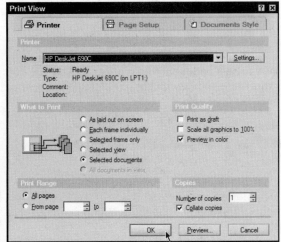

Figure 13-9:
Print documents from here.

This dialog box has a lot of stuff in it — and you may have even *more* options because what you see depends on the kind of printer that you use.

The most important options in the dialog box are the ones on the Printer tab in the What to Print area: Selected View and Selected Documents. Use these options (judiciously) to specify whether you want to print the view as it appears onscreen or print the actual documents you have.

Use the other options to determine which printer to use, which pages to print, the quality of the print job, how many copies to print, and whether to collate copies. Click the Documents Style tab to tell Notes how to separate the documents (new page, no separation, line), whether Notes should reset the page numbers for each document it prints, and whether to print using another form. Back on the Printer tab, I recommend clicking the Preview button to see onscreen what the printed page will look like. After you make your printing choices here, click OK to finish. Check out Chapter 5 for more information about printing.

Deleting documents

To delete documents, select the document (or documents) that you want to get rid of and press Delete. The documents don't actually disappear, but each document gets marked with an *X*, as shown in Figure 13-10.

To actually dispose of the marked document, do one of the following:

- Press F9
- Choose View⇨Refresh
- Close the database

When you take any of the preceding actions, Notes makes you confirm via a Yes/No dialog box that you do indeed want to delete documents. That's good because you can click No if you goofed.

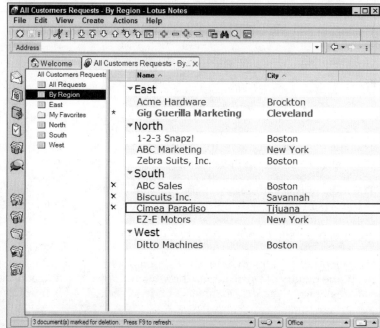

Figure 13-10: Documents marked for deletion have an *X* next to them.

When you mark a document to be deleted (but haven't used one of those three taken steps to finalize the deletion) and you decide that you don't want to delete it after all, select the document and press Delete again. The little *X* disappears, and you can stop worrying because that document's not going anywhere.

Of course, you can't necessarily delete a document just because you know how to use the Delete key. In fact, in most databases, you can delete a document only if you're the person who composed it in the first place. Not only are you prevented from deleting anyone else's documents, but you don't have to worry about anyone else deleting your documents, either. For more on permission to delete, read the upcoming section, "Wait — can I create?"

A Document with All the Fixin's

When you open a document, you may see all kinds of things: words, pictures, icons, tables, and buttons. If you want to be the resident Notes expert, read the following sections to find out what all these things are about.

What's the difference between a document and a form?

Good question! The difference between a form and a document is a little bit subtle, especially because you really don't ever see one without the other.

A form is a part of a database. *Forms*, created by database designers, are the part of the database that's used to read and edit documents. For example, if you need to add new information to a database, you do so by filling out a form. If you're like most Notes users, you won't create your own forms: You use the forms that have been added to databases by the database designers or systems administrators at your company.

A *document*, on the other hand, is the actual information that you enter. Most Notes users definitely do create their own documents, using the forms in the database to create them.

The bottom line? When you press Enter in a view to open a document, you're actually looking at two things: the documents and a form. The form is the thing that organizes the information, lists the document's field names, and so on. The document is the actual information that's in the database.

When you open a document, you're likely to encounter several different things. In the next few sections, I discuss what can show up on a form.

Static text

No, static text doesn't have anything to do with rubbing your feet on a rug in the wintertime. *Static text* just refers to words that are a permanent part of certain documents: You can't change it.

The person who created the forms in the databases that you use no doubt included some static text. Static text can be the title of the form, field names, or maybe some instructions about how to use the form. Take a look at Figure 13-11 to see some examples of static text. In this (overly-simplified) form, the static text is in bold, and the fields filled in by the user are plain text. (Of course, in the forms you use, the static text might not be bold.)

Fields

Fields are where the action is in a document. They contain the information that matters: that is, the information that you can add and change when you're composing or editing a document. Fields come in a number of different flavors (not quite 31). Here are some of the types of fields that you're likely to encounter:

- ✔ Text
- ✔ Keyword
- ✔ Rich text
- ✔ Date
- ✔ Numbers
- ✔ Names

If you have a PhD in Notes, you probably know about other fancy fields and speak official fieldname-ese. As for the rest of us, these six field names will do just fine.

When you fill out a new document, you may not be able to tell the data types of the various fields. In other words, it's hard to tell just by looking whether a field is a date field or a number field or even a text field. Just use common sense; if the field name is something like *Quantity* or *Price,* you can probably bet that Notes expects you to enter a number. If the field name is *Address,* you can bet that it's a text field.

Text fields

A text field is just what it sounds like. A *text field* can contain any combination of characters: letters of the alphabet, digits, punctuation, you name it. A text field can contain a customer's name, your colleague's street address, or a description of property for sale.

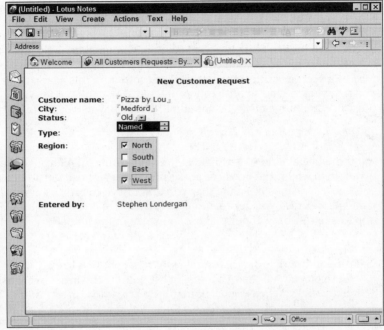

Figure 13-11:
Static text
makes a
form easier
to use and
understand.

A text field can contain a maximum of about 7,000 characters. That's more than most people ever need to put in a text field, so don't worry about running out of space!

Put away your calculator: Editable versus computed fields

In most cases, when you compose a new document, the fields are empty, and your job is to type the new name, address, and so on. However, you may occasionally encounter a computed field. A *computed field* is a field for which the program automatically calculates the contents.

For example, suppose you're using a database that tracks customer orders, and it has three number fields: Quantity, Price, and Extended Cost. The database manager has set up this

Extended Cost field as a computed field so that when you enter a value in the Quantity field and then enter a value in the Price field, Notes automatically multiplies the two and puts the answer in the Extended Cost field.

Computed fields are *non-editable*, which means you can't make any changes to them. That makes sense: If your computer automatically calculates a field, why would you want to change it?

You may encounter a special area in a document, called a *section*, which can hide certain information in a document. Onscreen, a section appears as a boldface title (sometimes a name) with a triangle to the left of it. To see the information hidden in a collapsed section, you must click the little triangle (twisty) next to the section title. Sometimes, despite clicking the little triangle next to a section's title, you just can't get into it. In this case, the section that you're trying to view is probably protected. You can't get into this section, but you can double-click the section title to see who can get in.

Keyword fields

Another special kind of text field is the keyword field. A *keyword field* is just a text field in which the possible entries have been chosen in advance. That's good news because it means that you don't have to type a keyword field's contents because you get to choose from a list of possible values, and you don't have to worry about making a mistake in the field. Here are all the different kinds of keyword fields that you're likely to encounter:

- **Dialog list:** The *dialog list field* looks an awful lot like a regular text field, but you can tell that it's a dialog list field by the little arrow to the right of the field. When you click that little arrow (or press Enter in the field), you get a list of the possible values.

  If the database designer chose to allow it, you may be able to choose more than one item or to enter an item not in the list. To tell whether you can choose more than one item, click one and then click another. If the first selection is unchecked, you're stuck with just one. If you are allowed to add new items, you see a text box below the list. You may also be allowed to enter values that aren't in the list.

  If you're using a dialog list field, you can press the spacebar to cycle through available options. (Using the spacebar is a little faster than using the list box.) You can also type the first letter of any of the options to choose it, which is even faster.

- **Radio buttons:** In a *radio button field,* you can choose only one of the options in the list. You select the value that you want by clicking it or using the arrow keys to highlight the option that you want and then pressing the spacebar to select it. You're stuck with the choices that the designer gives you.

- **Check boxes:** In a *check box field,* you can make more than one selection. Select as many of the values as you want or highlight them with the arrow keys and then use the spacebar to select them.

- **List box:** Only one choice from the list is visible in a *list box field.* The box containing the item allows the user to scroll up and down the list by two small scroll arrows at the right side of the box. The designer can allow you to choose more than one item.

✔ **Combo box:** The *combo box field* is a bit like the dialog list, but it's an empty box rather than field markers; it comes with a down-arrow at the right side of the field or outside of the field. When you click this arrow, the list appears, and the user makes the desired choice or choices. In this type of keyword field, the designer may decide to let you add items not in the list, but you can choose only one. The Region field in Figure 13-12 is a combo box.

Rich text fields

Rich text fields are what separate Notes from all the rest of the database programs in the world. *Rich text fields* are like regular text fields in that they often contain plain words and numbers. What's so rich about them, you ask? Well, in a rich text field (unlike a regular text field), you can use the Text menu to make words bold or italicized or a larger font. Just try that in a regular Notes text field, for that matter. Also, only in rich text fields can you create the magic of embedded objects, file attachments, and pictures.

How do you tell the difference between a rich text field and a regular text field? You probably can't, or at least you can't by just looking at it. When you're creating a document, text fields don't look any different from rich text fields. Here's a subtle trick to determine whether a field is a regular text or rich text field. Put your cursor in the field in question and look at the toolbar (at the top of the screen, if you forgot). If you see the font name, font size, and paragraph style there, you're in a rich text field.

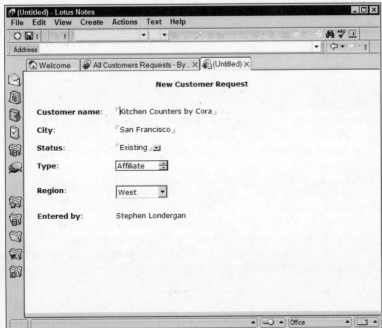

Figure 13-12:
Keyword
fields save
you typing.

It's default of de field

The person who creates your database can save you some time (and typing) by including *default* values in some fields.

Suppose that most of your customers are from Maine (ayuh). If you're lucky, someone has set up a default so that every time you compose a new Customer Profile, the State field already reads Maine. You can change the State field if you want to — after all, not *all* your customers are from Bangor — but think of all the typing that you *don't* have to do for the people who are in Maine. Think of default values as suggestions.

Many Notes forms have default values in fields that hold things such area codes, state names, and author names. These defaults can save you time and typing.

You can use the status bar to change the font, font size, and paragraph style in only a rich text field. So the status bar displays the font and font size only when you are in a rich text field.

Rich text fields can also contain attachments. You use attachments to include a computer file in a Notes document. In the old days, you would do your expenses in Microsoft Excel, print the spreadsheet, and then give the piece of paper to your boss for approval. Now, because you're using Notes, you can actually *attach* the spreadsheet to an e-mail message and get it to your boss electronically. We're one step closer to the paperless office! (But then we'll have to make paper planes out of old floppies.)

Any rich text field can hold many, many megabytes of information — you can send someone an e-mail and include in it a Lotus 1-2-3 worksheet, and a Microsoft Word document, and a copy of your resume, and a scanned picture of your new baby, and. . . .

Date fields

Date fields hold (you guessed it!) dates. You may be surprised to find out that you can also enter times in a date field. If you're using a database that tracks customer calls, for example, you may need to enter a date and a time.

The format that you use to enter a date or a time depends on the way that your computer is set up. When you try to save a document and you get the error message Unable to interpret time or date, you probably used dashes when you should have used slashes. Or maybe you used slashes when you should have used dashes. Sigh. Try one way or the other to see which your computer accepts. (***Hint:*** Your database designer can help with this by placing the dashes/slashes in the field for you.)

Number fields

Number fields hold numbers, pure and simple. Don't try to enter any non-number characters — such as slashes, dashes, letters, or smiley faces — in a number field. In number fields, you also don't have to enter characters such as currency symbols. Notes just strips them out if the database designer didn't want them there, or adds them there if the designer tells Notes that the contents of the field should look like money.

Name fields

Name fields are special because they hold a person's name for some kind of security reason. For example, most Notes documents have a computed field that automatically records the name of the person who composed the document. This feature enables people who read the document to know who wrote it, and it also reminds Notes itself who should be able to edit the document later. (In many databases, you can edit a document only if you composed it yourself.)

You may occasionally encounter *editable name fields*, such as in a database with a field in which you enter the name of the person who should receive your purchase requisition. In an editable name field, just type the person's name as it would appear on his or her business card.

Buttons

In addition to static text, fields, and sections, you can count on running across buttons during your adventures with Notes. Buttons help you do things quickly. If you've already delved into Notes mail, you've probably already used the buttons on the Action bar there. You're also likely to encounter such buttons on the forms in some databases, such as the ones at the top of the form in Figure 13-13. Customized buttons such as these are intended to help you with specific tasks, such as sending an e-mail message or a fax to a customer.

If you see a button and you want to use it, click it. (That's pretty easy, right?) You can also use your keyboard navigation arrows to select it and then press the spacebar to push (click) the button.

Of course, what happens when you click a button depends on what the database designer has programmed that button to do.

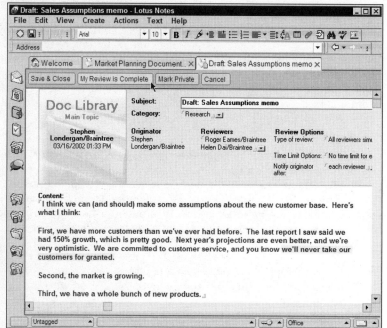

Figure 13-13:
Some forms
have
buttons.

Hotspots

A *Hotspot* is a special part of a document that does something when you click it, just like a button. Clicking a Hotspot might display some tidbit of information or open a different document in a different database. To use a Hotspot, click it, or select it with the arrow keys and press the spacebar.

Pop-ups

The most common kind of Hotspot that you'll encounter is a pop-up. *Pop-ups* usually appear as text enclosed in a green box that you can click to display a reminder, a hint, or more information about a particular word or sentence. Press and hold down the mouse button anywhere in the green box to see the pop-up. In Figure 13-14, you can see a Hotspot that explains the purpose of the Account Opened field.

Some pop-ups are used to take you somewhere. For example, some buttons and pop-ups may take you to a different document in the database, to a different database altogether, or even to a Web page.

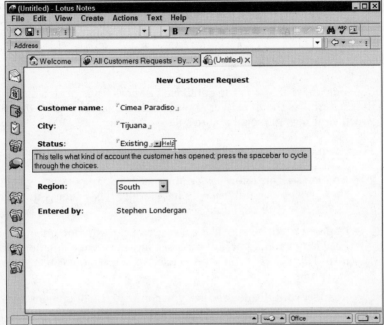

Figure 13-14:
Forms can
have pop-
ups, too.

Join the Party — Bring Your Own Document!

You've read a bunch of documents in a Notes database, and now you want to jump into the fray and make your own contribution — you're going to add your own new document.

You have to open the database in which you want to compose a new document before you start messing with the Create menu. More often than not, you'll already have a database open when you decide to create a new document — just make sure that you do, and that it's the database in which you want to create your document.

Wait — can I create?

Just because you *want* to add a document to a database doesn't mean that you *can* add a document to a database. Every single Notes that database that you use — even your own mail — has a set of rules that determines who can do what in that particular database.

In some databases, you'll find yourself on a strictly-need-to-know basis; whole areas of the database may be off-limits to you. In some databases, you have free rein to add and delete documents, while in others you may even be able to edit and documents that other people have created. The point here is that, well . . . it all depends.

Depends on what? — on the database's Access Control List, also known to the digiterati as the *ACL*. Every database has one, and this is the thing upon which your own personal abilities depend.

The seven levels of access in a Notes database are

- ✔ **No Access:** This one's pretty obvious. If you're personally set up to have No Access to a database, you have, well . . . NO access to it. There's just no other way to explain it.

- ✔ **Depositor:** With Depositor access, you can add documents to the database in question, but you can't see any of the documents, not even your own. This access level is often used in anonymous Suggestion Box type situations.

- ✔ **Reader:** With Reader access, you can read the documents in a database but you can't create your own. Imagine a policies and procedures database, perhaps, or any other kind of reference-type application.

- ✔ **Author:** This is one of the most common levels of access. If you're listed as an Author in a database, you can do four things:

  - **Read** documents that other people have added

  - **Add** your own documents

  - **Edit** your own documents

  - **Delete** your own documents

- ✔ **Editor:** With Editor access, you can do everything that an Author can do, plus you can edit and delete documents that have been created by other people.

- ✔ **Designer:** With Designer access, you can change the way that the database works by adding, deleting, and editing things such as forms and views. You use a whole different program to do this: Lotus Domino Designer.

- ✔ **Manager:** With Manager access, you are the king and queen of it all. You can do anything that you want in the database in question, including granting and denying access to other people.

So you have all these different databases you use in Notes, and you have your own personal standing in each database's ACL. How do you know what level of access you've been granted?

You can tell by trying to use options from the Create menu. If you go there and don't find any form names listed for you to create, it's a pretty safe bet that you only have Reader access in that database. Rats.

But because not all databases use the Create menu — some databases use buttons with which you add documents — you need a more fail-safe way to ascertain your personal level of access in a database.

Look at the bottom of the Notes screen for the Status bar. On the right side of it, look for the Security button — it usually looks like a left-facing key. This button is contextual; that is, it changes depending on the database you're in. For example, if you're in your mail database, you should see a key; if you're in a company mail directory database, you may see a quill-and-scroll icon. Click this button and then check out what level of access you have from the Groups and Roles dialog box that appears.

In most cases, you can't change your level of access to a database . . . which is kind of the whole point of having an access list, if you really think about it. If you need a different level of access to some database, speak to someone with Manager access to get your standing in the ACL changed.

Using the Create menu

When you choose Create, Notes gives you a list of the documents that you can create in that database, as shown in Figure 13-15.

Getting your inheritance from the right document

Does it matter which document is open when you compose a new one? The answer to that question is a definite maybe. Many databases have documents that rely on a feature called inheritance. *Inheritance* is a way for Notes to pass information from a document that's already in the database to the new one that you're about to compose.

Suppose you have an Orders database. In it, you can compose two types of documents: a Customer Profile and a Customer Order. The database is already set up so that when you compose a new Customer Order, Notes automatically fills in the name of the customer and other information about them. Notes accomplishes this feat by inheriting the values from the address fields of the Profile document that you selected when you composed your new order. If you don't have the right profile open (or highlighted in the View pane) before you try to compose a new order, you'll get the wrong address in your order.

You must have the right document open when you compose a new document if you're using a database that relies on inheritance to compute some fields.

The list of documents that you can compose from the Create menu varies from one database to the next. For example, in your mail database, you can compose a memo or a reply; in a different database, you can compose different kinds of documents. I can't give you examples of these because the names of the documents depend on the databases that you use.

Just finding the Create menu doesn't mean that you can actually compose documents in a given database. In some databases, you only have Reader access; you can't compose your own (Author). (Don't take it personally.) For more on Create menu access, read the previous section.

If you're not sure whether you're allowed to compose documents, open the database in question and look in the status bar. If you see a little picture of eyeglasses, you can forget about the Create menu — you have only Reader access to that database . . . consequently, you can only read the documents that other people have composed. For more on access levels, skip back to the earlier section "Wait — can I create?"

Call your administrator if you want to add documents to a database in which you have only Reader access.

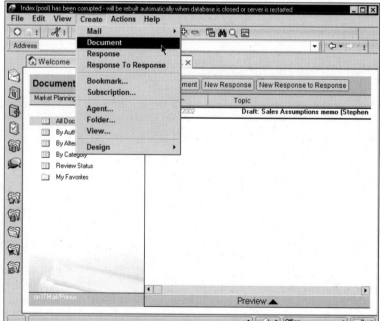

Figure 13-15:
The Create
menu
lists the
documents
you can
add to a
database.

Moving around in your new document

Moving around in a document is easy. As you enter values in your new document, press Tab to move from one field to the next. You can also use the arrow keys and the mouse to get from one field to the next.

You can't press Tab to move from a rich text field to the next field. You have to use the arrow keys or the mouse instead. If you press Tab in a rich text field, you move to the next tab stop in the field.

Saving your new document

When you've finished filling out the fields in your new document, press Esc. In the dialog box that appears, click Yes to save your document in the database, close the document, and return to where you were in the first place.

Save — and save often — any document that you're creating while you're composing it. In case you goof, the power fails, or your computer crashes, you're golden. Nothing worse than working on prize-winning stuff for hours to lose it needlessly. Argh. You can easily save a document anytime by choosing File⇨Save, by clicking the Save button in the toolbar, or by pressing Ctrl+S.

Abandoning your new document

If you start composing a new document and then change your mind and don't want to save it, just press Esc and click No in the Save dialog box that appears. Presto — it's gone!

Playing by the rules

The person who created the database may have set some rules for the fields: Perhaps you can't leave certain fields empty, or perhaps a rule ensures that you can enter only one of the approved two-character state abbreviations. When you save a document, Notes validates what you've entered in the various fields against the rules (if any) that the database designer has set up.

Don't be surprised if you get an error dialog box (like the one in Figure 13-16) when you try to save a document. Such a box tells you what rule you've broken and insists that it's not going to let you save the document until you correct the problem. No big deal; click OK, correct your mistake, and then try to save the document again.

Figure 13-16:
Some
documents
have rules
you have
to satisfy
before you
can save
them.

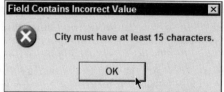

A Document Catches Your Eye

Besides reading documents and entering new ones, you can also print a document, edit it, delete it, mail it, or put it in a Personal folder.

Print it

To print the document that you have open, click the toolbar Print button, or choose File⇨Print, or press Ctrl+P. You get the Print Document dialog box, as shown in Figure 13-17. Here you can decide which printer to use, how many copies to print, which pages you want to print, whether to print in draft quality (a faster but uglier choice), and whether to print graphics at 100 percent of their size, even if you changed their shape or size in the document. You might also want to preview the document before you print it. After you check out the appearance and make up your mind about the choices, click OK. Out comes your document from your printer. (Read more information about printing documents in Chapter 5.)

Figure 13-17:
Print a
document
from here.

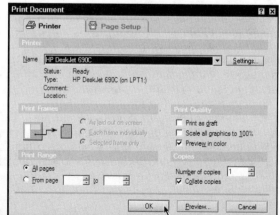

Edit it, maybe

If you want to edit a document, you must first either open it or at least highlight it in the View pane. Then click the Edit Document button on the toolbar, choose Actions➪Edit Document, or press Ctrl+E. Assuming that you are, in fact, allowed to edit the document, Notes puts you in *edit mode,* and you can change any field values. When you've finished making your changes, save the document just as if you were saving it for the first time. (Press Esc and then choose Yes.)

If you already have a document open, you can double-click it (anywhere) to get into edit mode. Or, the database designer may have included an edit button for you in the toolbar.

Being able to read a document doesn't mean that you can also edit it. In fact, most databases allow you to edit a document only if you are the document's original author. (You wouldn't want somebody else to edit your document and take all the credit for your great ideas, would you?) If Notes won't let you edit a document, it's probably because you aren't the person who composed the document in the first place. You need Author, Editor, or Manager access to edit.

Delete it, maybe

Press Delete to delete the document that you have open or highlighted in the View pane. If you have a document open when you press Delete, Notes closes that document, marks it as deleted, and then takes you to the next document in the database. Notes won't actually delete the document until you update the view (by pressing F9) or exit the database, so you have a chance to change your mind and not delete the document if you decide that you've made a mistake. Hop back to the earlier section in this chapter "So, What Can You Do with Documents?" to find out more about deleting and undeleting documents.

In most databases, after you compose a document, you (and you alone) control its destiny. You're the only person who can edit it and delete it. Otherwise, your rivals would be deleting your documents all day long. And that would make you look bad.

Hey Bob, check this out!

You can turn any Notes document that you see into an e-mail message — anytime, anywhere. If you're reading a document and decide that you want to forward it to your friend, choose Actions➪Forward. Notes takes the document and makes it the body of a new e-mail message that you can send to your associates. You address the e-mail as you would any other message and send it off.

Put it in a Personal folder

Some databases are set up with Personal folders. Use *Personal folders* to collect the documents in a database that interest you and gather them all in one place, which makes them easy to find later.

A good example of when you may want to use a Personal folder is in the Lotus Notes Help database. This database, chock-full of documents explaining every possible thing that you could ever want to know about Lotus Notes 6, has way, way more information than you could ever need! Suppose that you spend an hour in the Help database, trying to find out how to use the status bar. You don't want to waste an hour the next time that you want to check help on this topic, so you decide to put the document in your Personal folder in the Help database. That way, when you need to read the status bar help again, you can go right to your own Personal folder in the Help database.

Only you can see the contents of your Personal folder. Also, folders names have little folders next to them, but views have squares with mock text on them. You can't drag a document to a view.

You can drag the document that you want to put in your Personal folder from the View pane into that little folder in the Navigation pane. You know when you can let go of the mouse because the mouse pointer changes into a little cross.

If you're reading a document, choose Actions➪Move to Folder to put that document in a folder.

To see the documents stored in your Personal folder, click the folder icon in the Navigation pane.

When things get sensitive

I didn't exactly save the best for last in this chapter. Not that the following two features are bad; it's just that you'll hardly ever use them if you ever use them at all. In fact, you should read the rest of this chapter only if you absolutely have to — only if you've been told that you'll be *encrypting* fields and hiding documents.

Using encryption to make fields private

Notes has a feature called *field encryption* that is an extremely secure way to make certain field values private. And I mean private! If a field has been encrypted and you aren't one of the people allowed to see the field's contents, you can do nothing to spy on the field.

Okay, so why would you ever use encryption? Suppose that your company has a database that tracks information about employees. It has fields such as Employee Name, Office Location, Phone Number, and Yearly Salary. The whole company uses the database as a kind of corporate directory; people use it to look up other employee names and phone numbers and shoe sizes and other data of interest to the public.

Would you want your colleagues to be able to see how much money you make? (A high salary such as yours would breed all kinds of discontent and resentment if everyone could see it.) Your managers want the whole company to use the database, but they want to make the salary field protected so that only you, your boss, and the Human Resources department can see the salary field.

When a field has been encrypted, you need a special key to see the field's contents. If you read a document that contains an encrypted field and you haven't been given the key to the field, you can't see the contents of the field. Notes stores these keys in your user ID.

Hiding a document

When you compose a document, you can decide that you want only certain people to be able to read the document. By creating a Read Access List before you save a new document, you can be specific and particular about the people who are able to see your document. People who use the database but aren't listed in your document's Read Access List will never even know that the document is in the database.

Just before you save a document that you want to make private, choose File⇨Document Properties. From the Document infobox that appears, click the tab with the key on it. By default, the All Readers and Above check box is selected, meaning that anyone with access to the database can see the document that you're creating. Right off the bat, you have to clear that check box. Then you can click the names of the people whom you trust to read the document.

If you want to include a person whose name isn't in the list, click the upper Names button — the one next to the list of names of people who can read this document (with Notes' version of a silhouette) — to choose other names from the directory.

Figure 13-18 shows a Document infobox that guarantees that only Stephen and Helen are able to read this document.

After identifying the names of the people who can read the document, save it as you save any other document.

If you add a Read Access List to a document, don't forget to include your name in the list; otherwise, even you won't be able to see the document!

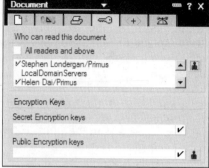

Figure 13-18:
Set up a
document
so that only
certain
people can
see it.

Searching

Databases — documents piled up in each one — crowd your servers, and hundreds of millions of documents are tucked in dusty corners of the Internet. Mountains of data are there for the reading. Now you need to find some important piece of information that someone entered somewhere. All you have to do is read every document to find it. Cancel your plans for the weekend because you have a lot of reading to do. Or do you? We live in the age of electronic miracles, so isn't there some way to find a text without having to read every document in every database?

Rest assured that I wouldn't raise the question if the answer were bad news. Notes has several ways for you to find information, from quickly searching a single document to full-text searching (a slick way to let Notes do the digging) to letting Notes search the net. Take my word for it — no matter how many speed-reading courses you take, Notes can find information faster than you could ever hope to.

A Full-Power Search

By using the Search icon in the toolbar, you have everything at your fingertips from a view to the world. Where you look, what you look for, how you want the search results displayed, and what specific search conditions you want to use are all contained somewhere in that Search icon. The choices that you're able to make, however, are determined by where you look.

The options available to you and the appearance of the search results depend on whether the database that you're searching has a full-text index (FTI). If the manager of the database didn't create an FTI, you can still search the database, but more elaborate features such as Searching by Form aren't available.

Searching through all the documents in the view

You just got a new job, and you're going to be taking business trips once or twice a month. The first thing that you need to do is to find out your company's policies for travel — what airline should you use, what hotels can you stay in, and, most important, do *you* get to keep your Frequent Flyer miles? So you open up that trusty Human Resources Policies database, but it must have at least 700 documents in it. How are you going to find all the documents that have the word *travel* in them? I mean the whole document, not just the title or whatever other text is displayed in a view containing the documents that you want to rifle through.

The Search icon in the toolbar comes to the rescue. Using the Search icon allows a *full- text search,* which is a nifty way for you to find all occurrences of a word (or of a few words) very, very quickly. You can search a huge database in no time at all. Most searches don't take more than two or three seconds. And, when you ask Notes to search for the word *travel,* it finds *all* the documents for you, no matter where (or how many times) the documents contain the word *travel.* Notes calls this a full-text search not because it finds full text (there's no such thing), but because it's full of neat features.

Hide and go seek with the Search bar

To do a full-text search, you need to see the Search bar to enter the criteria for your search. To display the Search bar, click the Search icon in the toolbar (looks like a pair of binoculars) or choose View⇨Search this View. See the Search bar in Figure 13-19.

Notes searches only documents in the current, open view. So you have to be careful to choose the right view, such as an All Documents view, before you start your search. If the view that you have open shows documents from only the first half of the year, for example, your search won't look through documents from the second half of the year.

Belly up to the Search bar

The Search bar contains several important parts. Starting from the left, the blank Search For text field is where you type the text you want to search for. Here are the types of things that you can enter:

✔ **A single word:** For example, type **gold** to find all documents containing the word *gold*.

✔ **A phrase in quotes:** For example, type **"gold and silver"** to find documents containing the phrase *gold and silver*.

✔ **Words connected by *and* without quotes:** For example, type **gold and silver** to find documents with both the word *gold* and the word *silver* in them.

✔ **Words connected by *or* without quotes:** Type **gold or silver** to find documents that contain either the word *gold* or the word *silver* — maybe both, but at least one of the two.

Get into conditions

Most of the time, you'll be happy to simply find documents containing some text. So enter the text that you want to find, click the Search button, and wait for the proper documents to appear. But suppose you search for *travel* in the Human Resources database and find 157 documents. You still have too much to read. If you can somehow refine your search, you can narrow the number of search results. You may, for example, know that the author of most of the travel policy documents is Dwight Morse in HR, so you could narrow the search to documents that he created that contain the word *travel*.

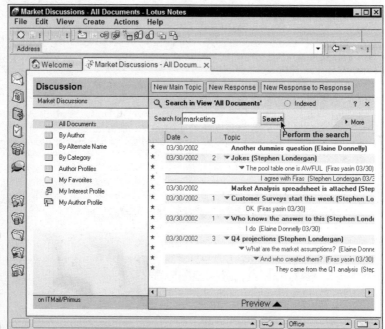

Figure 13-19:
Run a full-text search from the Search bar.

Click the More tab to the right of the Search button. In the tab field that drops down, click the Author button (in the Conditions field) and type the author's name. Check it out in Figure 13-20.

As you click the various buttons and specify conditions, each condition is added to the search window so that you can find specific documents: for example, written by Dwight Morse, and containing *travel*. In the Search bar, each condition is represented by a condition token, which is a gray box containing the specific condition. To see or modify the condition, double-click its token. To delete the condition, highlight its token and press Delete.

But wait, there's more, much more. In fact, too much to crowd into this chapter. I suggest that you spend a few minutes improving your search skills by clicking around the buttons in the Search bar to see all the options available to you. The more important options follow:

✔ **Date:** Click this button, and a dialog box appears in which you can enter a date to tell Notes to find documents newer or older than that date. You can find documents created between two dates, all documents not created between two dates, documents created in the last specified number of days, and on and on.

✔ **Author:** Click this button, and a new dialog box appears for you to enter the name of someone whose documents you would like to see or don't want to see.

✔ **Field:** Click this button, and a dialog box appears for in which you enter a field name and the data that you want that field to contain (or not) in the documents that you want to find.

✔ **Form:** Click this button to look for documents created in a single form. If the view that you're searching through has many types of main documents and responses, you may want only a certain type of document. For instance, in the travel policy example, you may want documents created only with the Policy form.

✔ **Multiple Words:** Click this button to refine your search when looking for several words: for instance, *travel* and *policy* and *employee*. Rather than entering words or phrases that you want to find in the Search For text box, you can enter them in the numbered boxes in the Search Builder dialog box. Click the Multiple Words button and then enter one word in each numbered space. Choosing Any is like using the word *or* in the text box between gold and silver; the resulting search finds all documents containing either of those words. Choosing All finds documents that contain every word in the list.

✔ **Fill out Example Form:** Click this button and then fill in specific fields in a specific form. Included among the options in this button is the famous query by form, which I explain in further detail in the next section because it's so important.

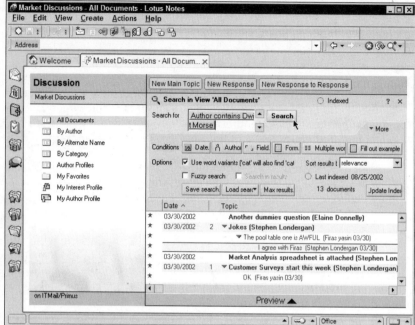

Figure 13-20:
Narrow
your Notes
searches.

Query by form

A way to make your life easier is to do a *query by form*. You use one of the forms in the database to tell Notes which words you're looking for and in which fields you want to find them. This method narrows and refines your query substantially.

Say that you want to search through a personnel database for a person's name, but that person is the author of many documents in that database. Complicating the problem is the fact that the documents in the view are of many different types (composed with different forms). You're interested only in documents in which the person's name is mentioned (not in documents that the person wrote), and you want only one type of document. You can use a query by form to tell Notes to be sure that the name occurs in the Body field of a particular form. (The name of the field may be different in the form you're using.)

Here's how you make a query by form:

1. **Access the Search bar by choosing View⇨Search this View.**

2. **In the Search bar that appears, click the More tab.**

3. **In the tab area that appears, click the Form button.**

   The Search Builder dialog box appears.

4. **Click the down-arrow at the end of the Condition text box and select By Form.**

5. **Click the form(s) that you would like to search in the Search for Documents which Use Form dialog box.**

6. **Move the cursor into the field where you want to find the word or phrase and the type the text that you want Notes to find.**

7. **Click OK to close the dialog box and then click the Search button in the Search bar to find the documents.**

Fuzzy search: The latest toy craze?

Don't go racing off to wait in line at 5 a.m. at your local Toyland for Kiddies store to buy a Fuzzy Search for that special child just yet. In fact, don't do it at all. We suspect that special child would be just as happy with a simple toy that you didn't have to risk being killed for. But wait, Fuzzy Search isn't a toy anyway; it's a search option.

In the Search bar, below the places where you place your order for search conditions, are some search options that you may want to choose before you send the search engine purring off into the database on a scavenger hunt. You can see the options in Figure 13-20. You can see them on your screen as well if you click the More tab.

Following are the options available to you when you have a full-text indexed database:

- ✔ **Use Word Variants:** Select this check box to tell Notes that you want to look for specific text and also its base word with possible prefixes or suffixes. Searching for *sneeze,* for example, also finds *sneezed* and *sneezing.* Bless you.

- ✔ **Fuzzy Search:** Select this check box to tell Notes to use not only the key word that you want to find but also corrected spellings if you misspelled your criterion, as well as similar phrases. For instance, searching for *travvel* will find *travel;* searching for *known problems* will return *known serious problems.*

Here are the choices in the Sort Results By drop-down list box:

- ✔ **Relevance:** The documents are arranged so that the ones with the largest number of examples of your criteria are at the top.

- ✔ **Last Modified or First Modified:** The documents with the most recent date of modification or the oldest date of modification, respectively, head the list that Notes gives you.

✔ **Keep Current Order (Sortable):** The documents are kept in the order that they were in the view; they aren't sorted by relevance. Only the search results are displayed in the view, and they appear with check marks. (Only available if the database allows column sorting.)

✔ **Show All Documents (Sortable):** All documents in the view are shown, but a check mark appears next to documents that satisfy the search results. If the database is designed to allow it, you can sort results by clicking the little triangles in the bars at the top of columns.

On your mark, get set, search!

After you set your conditions and choose your options, it's time to start the search itself. That part's easy — just click the Search button. If you have a lot of documents in the view, it may take a few minutes to find them. On the other hand, if you're searching a database with three small documents, the search won't take any time at all. The point? The amount of time a search takes depends on three factors:

✔ The **size** of the documents in the database

✔ The **number** of documents in the database

✔ The **complexity** of the conditions that you set

Seek and ye shall find

When the search is finally finished, Notes changes the view to show the search results in the way that you specify in the Sorts Results By list.

If the database is full-text indexed, Notes lists the documents that match your criteria in order of their weight. No, Notes doesn't measure a document's weight in grams or pounds or even bytes. Rather, in this case, *weight* refers to the degree to which each document satisfies the search criteria. It lists first the documents that have the most occurrences of your criteria and then the documents that have fewer occurrences of the criteria. The vertical bar, called the *marker bar,* in the left side of the view represents the relative frequency of your criteria in each document. The darker the bar, the more occurrences in that particular document.

With the Sort Results By option, you can choose to sort documents in ways other than by weight. Just be sure that you make the decision before the search.

You open a document uncovered by a search in the same way you open any other document: Double-click it, or highlight it, with the cursor keys and then press Enter. When you do, Notes shows you the document and highlights the words that you asked it to find.

While you read a document retrieved by a full text search, you can jump quickly to the next occurrence of the search word in the current document by pressing Ctrl++ (that's the Ctrl key and the plus sign). You use Ctrl+— (Ctrl and the hyphen, or minus sign, key) to jump quickly to the preceding occurrence of the word.

Resetting the stage

When you've read the documents that interest you, click the Clear Results button to clear the search and return all documents to the view.

If you want to conduct another search, it isn't necessary to click Clear Results first. Just type a new bunch of text and set your conditions; then click Search and off you go. Typing a new search word makes Notes forget all about the old search, returning only documents that satisfy the new set of criteria. You only need to use the Clear Results button when you're completely finished searching.

Part IV
Making Notes Suit You!

The 5th Wave   By Rich Tennant

"TELL THE BOSS HE'S GOT MORE FLAME
MAIL FROM YOU-KNOW-WHO."

In this part . . .

Reading and sending e-mail and even puttering around in a Notes database are pretty much standard Notes fare. In Part IV, I show you how to become a power Notes 6 user by customizing this powerhouse to fit your own needs, specifications, and predilections.

Up to this point in the book, I show you how to use Notes the way that it fell out of the box. From here on out, I show you how to take command. Reading this part of the book will make you feel as though you've stared down the beast and mastered it. No more intimidation; no more feeling like your computer is running you. It *is* supposed to be the other way around, after all. You're in charge here!

Chapter 14

Jazzing Up Your Text

. . . .

. . . .

*W*hen you send an e-mail or create a document, don't you want people to notice it? Of course you do. Otherwise, you wouldn't have bothered to write it. If one sentence or phrase is more important than other text, why not change it in some way so that it stands out? If a particular word needs attention, why not make sure that no one misses it?

Sure, you *could* make the text pink and huge (and in this chapter I show you how to do that), but perhaps something a bit more subtle will do the trick. Read on to discover how to jazz up the text of your messages in Lotus Notes 6.

Changing Characters

All documents are composed of individual characters. In Notes, you can change the appearance of those characters, either one at a time or in groups such as words, sentences, or paragraphs. For example, you can make characters **boldface** or *italic* or different colors and sizes. And you can determine the appearance of a bunch of characters before you even type them, or you can pour out your thoughts onto the screen and then go back and make the changes when you finish typing. Not surprisingly, the way that you change the appearance of characters works pretty much the same way as other prominent programs, such as Microsoft Word.

Changing the appearance of text is called *formatting*. You'll probably hear that term used.

Take full advantage of the text manipulation capabilities of Notes to dress your messages in creative ways. Just play by one rule: The text that you want to change has to be in a rich text field.

You can find out whether a field in Notes 6 is a rich text field by placing your cursor in it and then looking at the Navigation pane located at the top of your screen. If the formatting functions in the top Navigation pane are visible — if you *do* see the font name, font size, bold button, and so on — you're in a rich text field. If it is a rich text field, you can change the way the text and paragraphs are formatted. If it isn't a rich text field, you can't. It's as simple as that.

Selecting what you want to format

Many times after you type something, you later decide to go back and change it. Maybe what you typed is lackluster or difficult to read, or you want to spice up some headings. Before you can change its appearance, however, you have to let Notes know what it is that you want to change. That is, you have to select it first. Read upcoming sections of this chapter to discover what you can *do* to the text.

Three terms that you may as well get straight right now are I-beam, cursor, and insertion point.

- ✔ **I-beam:** This is the vertical line that moves around the screen while you move the mouse. Notes calls this line an *I-beam* because it looks like an I-beam used in building construction — a vertical line with little horizontal lines at the top and bottom. In fact, it kind of looks like a capital I.

- ✔ **Cursor:** This is the vertical line that blinks at the place where the next thing that you type will appear.

- ✔ **Insertion point:** Gotcha. It's the same thing as a cursor, but just has another name.

The mouse pointer is always visible onscreen, often in the shape of an I-beam; if you use the mouse to scroll up or down, however, the cursor may scroll off the screen. Don't fear. Press any cursor-movement key (such as an arrow key, Page Up, or Page Down), type something, click your mouse, or press the spacebar, and the screen display shows you where the insertion point is.

The easiest way to select text is to click and drag across it with the mouse. When text has a dark box around it, it's selected. The dark box is called *reverse video* (light letters on a dark background, rather than how text normally looks onscreen). To use your keyboard to select text, move the cursor to the beginning or the end of the text, hold down the Shift key, and press a directional arrow to move over the characters that you want to select. Press the left- or right-arrow key to stretch the highlighter one character to the left or right. Press the down- or up-arrow key to highlight to the same point in the next or previous line. Pressing Shift while using any cursor-movement key combination moves the cursor and highlights text on the way.

Here are some additional tips about selecting text that you can use to save you a lot of time:

- ✔ **Crtl+Shift:** Press the Ctrl key along with Shift and the cursor-movement keys to speed up the process of highlighting. Shift+Ctrl+← or → moves the highlight one word at a time. Shift+Ctrl+↓ or ↑ moves the highlight to the beginning or end of the next or previous line, respectively.

- ✔ **Double-click:** Double-click a word to select it.

- ✔ **Select All:** To select all the text in the current field, use the menu to choose Edit⇨Select All, click the Edit Select All button, or just press Ctrl+A. (See the Select All icon in the left margin.)

    When you use Edit⇨Select All in edit mode in a Notes database, for example, you select everything in the current field. However, if you use it in read mode, you select the whole document. (In the latter case, usually the only thing that you can do with selected text is copy it to the Clipboard.)

- ✔ **Selecting text in more than one field:** Sorry. If you want to select text in more than one field at a time while you're in edit mode, you're out of luck. Regardless of the method that you choose to select text, you can select text in only one field at a time.

- ✔ **Oops:** If you find that you selected the wrong text, simply select other text to correct the mistake.

- ✔ **Not quite enough:** If you selected some text but meant to select more, hold down the Shift key and then click at the farthest end of the additional text or use a cursor-movement key combination. Notes adds to the selected text all text between the currently selected text and the place where you click.

- ✔ **I want a lot:** To select a big chunk of text, put the cursor at the beginning of the text that you want to select and then use the mouse and scroll bars to scroll until you can see the other end of the text that you want to select. Press Shift while you click at the other end of the text, and Notes selects all the text in between.

- ✔ **Somewhere in between:** To select all text from the cursor to the beginning of the field, press Shift+Ctrl+Home. To select all text from the cursor to the end of the field, press Shift+Ctrl+End.

- ✔ **Remuneration:** Please pay for all selections at the cashier, no returns or refunds, have a nice day, and thank you for shopping with us.

I've made my selection; what now?

After you select a bit of text, you can change its appearance. You can remove it altogether, change how it looks, its formatting, location, move or copy it elsewhere, or check its spelling. Not only can you do lots of things with the text, you can usually do each thing in several different ways. Don't get nervous about trying to figure out all the different ways to do things; just figure out the method that works best for you and forget the rest.

The Ctrl key works with other keys to streamline the actions that you do most often. Don't be careless about whacking at these keyboard shortcuts, for one simple reason — if you choose the wrong one, you might be really sorry. For example, suppose you made lots of changes to some text and then accidentally use the Ctrl+B shortcut. You would make everything **bold**!

If you do use a keyboard shortcut by accident, remember a very useful one — Ctrl+Z. That tells Notes to Edit⇨Undo (reverse) the most recent action.

How about making your formatting life a bit simpler? Sure, you can take a few hours to memorize the various keyboard shortcuts. Or you can play it smart and use a magic box. Oooh! Yup, a lot of the things you can do to text — plus more — are included in the Text Properties box.

So when you want to change something about a paragraph or a word or even just a character, simply select whatever it is that you want to change and then either press Alt+Enter, Ctrl+K, or choose Text⇨Text Properties. Up springs the Text box, as shown in Figure 14-1.

Paragraph
Alignment

Paragraph
Margins

Paragraph
Hide When

Paragraph
Border

Font

Styles

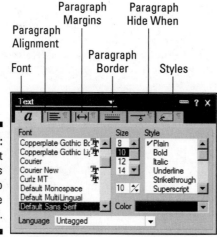

Figure 14-1: Use the Text Properties box to change formatting.

This special dialog box is chock-full of ways to change selected text, including giving it a bigger font size and coloring it pink. The Text Properties box has tabs to organize the different types of properties. Here's a brief list of the tabs for formatting text and paragraphs. Refer to Figure 14-1 to see these tabs. (I explain them in detail in upcoming sections later in this chapter.)

- **Font:** Make choices here to set the font; size; style (bold, italic, and so on); and color.

- **Paragraph Alignment:** Here, set the Alignment (left, center, right, full, or none); First line and paragraph indent; Spacing (between lines, above, and below the paragraph); and List options (bullets, circles, squares, numbers, checkmarks, and so forth).

- **Paragraph Margins:** Select here for Pagination options (for example, Page Break Before Paragraph, Keep Paragraph on One Page, Keep Paragraph with Next Paragraph); Left and Right Margins; and Tabs (for the whole paragraph).

- **Paragraph Border:** Here, set the style, effect, color, and thickness of a border around the text.

- **Paragraph Hide When:** Decide here whether to hide the selected text under certain conditions such as when the document is being previewed for reading, printing, opened for editing, and so forth. (Stay tuned if you want to know what these conditions are. Or hop down now to the section "The incredible disappearing paragraph.")

- **Styles:** Choose here to assign a style to the currently selected paragraph(s). Of course, you have to create styles before you can apply them. Coming soon to a page near you — an explanation of the use of styles, in the upcoming section "Formatting Paragraphs with Character."

At times, not using the Text Properties box is faster — for example, when you're setting the font, font size, or style. In these cases, get in the habit of using the toolbar. The next time that you're hanging around a rich text field, stop by the toolbar and click the box containing the name of the current font. In Figure 14-2, you can see a drop-down list of available fonts that appears when you click the font list in the toolbar. (The variety of fonts on your system may be different than what you see in this figure.)

The same fonts, sizes, and paragraph styles are available whether you use the toolbar, menus, or the Text Properties box. The toolbar is just a faster way of making a single selection.

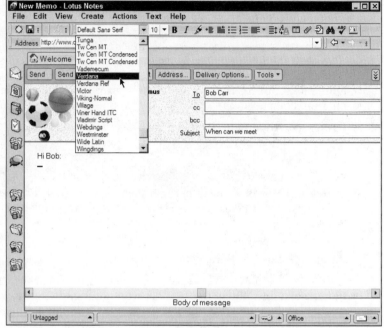

Figure 14-2:
Use the
toolbar to
quickly and
easily
change
common
text
properties.

If you select a bunch of text and then look at the status bar, you usually see the name of the font used in that selection. Sometimes, though, you may not see the font name. Why not? If the text that you select contains two or more fonts, the status bar doesn't show any font name or size. But don't fret — even if the font name or size box is empty, you can still use the status bar to choose one font for the whole selection. Click the box where you normally see a font name and then choose the font that you want from the list that appears.

The font styles and sizes that you see on the Web are very likely different from those you see in Notes. It's the result of the limitation of your browser, not Notes, so don't go blaming Notes. Browsers can display two fonts: one monospaced (a typeface in which each character is given the same width, as by a typewriter) and one of variable width (like in this book). Browser font sizes come in points (just a techie term for font size) of 8, 10, 14, 18, 24, and big. This book is printed in about 10-point type, if that helps.

Becoming a formatting guru

Suppose that you're writing a message to your whole department, inviting them to the annual company party on Saturday. You type the text first and then you decide to realign and enhance some of the text. Just putting your cursor at the beginning of a word and clicking the toolbar's Bold button is not enough. Selecting the text and then choosing bold is the only way to enhance text *after* you've typed it.

After you get the hang of enhancing text, you can make your messages more interesting and professional. See Figure 14-3 for an invitation before any extra formatting. With just a few keystrokes to change the font, font size, and style, you can transform boring text into the more appealing message shown in Figure 14-4.

You can improve the appearance of a message with a new font, italics, and centered lines by using only a few keystrokes. Just like you improve your party invitation with a little interior decorating, also make sure that you plan just as carefully the documents that you create for work. Choosing the right words is only half the battle: The other half is making a document look good so that it's readable and that people *want* to read it.

Be sure to think about what kind of audience your message is intended for before you go applying crazy colors and other wild formatting. A little enhancing goes a long way. If too many words in a document are boldface, they don't seem so important anymore. And if you plaster lots of different fonts and different font colors and sizes around the page, your document could end up looking more like a circus poster rather than an official announcement.

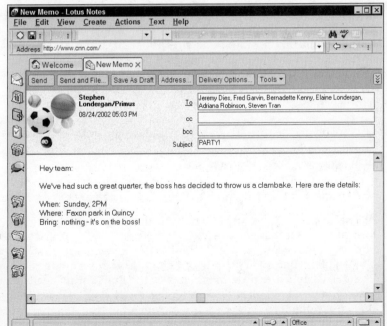

Figure 14-3:
Your basic, boring message. Yawn.

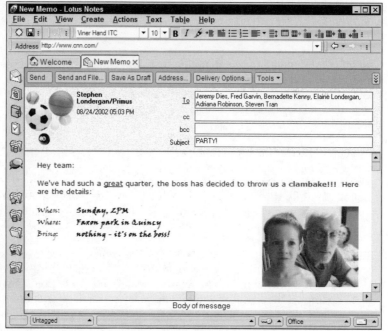

Figure 14-4:
Wow! Your
message
after
formatting.

It's hard to be bold when you don't exist

Here are some of the more frequently asked questions about enhancing text:

Q: How can you select text you haven't even typed yet?

A: You can't.

Q: Can you decide to enhance text before you type it?

A: Yes.

Q: What do you do to enhance text that you haven't typed yet?

A: The keyboard shortcuts and buttons that I describe throughout this chapter work for text that you are about to type as well as for text already typed. If you're typing a sentence and know that the next few words should be bold, click the Bold button first (or use one of the other techniques for bolding like Ctrl+B), type the text, and then click the Bold button again (or Ctrl+B or Ctrl+T) to turn bold off and finish typing. If you want to center the next line that you're about to type, click the Alignment button located in the Text box (or in your toolbar if available), select Center from the menu, and type. Voilà! (Or is it viola?)

If your keyboard doesn't have 600 keys

Our world is shrinking fast. Maybe that's why so many people are trying to lose weight. You can be in New York for lunch and France for dinner. Of course, all that eating won't do much for your weight in this shrinking world, but that's beside the point. The point, in case your mind is wandering, is that we are increasingly called upon to use words and symbols in our writing that come from other languages. You ignore the subtle differences between alphabets at your own peril — one wrong character can easily set off an international incident between co-workers. After all, *E* and € mean very different things.

You may be wondering how you're going to type a U with an umlaut (ü), especially if you don't have such a key on your keyboard. Typing **u"** instead is pretty hokey. Notes, recognizing that you might need to type some non-English characters, has a large number of extra characters not available on your keyboard (or in stores). To find these *compose sequences* for a particular character, look in Help or in the documentation.

For example, here are the keystroke sequences used to type *é*. On the IBM-style English keyboard, first press Alt+F1, type the letter **e**, and then the apostrophe. Or, to type ˜i, press Alt+F1, the letter I, and then an apostrophe. (This is almost as bad as dialing a long-distance number with your credit card, isn't it?)

After you create the character, you can copy and paste it if you need it again using the Edit⇨Copy and then Edit⇨Paste commands (or Ctrl+C and Ctrl+V, respectively).

Formatting Paragraphs with Character

Armed with the skills necessary to change bits of text here and there, I turn my discussion to paragraphs. After all, sometimes you want an entire paragraph to have a unique appearance so that it stands out from the others around it.

Here are a few things that you ought to keep in mind as you work with paragraphs:

- **Format an entire paragraph:** You can select an entire paragraph and change the appearance of all its characters in the same way that you change individual characters, words, or groups of words. (See the preceding section "Changing Characters" for the lowdown on formatting.)

- **Formatting, other than text:** Summon the Text Properties box (choose Text⇨Text Properties or Ctrl+K) to make changes to the format of the paragraph other than the appearance of its text such as center alignment, incorporating a bulleted list, or altering the spacing between paragraph lines.

- **Rich text only:** You can apply paragraph formats only to text in rich text fields. (To read more on rich text fields, go back to the earlier section "Changing Characters.")

- ✔ **Change one paragraph at a time:** You can change the characteristics of one paragraph at a time simply by putting the cursor in that paragraph. You don't have to select the entire paragraph.

  If you change one paragraph, only that paragraph contains the changes. For example, if you set tabs in one paragraph, only that paragraph has those unique tabs.

- ✔ **Change more than one paragraph:** If you need to change several paragraphs at once, you must select them all.

- ✔ **Change all paragraphs:** If you need to change all the paragraphs, choose Edit➪Select All (or Ctrl+A).

- ✔ **Format before typing:** If you haven't typed anything yet, use the Text Properties box to set the characteristics you want all paragraphs to have; then start typing. All paragraphs will have those characteristics until you use the menu to set some new characteristics.

All margins great and small

Use the Paragraph Margins tab of the Text Properties box to change a paragraph's left or right margins. (The margins at the top and bottom of the page have nothing to do with paragraphs, so they don't appear here. Rather, they're in the File➪Page Setup menu.) To keep you as confused as possible, Notes offers you the chance to set your margins in absolute terms (measured in inches or centimeters, depending on what part of the world you're in) or relative terms (percentage of the width of the page).

You can switch from inches to centimeters by changing the Unit of Measurement setting on the International tab of the File➪Preferences➪User Preferences dialog box.

If you choose a relative margin of 14, which is 14 percent of the width of whatever you're printing to, the margin will be about 1 inch on an 8 ½-inch sheet of paper — and really, really teeny if you're printing on a postage stamp. As you can see in Figure 14-5, you can adjust the left and right margins:

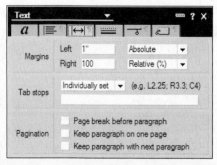

Figure 14-5:
Use the Text Properties box to set paragraph margins.

✔ **Left Margin:** The default is 1 inch if you're using imperial measurements, or 2.54 cm if you're using metric measurements. If you want the first line to be indented differently, switch to the Alignment (second) tab in the Text Properties box and choose whatever first line option suits your fancy.

✔ **Right Margin:** The right margin is the distance from the *left* edge of the paper to the right edge of the paragraph. That's the left edge of the paper. Paying attention? For a 2-inch right margin on a sheet of paper 8 ½ inches wide, the right margin should be 6.5 inches. The default is 1 inch.

Notes doesn't show text onscreen the same way that it shows text when printing, so you can't always see how the document will look on the page. Use File➪Print Preview to see what you're gonna get from your printer.

Keeping tabs on your paragraph

Back at the factory, paragraphs automatically have their own tabs set at every half inch. This may be fine for you, in which case you don't have to set any tabs at all. But if you're not happy with the preset tabs, you can use the Pagination option in the Paragraph Margins tab of the Text Properties box to set new ones.

In the Tab Stops area, choose Evenly Spaced and choose a distance between tabs, such as .75 inch. Or you can choose Individually Set and then type the location of each tab, as I did in Figure 14-6. Just type the distance (measured from the left edge of the paper) for all the tabs that you need. For that extra touch of variety, you could even enter some tabs in inches and others in centimeters. If you're using inches, you don't have to type any symbol; if you want centimeters, just type **cm** after the number. You can't use yards, miles, quarts, or kilometers, though. Here are a few things to remember:

✔ Four types of tabs are available: Left, Center, Right, and Decimal. Choose Decimal to align a column of numbers by their decimal points.

✔ The little example box shows you how to set the different tabs, but you're given a bum steer: The example box shows the setting as 4D (the number comes first), but it's D4 for a decimal tab at the 4-inch mark.

✔ Between each separate tab setting, put a semicolon, not a comma. Notes complains if you use commas.

✔ Per usual, tabs work only in rich text fields.

You may find it easier to use the onscreen ruler to set margins and tabs. If you're rubbing your eyes trying to find a ruler onscreen, try using View➪ Ruler or pressing Ctrl+R. A ruler much like the one in Figure 14-7 appears at the top of your screen.

Click in the ruler where you want a tab, and an *L* appears. To get rid of an unwanted tab, click it to remove it. The *L* means that the tab is a left tab. To change it to another type of tab, right-click the tab and then choose the type. (You can also choose to delete the tab if you goofed.)

You can add a tab in another way that's especially handy if you don't want the default left tab. Right-click in the ruler where you want a new tab and then select the one you want from the list that appears.

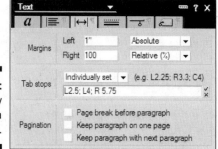

Figure 14-6:
Manually set tabs in a paragraph.

Figure 14-7:
Press Ctrl+R to use the Ruler to set tabs and margins.

One paragraph, indivisible

When Notes calculates that the bottom of a page is at hand, it inserts a page break automatically so that the printer will start a new page. The place that it chooses to make a page break may not always be where you had in mind. You may prefer to have a paragraph stay together, even if it means that a bit of white space is left at the bottom of the page. To protect a paragraph from being split, click the Paragraph Margins tab of the Text Properties box (refer to Figure 14-6). Then choose one of the following:

- ✔ Select the Page Break before Paragraph check box if you definitely want the current paragraph to start a new page. This is useful when you want to start a new section on a new page.

- ✔ Select the Keep Paragraph on One Page check box to prevent Notes from breaking up a paragraph somewhere in the middle. Notes will either keep the paragraph on the current page or shove the whole thing to the next page.

- ✔ Select the Keep Paragraph with Next Paragraph check box to be sure that a paragraph is always on the same page as the paragraph following it.

The incredible disappearing paragraph

The time may come when you need to hide a paragraph. Why? Well, here are a few reasons:

- ✔ You want to save some space by hiding a paragraph when a document is being previewed.

- ✔ You want text to be visible only when people are editing a document, not when they are reading it . . . perhaps because the text contains editing instructions.

- ✔ You want to hide it from certain readers. (Yes, you can rub your hands and chuckle over your power.)

- ✔ You have a button that executes a command in a document, and you want to hide it when you print the document so that some poor chump doesn't try pushing the button on the paper.

You have 11 choices for hiding a paragraph — all listed in the Paragraph Hide When tab of the Text Properties box, as shown in Figure 14-8. You can tell Notes to hide a selected paragraph by choosing any of the following check boxes.

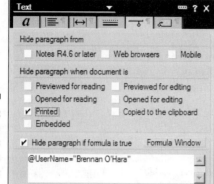

Figure 14-8:
Hide
paragraphs
in Notes
documents.

✔ **Notes R4.6 or Later:** Select this in the very, very quite unlikely, event that you're sending a message to someone who you know still uses Lotus Notes R4.6, and you have to hide something from them. (Lots of new features have been added to Lotus Notes since R4.6, and so occasionally separate information may need to be hidden from or shown to people who use different versions.) Please note that when you select Notes R4.6 or Later, you can view what paragraphs are hidden by choosing View⇨Show⇨Hidden from Notes.

✔ **Web Browsers:** If the item or text doesn't work for or apply to folks viewing the information from the Web, it makes sense to hide it from them. Best to avoid confusion.

✔ **Mobile:** If you know that someone reading your document will use a Palm Pilot, cell phone, or other mobile device, select this check box to hide the stuff that they don't need to see.

✔ **Previewed for Reading:** A document highlighted in a view is sometimes somewhat visible in the Preview pane (if you make the Preview pane visible), but a paragraph set with this attribute is not visible. (Selecting this check box saves valuable screen real estate when space is limited.)

✔ **Opened for Reading:** Select this and the hidden paragraph is visible only when you're in edit mode. It is also hidden for printing.

✔ **Printed:** If you check this box, the selected paragraphs do not print. This is useful for suppressing the printing of paragraphs that you want to be visible only onscreen. You may also want to select this check box when the paragraph contains graphics that slow down your printer.

✔ **Previewed for Editing:** A paragraph set with this attribute selected is not visible if the document is in edit mode in the Preview pane.

✔ **Opened for Editing:** When you select this, the paragraph is visible when the person looking at it is not in edit mode, but it disappears whenever someone tries to edit the document. This is a way to protect a paragraph from being changed by people who can edit documents. Be careful — after making this choice, *you* may never be able to edit the paragraph again.

✔ **Copied to the Clipboard:** If you try to copy a paragraph with this attribute selected while you're in edit mode, you find that you have nothing to paste.

✔ **Hide Paragraph if Formula Is True:** In Figure 14-8, I insert a formula in the formula window and select this check box. Notes first looks at the formula; if its condition is met, Notes hides the paragraph. If the user is Brennan O'Hara, he won't see this paragraph under any circumstances.

The preceding Paragraph Hide When tab choices are created to work for the *entire paragraph or individual line items,* not for individually selected text. In fact, many text options work on the entire paragraph or individual line items — specifically, spacing, list options (bullets and numbering), margins, tabs, hide-when options, pagination, alignments, and styles.

Get in align

Alignment refers to the arrangement of text in each line, relative to the margins. You have five choices from the Paragraph Alignment tab of the Text Properties box:

✔ **Left:** The text lines up with the left margin and has a ragged-right edge.

✔ **Center:** Want to guess what this does? If you guessed that it centers the text on each line and gives lines ragged-right and ragged-left edges, add ten points to your score and advance three spaces.

✔ **Right:** The text lines up with the right margin and has a ragged-left edge.

✔ **Full:** The text stretches from margin to margin so that the paragraph has no ragged edges. Full won't work if you type a really short line or if you press Enter at the end of a line.

✔ **None:** Text starts at the left margin and displays the text on one line — it doesn't wrap. Often, when you import documents from other programs, you may be shocked to see that lines stretch off the screen. You have to scroll to the right until you reach the end of the paragraph and then scroll back to the left to see the next paragraph. Change the alignment to Left or Full to correct the problem.

Use the toolbar Paragraph Alignment button (shown below) to change a paragraph's alignment.

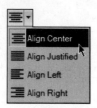

Give me some space

Feeling cramped, squeezed, closed in? Do your messages seem to have too much stuff and not enough open space? Then you need to space out. Use the Paragraph Alignment tab in the Text Properties box to s-p-r-e-a-d your paragraph(s) out over more space or to show more white space. You have three choices under each of the three types of spacing. You can use 1, 1 ½, or 2 to determine the distance in each of these ways:

- **Interline:** Between lines of the paragraph
- **Above:** Between the current paragraph and the one above it
- **Below:** Between the current paragraph and the one below it

Choosing all three can be a heck of a mess; you may wind up with too much spacing. Practice a bit so that your screen isn't mostly white space with a line or a paragraph appearing once in a while like an oasis in a desert of white sand. If you make a selection that you're not happy with, don't forget the Undo feature.

You can also use the toolbar Spacing button (see it in the left margin) to change a paragraph's alignment.

Don't press Enter at the end of every line in a paragraph to achieve double spacing. Take my word for it: This is never a good idea. If you don't use the spacing choices, you'll wind up with gaps all through your document when you print or change the size of the window.

Puttin' on the style

You have to make the coffee, you have to put paper in the copier, and now you have to jump all around your documents applying the same formatting, one paragraph at a time. It's enough to raise your hackles.

Calm your hackles. You may still have to make the coffee, but you don't have to go through all those keystrokes again and again to format paragraphs scattered around your document. Imagine that you wrote a report with lots of sections and each section had its own title. You want the titles to be centered and boldface, to have one line of space after them, and to have a larger font with blue text. All you have to do is format one title, turn that format into a *style,* and then use that style for all the other titles, thus saving you lots of time and getting you home for dinner.

Applying styles also guarantees that you are consistent. After formatting 15 titles, you're bound to get bored and careless, and you may forget to add boldface along with all the other formats to a title. Using styles guarantees that the same characteristics are applied to every paragraph you select.

After you've written a title, centered it, colored it blue, boldfaced it, added the spacing, and changed the font — pshew! — keep the cursor in the title, open the Text Properties box, click the Paragraph Styles tab (the last tab), and then click the Create Style option. In Figure 14-9, you can see the Text Properties box with the Paragraph Styles tab selected — and for the same low, low price — the Create Paragraph Style dialog box that appears when you choose to create a new style.

Figure 14-9: Use Paragraph Styles for easy and consistent formatting.

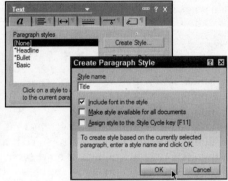

You name your new style in (wonder of wonders) the Style Name text box. You can then select Include Font in the Style, Make Style Available for All Documents, and Assign Style to the Style Cycle Key [F11]. Selecting the latter means that when someone highlights a paragraph and presses F11, the paragraph shows each available style in succession. Click OK to get out of the dialog box and finish with the current style.

After you create your styles, you can apply them to the current paragraph (the one where the cursor is) or to all selected paragraphs. Press F11 to cycle through all the styles that you've created and stop when you find the one you want. Or you can apply one of the styles by clicking the toolbar Paragraph Style button. (See left margin.)

Permanent Pen — Does It Stain?

Not to worry, the Permanent Pen has nothing to do with ink that won't wash out. It has everything to do with editing, though. Have you ever read a document and wanted to add some comments of your own scattered throughout the paragraphs? The problem is that the next person who comes along won't be able tell the difference between the words that were on the original document and those that you add as editorial comments.

So, fairly quickly, most people figure out what they should use to make the text they use for their comments different enough to stand out — maybe bold, or a different color, or bigger, whatever.

This Permanent Pen thing that Notes has is just a quick way to remember a combination of text attributes that you like to use to make your comments stand out from the rest. All you have to do is designate the different text properties as the Permanent Pen. Then, whenever you want to edit a document, you activate the Permanent Pen and enter your comments.

Check out Figure 14-10 to see what a document could look like after a couple of people have chimed in.

To choose your Permanent Pen settings, you don't need to type anything. Choose Text⇔Text Properties, choose the settings (font, size, color, and so on) that you want to call your own. Then choose Text⇔Permanent Pen⇔Set Permanent Pen Style. Fini.

Now open the document you want to edit and find something that you want to comment on. Click the toolbar Permanent Pen button (see left margin) or choose Text⇔Permanent Pen⇔Use Permanent Pen and start typing. (You'll notice that the words you type automatically have the settings you chose in the previous step, which is the whole point here!) To turn off the Permanent Pen, click the Permanent Pen button again, or choose Text⇔Permanent Pen⇔Use Permanent Pen again.

After you choose your own Permanent Pen settings, you can use them anytime by clicking the Permanent Pen button in the toolbar.

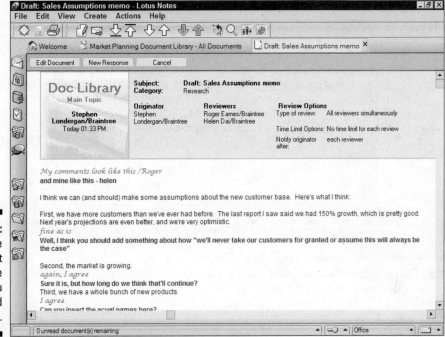

Figure 14-10:
Use
Permanent
Pen to make
what you
type stand
out.

Highlighter — Does It Stain?

Notes highlighters come in three colors: pink, yellow, or blue. Just like those fat smelly day-glo markers that you probably used in college to call out the parts of a text book page that were going to be on the test, you can use the Highlighter function in Notes to draw a reader's attention to a particular part of the document.

This is the one feature of Notes that works a little different from all the rest — so pay attention!

When you want to highlight some text, you do *not* first select the text. Instead, you just choose Text⇨Highlighter and then choose the color that you want. When you do, the cursor changes to a little pen, as you can see in Figure 14-11. Now it's just a matter of dragging the mouse over the text you want to high-light, from left to right. If you want to un-highlight, click and drag the cursor from right to left, instead.

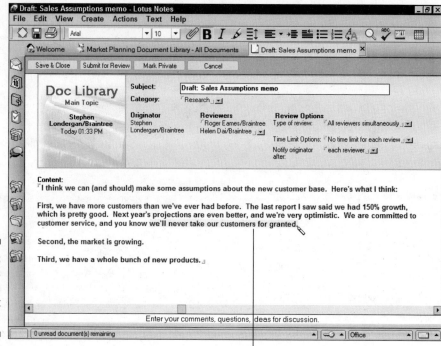

Figure 14-11:
Use Notes
highlighting
to make text
stand out.

Highlighted text

Choose Text⇨Highlighter and then the color you want again when you're done and want to turn the highlighter off.

Chapter 15

Doctoring Your Documents

• •

In This Chapter

▶ Inserting page breaks

▶ Creating tables

▶ Modifying tables by adding and deleting rows and columns

▶ Adding headers and footers

▶ Changing the page setup

▶ Searching and finding and (just maybe) replacing

▶ Checking spelling

• •

*I*f you've already read Chapter 14 of this book, your characters now have character, your sentences make sense, and your paragraphs punch like never before. Now, what about whole pages and entire documents? In this chapter, I take you from concentrating on the individual characters to having a global view, seeing the big picture, and making your single- or multi-page document a complete, professional, and well-crafted entity of which you, your colleagues, and even your family, can be proud. Read here for the Lotus Notes 6 lowdown on page breaks, creating tables, changing page setup, and more.

When you make nifty adjustments to individual pages and sweeping modifications to the whole document, you may not see a single change on your screen. Don't lose your temper yet: You'll see your changes if and when you print the document. For example, you won't see onscreen where one printed page begins or ends unless you choose View⇨Show⇨Page Breaks. You don't see headers or footers, either. The only way to see what a page will really look like prior to printing it is to view it in Print Preview. Hang tight; I explain all this here.

Break It Up!

Notes is a very smart program; and just like any word processor worth its salt, Notes knows when the text that you're typing has reached the bottom of a page. When you print a document, Notes automatically puts a *page break* in the proper place. That way, you don't print text off the page and into thin air.

However, you might want to insert a page break where Notes normally wouldn't. For example, if a paragraph starts a new section and you want it to appear on a new page even if the previous page isn't full, you can insert a page break in one of these two ways:

✔ Press Ctrl+Shift+L

✔ Choose Create➪Page Break

What you see onscreen after you insert a page break is a thin, horizontal line running from one side of the document to the other. Everything above that line gets printed on that page, and everything below the line gets printed on the page after that.

To remove a page break that you don't want anymore, simply place the cursor on the first character after the page break and then press Backspace. If you delete a page break and it comes right back again, maybe one line before or after the place where it used to be, you're trying to remove a break that Notes put there itself because the text is at the end of the page. That's a page break that you're going to have to live with. (Check out the pagination options that I cover in Chapter 14.)

Putting Your Cards in a Table

If you're having dinner, a table is something that you keep your elbows off. When you're using Notes, a table is something that makes it a whole lot easier for you to keep rows and columns of information lined up without having to set a million tabs — and they can be pretty with borders and colors.

A *table* is simply a spreadsheet that you can place in your document, complete with rows and columns of cells into which you type information. One of the advantages of using a table to align data instead of tabs is that tabs normally allow text to wrap back to the beginning of the next line whereas tables keep text aligned in columns.

You can put a table in only a rich text field, such as a document or the body of an e-mail message.

Building a table

Suppose that you need to send a message that includes a schedule. The schedule itself would be a great candidate for a table because it houses small bits of data that are best presented in rows and columns.

Tables lend themselves to any kind of Notes documents, so you'll find yourself using them in e-mail messages, in a discussion database, and so on — really anywhere.

Tables work only in rich text fields.

When you get to the place in a document where you want to insert a table, choose Create⇨Table or click the Create Table button in the toolbar. In the Create Table dialog box that appears, as shown in Figure 15-1, you have essentially three decisions to make about the new table.

Figure 15-1:
Set table
size,
dimensions,
and type
here.

First, you need to enter the number of rows and columns that your new table will have. You can always add or delete rows and columns later. Enter the appropriate numbers in the Number of Rows and Number of Columns text fields, respectively.

Second, you have to make a decision about the table's width. Select from one of these three radio buttons:

- **Fit with Margins:** Select this radio button to create a table with width that automatically changes depending on how the document's margins are set.

- **Fit to Window:** Select this radio button to create a table with width that automatically adjusts based on the size of the window in which it's being displayed.

- **Fixed Width:** Select this radio button to create a table of the width that you specify regardless of the window size and regardless of the size of the paper on which it's printed.

People who view your table might see something slightly different than you expect based on the kind of monitor they have, whether they have multiple windows open when they see your table, and so on. That's why selecting Fit to Window is usually the best choice — it pretty much guarantees that someone looking at your document is able to see your entire table, no matter what.

Finally, you have to choose the type of table. Pick from these five types, which I present here as they appear left to right in the Create Table dialog box:

- ✔ **Basic:** All rows and columns are visible all the time.
- ✔ **Tabbed:** Only one row is visible at a time, and each row is represented by a clickable tab.
- ✔ **Animated:** Displays each row for two seconds.
- ✔ **Caption:** Displays each row as a clickable caption.
- ✔ **Programmed:** Displays one row based on a field value.

To choose your table type, just click the button for whichever type that you want.

You'll almost always want to use Basic tables because they're the simplest and easiest to use — and also because the other kinds of tables usually aren't worth the trouble (unless you want to show off). For that reason, this chapter focuses on the creation of Basic tables.

See Figure 15-2 for a table that organizes a course schedule. A schedule is just one example of a good reason to use a table. (Try hard, and you'll think of lots of other examples.) When you add a new table, Notes will usually fit it to your screen according to your specifications, making each column the same width. You can change the column widths, too, as you can read in the upcoming section "Changing column widths the easy way."

Whenever you put the cursor in a table that you add to your document, Notes is smart enough to change the menus. (Did you notice?) When your cursor is in a table, you see a new menu command called (appropriately enough) Table. It's located in the toolbar right after Text and right before Help. You use this menu choice to do things such as change the table's properties and add, insert, or delete rows and columns.

As I recommend earlier, most new tables are set to Fit to Window, which means the table size and column widths change depending on the size of the window that the reader is using to read the document. Two other choices in the Create Table dialog box are available in addition to fitting your table to the size of the window: Fit with Margins and Fixed Width.

Choosing Fixed Width causes the table and its columns to be the same width that you specify no matter how big or small that you or your reader make the document window.

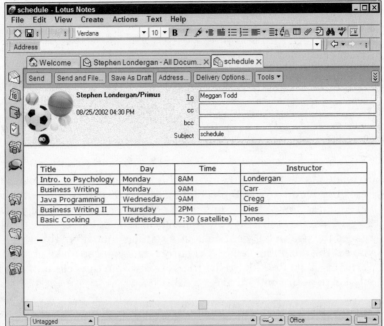

Figure 15-2:
Tables work
great for
schedules.

Setting the table

After you create a table, you may decide to change its appearance or the way that it behaves. When you do, the time has come to call to the screen the Table infobox. The tabs and the pages of the Table infobox contain many options to transform a plain table into one that will really catch your readers' eyes. You can help create more readable and attractive tables with a few formatting tricks, such as table and column width, cell borders, cell color, table borders, and table margins.

One size fits all . . . sometimes

If you want to create your new table so that it's the same size no matter who views it, make sure that the cursor is in the table and choose Table⇨Table Properties. In the Table infobox that opens, make sure that the first tab (Table Layout) is visible. Then select the Fixed Width check box located in the middle of the tab. In Figure 15-3, you can see the Table infobox open with the Table Layout tab chosen.

You can also use this dialog box to set the space between rows, the space between columns, the table's left margin, a particular column's width, and lots of other stuff. I recommend accepting the defaults simply because Notes sets the table attributes for best appearance.

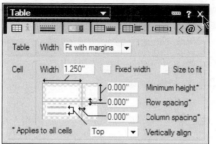

Figure 15-3:
Change
table width
here.

To manually set any or all of your table's dimensions, use choices from the Table Layout tab of the Table infobox. Here you can set the width of individual columns; however, the minimum height (which changes if you add more lines of text in a cell), the row spacing, and the column spacing (which spaces the text in adjacent cells) are settings that affect the whole table. If you set the minimum cell height fairly large, you can make choices from the Vertically Align drop-down list to put text within the cells at the top, in the middle, or at the bottom of each cell.

The one setting that you'll most often want to change is the width of different columns. You have two options for changing the column width. The first option is to use the ruler. I explain how to do this in the upcoming section "Changing column widths the easy way."

The second option involves using the Table infobox. (Access this by choosing Table⇨Table Properties.) Go to the Table Layout tab, and enter the column width that you want in the Width text box. Express your desires either in inches (the default) or in centimeters (enter **cm** after the number). The table changes dynamically as you alter the dimensions.

Formatting cell borders

Cell borders aren't people who live in jail; they're the lines that surround each table cell. To change the appearance of these, choose Table⇨Table Properties. From the Table Property box that appears, click the Cell Borders tab (the second tab from the left, as shown in Figure 15-4) to make choices to change the appearance of your table's cell borders. Here you can change the following:

- ✔ **Cell Border Style**

  - **Style:** Choosing any of these three styles (Solid, Ridge, or Groove) applies to all cells.

  - **Color:** Choices from the many colors here applies to all cells.

- ✔ **Cell Border Thickness**

  - The thickness choices range from none to a thickness of 10. You can change the thickness of individual cell borders by clicking the up- and down-arrows in each Cell Border Thickness text box (Left, Top, Right, and Bottom), or you can set a uniform thickness for all the selected cells.

- **Set All To 0:** Clicking this button makes table cells have no border.

- **Set All To 1:** Clicking this button makes the cell borders visible again.

- **Outline:** Clicking this button outlines a selection of three or more cells in a table.

Cells within your table change dynamically while you make alterations to dimensions.

If you want to change part of a table — such as just a certain cell's border or perhaps the width of a column — put the cursor in the cell, column, or row in question before using the Cell Borders tab in the Table menu or the Table Properties box. First select several cells in order to change their border.

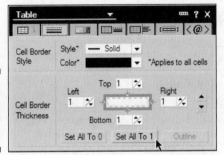

Figure 15-4:
Set table
cell borders
here.

Changing cell colors

Use the third tab of the Table infobox, Table/Cell Background, to change cell colors. This tab offers a lot of choices, and I'd be here all week (and bore you to tears in the process) if I showed you every single choice and described every possible combination of choices. Instead, here's an overview. I recommend that you create a table and experiment to find all the nuances of coloring the cells.

Figure 15-5 shows the Table Properties infobox Table/Cell Background tab.

Here are a few of the myriad changes that you can make:

✔ **Table Color:** Color groups of cells — all cells, certain border cells, or alternate rows or columns. You need to choose two colors from the Color field.

 ✔ **Cell Color:** Color the selected cells with a solid color or with two colors fading into each other vertically or horizontally. To apply color fading to your entire table, click the Apply to All button.

 ✔ **Cell Image:** Add wallpaper to the cell or cells and then use it once or repeat it throughout the cells. To insert an image, such as a GIF file, select the folder icon to the right of the Source field.

Figure 15-5:
Change
table cell
colors here.

Making a run for the (table) border

In the fourth tab of the Table infobox, Table Borders, you can change (surprise!) the settings for your table borders, as you can see in Figure 15-6. Don't confuse table borders with cell borders. *Table borders* are the halo around (outside) the entire table. The settings on this tab include, but are not limited to, the following:

 ✔ **Border Style:** Not too surprisingly, this option allows you to choose the type of border. Choose from several options, including Dotted, Solid, Double, Dashed, Ridge, Groove, and the ever popular None. Just to the right of the Border Style option is the place to set the table border color.

 ✔ **Border Effects:** This option is simple: Use it to add a drop shadow to the right and the bottom of the table so that the table looks like it's floating a bit above the page. The wider you set the width, the higher the table appears to be floating. Set it wide enough, and your readers will have to get a ladder to see what's in the table. ***Note:*** You can set the width by typing a number in the Width field as well as by clicking the little up- or down-arrows there.

 ✔ **Thickness:** Change Thickness to determine the thickness of the border. You can set each measurement separately by changing just Left, Right, Top, or Bottom. To save time, click the larger arrowheads to the right of the little table and change the entire border at once.

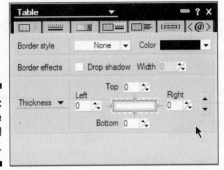

Figure 15-6:
Change
table cell
colors here.

Setting table margins

The Margins tab (the fifth one) of the Table infobox, which you can see in Figure 15-7, is where you make the settings that tell the table how to fit in with whatever surrounds it and still fit into the page. First you set the left and right margins. You can set table margins the same way that you set margins for any line of text.

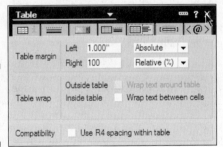

Figure 15-7:
Set table
margins
here.

The next setting on the Table Margins tab is for wrapping text around the table. The first option, Wrap Text around Table, is available only if you set the table to Fixed Width on the first tab (Table Layout) of the Table infobox. By selecting the Wrap Text around Table option, you make it possible to type text beside the table. You can't just type text and expect it to start wrapping, though. You need to place the cursor beside the table to be able to enter text there. When text is even with the bottom of the table, it begins to wrap around it.

The other wrap setting, Wrap Text between Cells, has to do with what happens *inside* cells. Pay attention here or you might get hurt. When you select Inside Wrap Text between Cells, an At Height box appears in which you enter a number (in inches, in this case) representing the maximum height that you want for the row. When you type enough stuff to cause the cell to reach that height, the new text spills into the cell to the right.

When you select the Wrap Text between Cells check box, all existing text in the cell to the right is moved into the current cell so that the cell to the right is empty and ready to receive the extra text that you may type. Choose this and you may have a lot of re-arranging to do unless the cells to the right are already empty.

Selecting the last choice, the Use R4 Spacing within Table check box, uses the slightly larger cell and spacing settings from Release 4 of Notes.

Entering data in a table

After you format your table to your satisfaction, feel free to close the Table infobox, put the cursor in a cell, and start typing. When you're finished with one cell, move to the cell above or below by pressing the up- or down-arrow key. To move to the right, press Tab; to move to the left, press Shift+Tab. Of course, you can click a cell to move to any cell in the table.

All you have to do to change the height of a cell is type. If you have too much text to fit on one line in the cell or if you press Enter while typing, the height of the cell increases to accommodate the additional text. The whole row becomes as tall as the cell with the most text in that row. If you want to change the width of a column, however, you have to mess with the menu, the ruler, or an icon. Read the section "Changing column widths the easy way" later in this chapter for more information.

A cool new feature in Notes 6 lets you reorder row items dynamically by pressing Ctrl+↑ or Ctrl+↓.

Open table, insert row

You finish formatting a table and you're about to send it when — "Eeek!" — you cry in frustration and disbelief. You forgot to include a column. Is it tragic? Sad? Are you out of luck? Is it difficult to add a column? Nope! You can add a new column or row as quickly as you can choose Table⇨Insert Column (or Table⇨Insert Row, depending on the circumstances).

Be sure that your cursor is in the column where you would like the new blank column to be. (The column where your cursor is located is pushed to the right.) To insert a row, put your cursor in the row where you want the new row to appear. (The row where your cursor is located is pushed down.) In other words, when you insert a column, the new column appears in the column where you have the cursor, and all other columns move to the right to make room for the new one. When you insert a row, all other rows in the table move down to make room. Choose the Table⇨Insert Special command to insert multiple rows or columns. You can alternatively choose Table⇨Append Row or Table⇨Append Column. Unlike inserting, which adds columns or rows where the cursor is, appending them adds them at the bottom of the table (for rows) and the far right (for columns).

No more row four

What if you don't need a row anymore? Time to smear white correction fluid on the screen? Wait a minute, this is the computer age. There has to be a better way of getting rid of a row or a column.

To delete an existing row, be sure to start by placing the cursor in the row that you want to delete. That sounds like a simple enough suggestion, but if you aren't on your toes, you'll wind up deleting the wrong row. Choose Table⇨Delete Selected Row(s). When you do, you'll get a warning that the action can't be undone. It's a one-way street. Likewise, to delete a column, choose Table⇨Delete Selected Column(s).

If you have the cursor in the wrong row or column, or if you choose to delete a row when you meant to delete a column, you could end up in big trouble! So *be careful.* Because an ounce of prevention is worth two in the bush, here's a piece of advice: Save the document first and then do your deleting. If you goof, you can close the document — without saving it — and reopen it. Now try again, and please be more careful this time!

More than one cell at a time

I often offer some pithy instruction such as "Make sure that you're in the right cell" or "Click the cell whose border you want to change and then. . . ." So, the burning question is: What if you want to make some kind of change to more than one cell (or row or column) at a time? Easily done.

To make changes to more than one cell, just use your mouse to click and drag from the first cell to the last cell you want to change. After you highlight a bunch of cells (by pressing the left mouse button and holding it down while you highlight the cells), you can make any kind of change that you want to those cells; a new font, italics, or even a new cell border are only a menu choice away.

Always make sure that you select the correct cell (or cells) in a table before you try to make a change to the table.

To merge cells, highlight the cells that you want to merge and then choose Table⇨Merge Cells. If you merge some cells and want to split them back to the way they were, use the Table⇨Split Cells command. You can't split a single cell unless it was first merged, and you can't merge a single cell, period.

Changing column widths the easy way

Skip back to see Figure 15-3, where I discuss how to change column width by using the Table Layout tab on the Table infobox. That's great if you know exactly how wide you need a column to be or if you want to autosize the column. But what if you want to eyeball it? In other words, you're not sure of the exact column width, but it's obvious by looking that the column in question is too wide (or too narrow), and you want to make it smaller (or bigger), and you want to do it now (not later).

First, make sure that the cursor is in the column that you want to change. Then choose View⇨Ruler (or press Ctrl+R) to activate the ruler above the rich text field. In Figure 15-8, the ruler (the vertical line in the left third of the screen, in this example) contains square symbols indicating the left and right margins of the column (that's column, not cell) and pentagon-shaped pointers indicating the text indents for the cell (that's cell, not column).

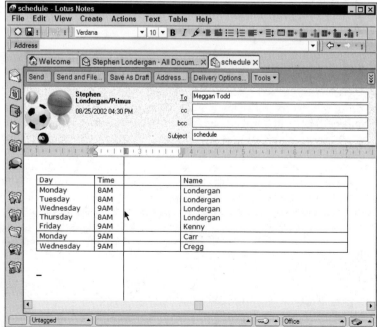

Figure 15-8:
Use the
ruler to
change a
column's
width.

Deleting a table

Getting rid of a table once and for all is a little tricky. You can't just select all the cells and then press Delete. If you do, you end up deleting all the table's contents, but the empty cells still remain.

Instead, first select the entire table by putting the cursor at the end of the line just before (and outside) the table; then press Shift+↓. Then, and only then, can you press Delete to get rid of the whole thing.

You set the width for the whole column with the ruler, but you have to change the text indents for each cell in the column individually. The moral? Highlight all the cells in the column if you want a consistent text indent.

Finally, grab that little square symbol to change the column's size. Most people find this method easier than using the Table Properties box, but if you would rather use the properties box to enter a column's width manually, go right ahead. All that clicking and typing . . . you could break a nail.

Remember that two of the table types — Fit to Window and Fit with Margins — are specifically designed to control the table size and that these settings will possibly override any changes that you try to make to a column's width. If you have trouble trying to change a column's width, you may need to change the table setting to Fixed Width. Go to the Table Layout tab of the Table Properties box to do that.

Trying to Get a Header the Situation

Imagine this heartbreaking situation: You print a 50-page monster report that you found in a Notes database. Just as the printer finishes, a strong, unseasonable breeze comes up, blows through the open window just as the last page comes out of the printer, and your document blows all over the place. You pick up the pages and try to put them in order. You have a tough time, though, because the pages aren't numbered. Sad, isn't it? What's a body to do? Next time, create a header (or a footer) and put page numbers there.

One doc, one header

Page numbers can appear in headers or footers, which are simply bits of text at the top *(header)* or bottom *(footer)* of each printed page. You can choose to put other information in a header or footer (or both) if you want. For example, if a document is urgent or contains the kind of information that spies and bad guys could use against your company, put that information in the header. If every page reads *URGENT!* or *Don't Show This to Bad Guys*, the reader is likely to get the message, even if one page is separated from the others.

To create headers and footers, choose File⇨Document Properties. From the Document properties box that appears, click the Printing tab that has the cute little printer (the fourth one), as shown in Figure 15-9. If you want to enter the text that's destined to appear at the top of each page, select the Header radio button. You don't have to be Einstein to figure out that you have to select the Footer radio button to enter text for the bottom of every page.

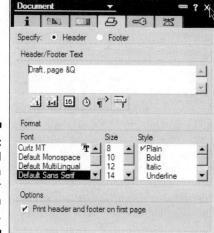

Figure 15-9: You can add a header, a footer, or both on every page.

Remember, you won't see headers or footers onscreen because they only appear on hard copy: that is, when the document is printed. You can preview what your headers or footers will look like by choosing File⇨Print Preview.

You can put all sorts of info in a header or footer and format it as well. Just type anything that you want. If you want the header (or footer) to be several separate lines of information, such as an address, press Enter at the end of the first line, the second line, and so on. Then use the following six buttons, located in the Header/Footer Text area of the Document infobox, to modify header/footer text. From left to right, they are

✔ **Insert Page Number:** Click the Insert Page Number button to automatically include a page number in the header or footer. The header or footer looks like this: Page &P. The &P turns into the proper page number when you print; for example, on the fifth page, you see *Page 5*.

✔ **Insert Total Number of Pages:** Click the Insert Total Number of Pages button if you want to display how many pages there are altogether. Now, if the document gets blown around, putting its pages in order is much easier. Of course, you can close that drafty window and avoid the problem altogether.

- ✔ **Insert Date:** Click the Insert Date button to automatically insert the date in a header or a footer. Printing the time or date in a header or footer is handy if the reader needs to tell which is the most recent printout among a lot of printed copies of the same memo.

- ✔ **Insert Time:** Click the Insert Time button, and the header or footer shows the current time (according to the computer's clock) each and every time that you print your document. Notes prints the time in this format: 03:48:42PM.

- ✔ **Insert Tab:** When you click the Insert Tab button, Notes moves the next part of the header over to the right, just as if you pressed the Tab key (on your keyboard) when typing a document. Clicking this Tab button enables you to make more complete headers and footers with, for example, the date in the lower-left corner of the page, the time in the middle of the bottom of the page, and the page number in the lower-right corner of the page.

- ✔ **Insert Title:** When you click the Insert Title button, Notes puts the title of whatever document you're working on in the header (or footer) for all to see.

Use the Font, Size, and Style format lists to determine how the header or footer looks. Note, though, that you can't mix and match these options. For example, all text in a header must be the same font, the same size, and the same style. How boring!

Imagine that you're working in the Daily Schedule document and you type this in the header:

```
Company Confidential|Page &P|&W
```

When you print the document, something like this appears at the top of page 6:

```
Company Confidential        Page 6 Daily Schedule
```

Here's a key to understanding the Notes header/footer symbols.

This	*Means This*
&P	Insert Page Number
&Q	Insert Total Number of Pages
&D	Insert Date
&T	Insert Time
		Insert Tab
&W	Insert Title

Headers and footers appear on every page except the first page unless you select the Print Header and Footer on First Page check box, located at the bottom of the Document infobox.

A chicken in every pot and a header for every doc

Creating a header or a footer is just fine and dandy, but doing so affects only the current document. To circumvent this limitation, you may instead prefer to create a header or a footer for any document that's printed in a particular database. *Note:* You can create one header or footer for every document that you print in the current database. Documents printed from other databases won't have a header unless you create one for that database, too.

To create such a universal header or footer, first choose File➪Database➪ Properties. From the Database dialog box that appears, click the little tab with the picture of the printer, and you're in business! You enter the text and formatting choices as I discuss in the previous section. The only difference is that the header (or footer) decisions you make in the Database dialog box apply to all the documents in the database.

The Document dialog box that you use to create a document header/footer looks remarkably like the Database dialog box that you use when creating a database header/footer, so be careful and pay special attention to the title of the respective properties box.

Set 'em Up, Boys

Setting up any printed page is an art. So put on your beret and choose File➪ Page Setup to open the Page Setup dialog box, as shown in Figure 15-10.

Hint: The full name of this dialog box changes depending on what type of printer that you use.

You'll use this dialog box most often (if you use it at all) to adjust the page margins by entering numbers in the appropriate fields. Although you can set margins for individual paragraphs, use the Left and Right fields when you need to add even more space to your paragraph margins.

If you include page numbers in a header or a footer, tell Notes to start with a page number other than 1 by entering a numeral in the Start Page Numbers At field. You may find this option useful if you're printing a report from Microsoft Word and you want to include a few pages from a Notes database. For example, you can print pages 1–5 in Word and then print pages 6–11 in

Notes. Use the Start Page Numbers At field to make your reader think that all the printed pages came from the same place.

If you intend to send your printed pages to a printing service to be reproduced, you could make the job easier for the printing service by using the Print Crop Marks feature. On the other hand, if you're like most people and don't often send material to a professional printing company, you probably won't use this tool.

In the Paper Source section, click the triangle to the right of the First Page field. This tells Notes which paper tray in your printer to use for the first page when printing. Now click the inverted triangle to the right of the Other Pages field to pick which tray to use for all the rest of the pages. Obviously, if you don't have one of those fancy printers with more than one paper tray, you won't spend too much time with this feature. But if you do have a fancy printer (lucky you!), this is a nice way to have the first page print on that fancy company letterhead.

Figure 15-10:
Set up
printing
here.

Search and Rescue

Everybody makes mistakes. Remember: To err is human, to forgive is divine, and to make the same mistake again is inevitable. So, in the spirit of mistake making, suppose that you type a long memo and then find that some of the text that you typed is wrong. Of course, you made the mistake over and over again. You might, for example, have referred to *Sue* when she prefers to be called *Susan*.

The time has come to find all the Sues in the document and change them to Susans. Choose Edit⇨Find/Replace or press Ctrl+F. Watch for the Find Text in Document dialog box to appear, as shown in Figure 15-11, which I tailor to make this global change.

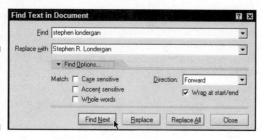

Figure 15-11:
Seek, find,
and replace
from here.

Searching for text to rescue your document takes a bit of planning if it's to work correctly. Use the Match check boxes within the Find Options section to your advantage.

- ✔ **Case Sensitive:** Select this check box so that if the document includes the word *sue* (the legal action), Notes won't replace that with *Susan*.

- ✔ **Accent Sensitive:** Select this check box to search for a word that contains a diacritical mark such as an accent (`), a circumflex (^), a cedilla (~), a freckle, or a mole. When you choose Accent Sensitive, the Find Text in Document feature looks specifically for that mark and ignores any occurrences of the word without it.

- ✔ **Whole Words:** You could select the Whole Words check box so that Notes doesn't go around changing *suede* into *Susan*de.

To be sure that you find all occurrences of a word that you want to replace, it's best to put the cursor at the beginning of a document before you start beating the bushes for that special word. Notes allows you to begin your Find/Replace search in the middle of the document; it will go back to the beginning of your document later for the parts that it hasn't scanned yet.

Enter the text that you want to find (in the Find text field) as well as the text that you want to use as a replacement (in the Replace With field) to start the process. You can choose one of the following in the Direction drop-down list:

- ✔ **Forward:** Begin at the cursor and go forward through the document to the first or next occurrence of the search text.

- ✔ **Backward:** Search from the cursor back to the beginning.

After you decide which direction to search, click any of these three buttons to search and/or replace.

- ✔ **Find Next:** Click this button to leave the current occurrence alone. Notes then looks for the next occurrence.

- ✔ **Replace:** Click this button to replace only the current occurrence of the found text.

✔ **Replace All:** Click this button to do the job quickly by replacing every occurrence of the search text with the replacement text without checking each time.

Use this choice carefully because strange and unpredictable things could happen. For instance, look what happens if the word Sue starts a sentence: *Sue us at your peril* becomes *Susan us at your peril*.

Select the Wrap at Start/End check box to cycle through the document repeatedly. For example, if you begin a forward search for text from a position in the middle of a document, Notes won't stop searching when it reaches the end of the document (as it otherwise would) but will continue the search at the beginning of the document.

The clever little searcher might find an occurrence of the search text behind the Find/Replace dialog box, which means that you sometimes have to move the dialog box out of the way to see the highlight. Just drag the dialog box out of the way by the scruff of its title bar.

Click the Close button when you're finished looking for and replacing text.

If Your uh Bahd Spellar

Even if you're a really good speller, you're bound to make the occasional typographical error sometime in the next few years. You need to be ever vigilant for that eventuality — ready to pounce on an error and correct it before it gets sent to thousands of recipients who will laugh quietly up their sleeves at you for an easily correctable oversight.

In the Spell Check dialog box in Figure 15-12, you can see that the person who knocked out the memo didn't notice that *corporate* was spelled incorrectly. Then again, maybe he or she didn't know how to spell it. No matter, the writer was able to find this mistake by running the Notes spell checker.

Figure 15-12:
Check your
spelling
here.

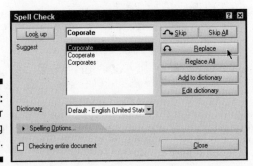

To run a spell check, save your document (just to be safe) and then choose Edit⇨Check Spelling or click the Spell Check button in the Toolbar. Regardless of where you last saw your cursor, the spell checker starts at the beginning of the document. If the spell checker finds a word that it doesn't recognize, it highlights the word (sometimes behind the dialog box) and waits for you to take some sort of action.

The word in question also shows up in the Not in Dictionary field, and substitution suggestions (some helpful and some hilarious) are offered in the Suggest list. Proper names usually give spell checkers fits. Sometimes the Notes dictionary won't offer a replacement suggestion; in those cases, the Suggest list is empty.

As the spell checker moves from word to word, you can click any of these buttons:

✔ **Skip:** Click this to not change the word that Notes think is misspelled but still have Notes continue to watch for it in the rest of the document.

✔ **Skip All:** Click this button to ignore every occurrence of the word in this document.

✔ **Replace:** In the Suggest list, highlight the one that you want (or type in a replacement in the Not in Dictionary field if it's not an option) and then click the Replace button to substitute the good for the bad.

✔ **Replace All:** Click this button after you choose one of the suggestions in the Suggest list (or type in a replacement in the Not in Dictionary field if it's not an option) to replace every occurrence of the misspelled word with the one that you chose.

✔ **Add to Dictionary:** Click this button to essentially teach Notes a new word by adding it to the Notes dictionary so that Notes will never, ever question the word again. This is useful, for example, when dealing with names and addresses.

✔ **Edit Dictionary:** Click this button to peruse and correct the words that you've previously "taught" Notes.

Click the Close button at the bottom of the dialog box if you're not prepared for the shock of seeing what you spelled wrong . . . or if you're done being editorial.

If you just want to spell check a small section of a document, highlight all the text that you want to spell check and then kick off the spell checker.

Use the Add to Dictionary button carefully because adding a misspelling to the dictionary can be very embarrassing. Forevermore, Notes will ignore that misspelling, and you'll look foolish.

Document Locking

One of the new features of Notes 6 is the ability to lock a document. Imagine a database that's used by your whole department and to which everyone has Editor access. (That is, when users are allowed to create and edit documents in a database.) You can imagine the trouble that could be brewing — what happens if more than one person edits the same document at the same time?

Document locking is the solution to this conundrum. When you lock a document, you tell Notes that you want to make changes to the document *and* you want Notes to prevent anyone from editing the same document at the same time.

The good news is that document locking is an automatic feature; you don't have to do anything. When you press Ctrl+E to edit a document, Notes automatically locks it to prevent anyone else from trying to edit it at the same time. When you close and save the document, Notes also automatically unlocks it so that someone else can then edit it.

Document locking is a feature new with Notes 6, which is set by the database's owner on the Database box, as shown in Figure 15-13. Access the Database infobox by selecting File⇨Database⇨Properties. Because you might not be the manager of all the databases that you use, you may need to ask someone (the database owner or your administrator) if you think that you need this feature turned on for you. Otherwise, simply select the Allow Document Locking check box and you're good to go.

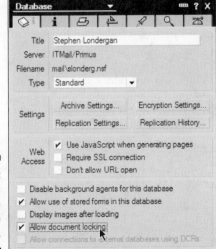

Figure 15-13:
Make a
database
lockable
here.

Chapter 16

Notes the Way You Want It

. . . .

. . . .

Some people are happy with the world the way that it is — other people, well, aren't. If you fall into the latter category, this chapter's for you.

If you think that Lotus Notes 6 works just great just the way it is, maybe you can skip this chapter. But if you're one of those people who likes to have things her own way, or one of those people who always wants to know just a little bit more, read on.

Read here to discover how to customize Notes, create links, and set preferences for how you want Notes to behave, including the Mail and Calendar features.

The Notes Welcome Page

When you start Notes, you see the Welcome Page, as shown in Figure 16-1. (For more on the Welcome Page, read through Chapter 2.) What you see on the Welcome Page is determined by a few things. For example, although you can change the Welcome Page layout and contents, you should also know that your administrator has some control over what you see so that he can make sure that you see important announcements and so on.

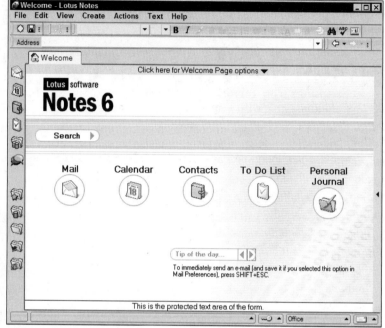

Figure 16-1:
Begin at the
default
Notes 6
Welcome
Page.

Changing the Welcome Page

You can easily change the layout of your Welcome Page. Look at the top center of the Welcome Page for a little triangle immediately preceded by the words *Click here for Welcome Page options.* Well, you can probably guess that this is what you click to change the look of your Welcome Page, and that's exactly what I am about to do in Figure 16-2. As you can see, there's a plethora of things you can do to make your Welcome Page your very own.

In Figure 16-2, I also clicked the Current Welcome Page Selection drop-down list. As you can see in this list, Notes 6 has six Welcome pages to choose from.

- ✔ **Basics:** This configuration is the simplest Welcome Page of all, with those five round main buttons: Mail, Calendar, Contacts, To Do List, and Personal Journal. This is the setup that I discuss throughout this book, and it's the one shown in Figure 16-1.

- ✔ **Basics with Calendar:** This layout is the same as the Basics except that it also shows your Calendar right in the Welcome Page.

- ✔ **Headlines with My Lycos:** This configuration combines your Inbox with your Calendar as well as a special page from the My Lycos Web site.

- ✔ **Headlines with UK My Lycos:** This layout is the same as Headlines with My Lycos except that the Lycos Web page shows items of special interest to Notes users who are in the United Kingdom.

- ✔ **Headlines with Terra:** This configuration combines your Inbox and your Calendar along with a special Web page from Terra (which is in Spanish).

- ✔ **Basics Plus:** This layout combines your Inbox with your Calendar; it also shows those five big round basic navigation buttons that are on the default Welcome Page as well as a special box that lets you conduct searches.

Your Welcome Page choice is really up to you — you can choose whichever one appeals to you. And because it's so easy to change from one to the other, I recommend that you use one Welcome Page for a few days to see whether you like it and then switch to another Welcome Page to give it a try, too.

Figure 16-3 shows my favorite Welcome Page, Basics Plus, which is my favorite because it shows at a glance the things that I do most often.

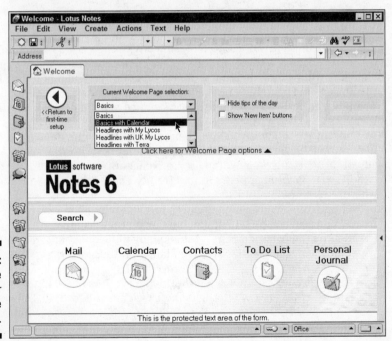

Figure 16-2:
Customize your Welcome Page.

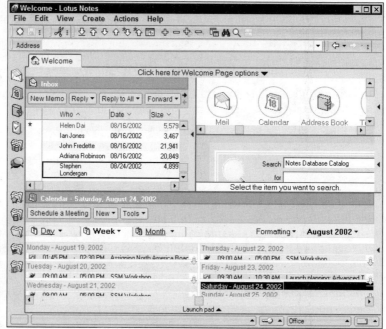

Figure 16-3:
The Basics
Plus
Welcome
Page.

The one distinct advantage to choosing any of the various Welcome pages other than Basics is that you can further customize these other pages by changing what's included in the page. For example, you might decide to use the Basics Plus page but change the contents of the page itself to use your To Do list or perhaps a database that you use instead of the Calendar.

As you can see in Figure 16-3, each area of the Welcome Page (called *frames*) has a little triangle (it's blue) midway down its right border. When you click any of these triangles, a Switch Frame To list appears from which you can choose exactly what appears in that frame. That's what I do in Figure 16-4, where I select my To Do list.

As you can see in Figure 16-4, you have several alternatives to choose from the Switch Frame To list. Here's the blow-by-blow on what you can have in a Welcome Page frame and why you might want these items:

✔ **Everyday Tasks:** This is another name for those five, big round basic buttons that are part of the default Welcome Page: Mail, Calendar, Contacts, To Do List, and Personal Journal. You can see such a frame in the upper-right corner in Figure 16-4.

✔ **Inbox:** The most common addition to a Welcome Page, this is where your mail comes in. You can see such a frame in the upper-left corner in Figure 16-4.

- **Trash:** Select this to display the e-mail messages that you've recently deleted.

- **Calendar:** Choose this when you want your Welcome Page to show you where you're supposed to be . . . you know, your schedule. You can see such a frame in the bottom half of the screen in Figure 16-3.

- **To Do:** This includes your exhaustive list of action items in the Welcome Page.

- **Subscriptions:** Choose this to mark certain databases and documents in which you're interested; selecting this also automatically displays updates in real-time when these monitored items change. For more on this, read the sidebar "Creating a subscription" elsewhere in this chapter.

- **Web Page:** Select this to include any page — either from the Internet or your company's intranet — in your Welcome Page.

- **Database:** Choosing this enables you to include any Notes database.

- **File Folder:** This one is way, way cool: Select this to include a window into one of the folders on your own computer, right in the Welcome Page — what an easy way to get to the files that you use most often. For an illustration of this, check out the middle-right frame of the Welcome Page in Figure 16-4.

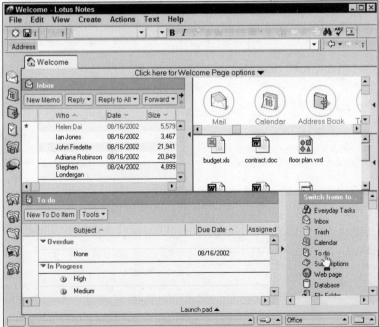

Figure 16-4:
Further refine your Welcome Page by changing a frame's contents.

Creating a subscription

One of the things that you can choose to display on your Welcome Page is a subscription. Suppose that every morning you check a discussion database to see whether anyone has added anything since yesterday. Using a subscription is an easy way to let Notes' fingers do the walking; it will check to see whether new documents have been added and then (optionally) display them on your Welcome Page. You can subscribe to any Notes database.

To have Notes track a database for you, first open that database and then choose Create⇨ Subscription. From the Doc Library Subscription form that appears, tell Notes what you want to track. For example, you can ask Notes to notify you whenever documents have been added to a certain database, when documents are added by a particular person, or when documents are added that contain a particular category. Click OK when you finish defining the subscription.

You can also change the layout of a Welcome Page by changing its frame widths and heights much the same way you would change the width of a column in your Inbox. (**Hint:** Think click and drag.)

If you really aren't smitten with any of the standard six Welcome Page configurations that Notes offers, just create your own. Instead of modifying one of the existing Welcome Page's contents, create a brand new Welcome Page, with almost any layout and contents that you can imagine, by clicking the Create a New Welcome Page. To find this option, just go to the Welcome Page and click the heading Click Here for More Welcome Page Options.

Creating Links

Very often you need to direct someone's attention to a particular Notes document, database, or view. Perhaps you've posted a new document in your company's expense reporting system, and you want to alert your boss so that she can approve it and you can get reimbursed. Or perhaps you've found a new database that's chock-full of marketing analysis, and you want to tell a friend about it.

To accomplish this, you need to create a DocLink. Figure 16-5 shows what a DocLink looks like. As you can see, all your reader has to do is click the link, and he's whisked away to the document in question.

You can create a link to a document, a specific part of a document, a view, or a database.

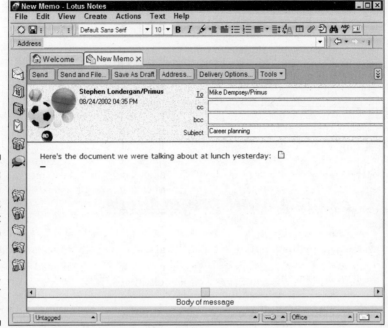

Figure 16-5:
Using a
DocLink
makes it
easy to
go to a
particular
document,
view, or
database.

Here are the steps to create a link:

1. **Open the document, view, or database that will be the target of the link.**

2. **Choose Edit⇨Copy as Link.**

3. **From the options that appear, choose Document Link, View Link, or Database Link.**

   This step copies the link to the Clipboard.

4. **Close the document, view, or database that will be the target of the link.**

5. **Open the document (or e-mail message) that will contain the link.**

6. **Choose Edit⇨Paste to insert the link.**

7. **Save or send the document or message.**

Setting All those Myriad Preferences

If you had to pay for Lotus Notes 6 by the pound and you weighed all the preferences and customization settings that Notes has, you'd sure have to pay a lot. That's a terrible metaphor, but realize that you literally have a few hundred different buttons and boxes that you can use to customize how Notes 6 works.

The good news is that you most likely don't care about most of them, so my goal in this section is to show you, dear reader, how to get to the various and sundry dialog boxes that are used to change Preference settings. Then I draw your attention to those that are the most important.

Just because you can change a Preference setting doesn't mean that you should.

Changing Mail preferences

I recommend that you live with the default Mail settings that Notes provides to see what you do and don't like. Then when you can't resist the urge any more to fiddle with them, fix them how you want. To change the way your Mail works, do the following:

1. **Open your Mail.**

2. **Choose Actions⇨Tools⇨Preferences to open the Preferences dialog box, as shown in Figure 16-6.**

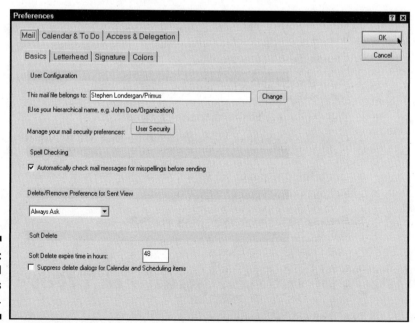

Figure 16-6:
Set Mail preferences here.

As you can see in Figure 16-6, the Mail tab in the Preferences dialog box has four tabs of its own: Basics, Letterhead, Signature, and Colors. For a discussion on the Colors settings, read Chapter 7. Here I focus on the Basics, Signature, and Letterhead tabs.

Basics tab

Adjust the features here for basic mail preferences, such as checking spelling and deletion.

- ✔ **User Configuration:** The first field on the Basics tab — This Mail File Belongs To *xx* — is used to determine the name of the person who owns the mail file in which you're setting the preferences. In almost all cases, your name goes in that field; you'd only change this if the mail file was set up for use by one person (like the CEO of your company perhaps) and was actually used and managed by a different person (like the CEO's assistant). Bottom line: Change this field only if you are really, really sure that you need to.

- ✔ **Spell Checking:** Refer to Figure 16-6 to see that the default setting is for Notes to automatically check the spelling of a mail message just before you send it. If for some unimaginable reason you don't want Notes to automatically spell check your messages (you'd certainly be exhibiting rather extreme confidence in your spelling abilities), you can turn this feature off — but I recommend that you leave it on. Just leave the Automatically Check Mail Messages for Misspellings Before Sending check box selected. To discover how to add or edit this user dictionary, see the upcoming section "Setting user preferences."

- ✔ **Delete/Remove Preference for Sent View:** A relatively common mistake that people make in Notes (and have been making for years) is that they try to *delete* messages from a folder in their mail when they really mean to *move* the message somewhere. In order to warn people that they probably don't want to do this, Notes displays a warning when you try to delete a message from the Sent view. If you want to turn this warning off, select Always Delete from the Delete/Remove Preference for Sent View drop-down list.

- ✔ **Soft Delete:** Deleting a message really just moves it to the Trash bin, from whence messages are really, permanently deleted every 48 hours (the default). This scheduled Trash-emptying feature — which is new in Notes 6 — is called *soft delete*. You can adjust this deletion timer in the Soft Delete Expire Time in Hours field. Not that I recommend it, but you can change this field if you want more (or less) time to change your mind between when you delete a message and when the message actually gets removed from the Trash bin.

To accept any changes that you make in the Mail/Basics tab of the Preferences dialog box, click OK.

Signature tab

The idea behind a message signature is that you may want to have a rote, standard closing for all your messages. If you find yourself typing the same thing at the bottom of every message you send — maybe just the word *Thanks*, or perhaps a more involved signature block of text that has your phone number and e-mail address in it — you can save yourself some valuable time (and typos) by using the Preferences dialog box to set up a signature. That way, every time that you start a new message, your signature block is automatically inserted at the end of the message.

To set this preference, go to Mail tab of the Preferences dialog box; then click the Signature tab there. See Figure 16-7 for the options of the Signature tab. On this tab, first select the Automatically Append a Signature to the Bottom of My Outgoing Mail Messages check box. Make sure that the Text radio button is selected and then enter your signature text in the Signature field. You can alternatively select the HTML or Image File radio button if you instead want your signature to come from an external file.

Click OK when you're finished setting up your signature.

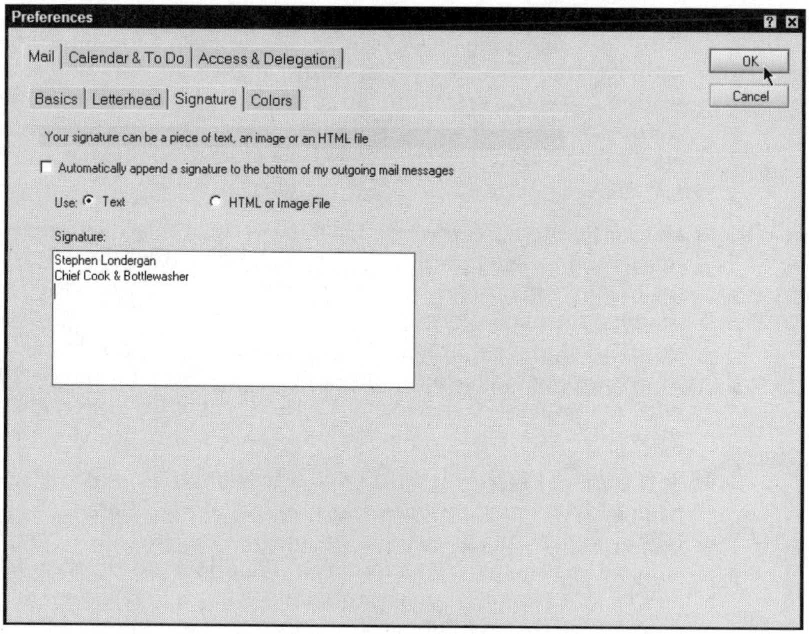

Figure 16-7: Define a signature for the bottom of every message that you send.

One of the most common things that people put in their signature block is their e-mail address, which always strikes me as being, well, dumb. If you send someone an e-mail message, you don't have to tell the person what your e-mail address is because that person can just click the Reply button to send you a message. And don't forget that your e-mail address is already displayed at the top of every message that you send, anyway.

Letterhead tab

Ever since the days of Notes R4, you've been able to choose your own letterhead — those cool graphics that appear at the top of the e-mail that you send. Letterhead is back in Notes 6, but it's better than ever. (Pony Express is still my favorite, however.) To select the image that appears at the top of the e-mail that you send, open your mail and then choose Actions⇨Tools⇨Preferences⇨Letterhead. Select your letterhead from the drop-down list, and check out how it looks in the Preview window.

Setting Calendar preferences

Here's how you use the Preferences dialog box Calendar settings to customize Notes to your own taste:

1. **Open your Calendar.**

2. **Choose Actions⇨Tools⇨Preferences to open the Preferences dialog box.**

   The Preferences dialog box opens.

3. **Click the Calendar & To Do tab of the Preferences dialog box, as shown in Figure 16-8.**

Don't be intimidated by all the tabs in Calendar & To Do because some of them don't merit much attention. That said, here are the ones that do:

✔ **Basics:** On the Basics tab (see Figure 16-8), use the first field to determine what's going to happen when you double-click a time slot in your Calendar.

✔ **Display:** Use the fields on the Display tab to determine which days of the week appear on your Calendar and what time your workday starts. If, for example, you work the graveyard shift, you can change your workday to begin at 12 a.m. (yawn).

✔ **Scheduling:** Use the fields on the Scheduling tab to tell Notes about your workday. This setting is especially important if you let other people see your Calendar in advance of sending you invitations. For example, if you never work on Fridays, you'd use the Friday setting on this tab to make yourself unavailable; that way, no one will even try to schedule you for something on your day off. You can also use the Scheduling tab to specify whether you only want certain people to be able to see when you're free.

✔ **Autoprocess:** You can use choices on the Autoprocess tab to have Notes automatically reply to invitations for you based on whether your settings say that you're available. For example, you may decide to enter the name of your manager in the fields on this tab because you'll probably always show up to the meetings that she invites you to . . . if you're smart. The only downside to accepting invitations with Autoprocess is that it means you have to be extra-specially conscientious about checking your Calendar when you arrive at work each morning; otherwise, you might not be aware of meetings that Autoprocess has booked for you without your knowledge.

✔ **Colors:** Finally, use the Colors tab to decide what color combination Notes will use for each type of entry on your Calendar. For example, if you want all your meetings to appear in purple and your appointments in lime green, you can do it here.

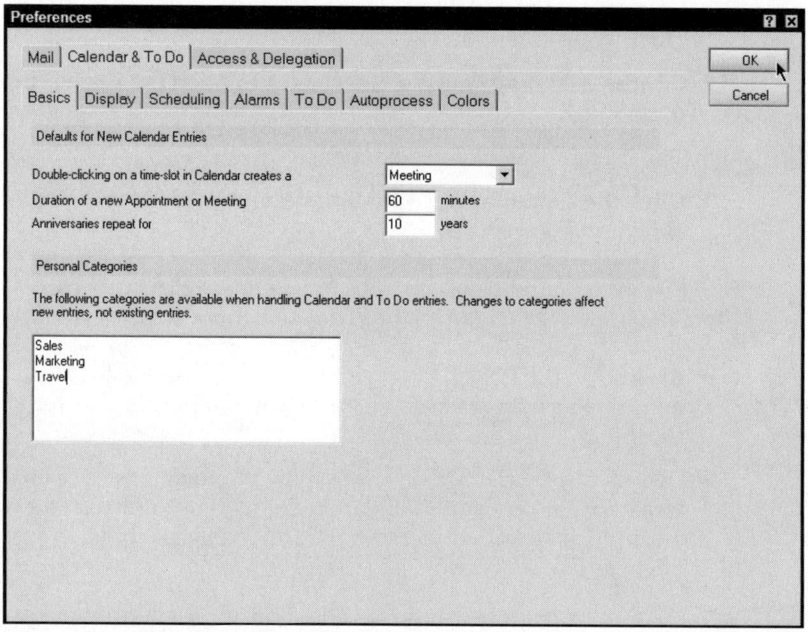

Figure 16-8:
Set
Calendar
preferences
here.

Setting User Preferences

Here's how you use the User Preferences dialog box to customize Notes to your own taste:

1. **Arrive at work.**

2. **Turn on your computer.**

3. **Go get some coffee (no sugar).**

4. **Return to your office.**

5. **Start Notes.**

6. **Choose File⇨Preferences⇨User Preferences.**

The User Preferences dialog box has five tabs: Basics, International, Mail, Ports, and Replication.

See the Basics tabs of User Preferences dialog box in Figure 16-9. Many of the items are self-explanatory. You don't have to be a rocket scientist to figure out what's going to happen when you change the Bookmark icon size from small to large. (*Hint:* Think big.) It's also worth mentioning that probably 90 percent of the buttons and check boxes in the User Preferences dialog box have such specific use and narrow focus that there's a pretty good chance that you don't need to change them.

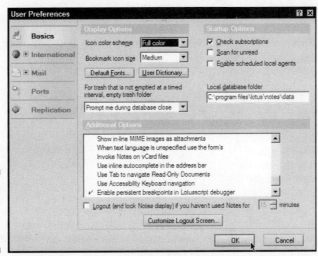

Figure 16-9:
Set User
Preferences
here.

Messing with some of the User Preferences settings can have fairly disastrous consequences, so be careful. Many of them require your administrator's approval.

A few things in this dialog box warrant special consideration and attention. To wit, in the Basics tab:

- **User Dictionary:** Click the User Dictionary button to see all the words that you've added during spell checks. You can also use this button to add new words to the dictionary or to remove a word that you added by mistake.

- **Scan for Unread:** If you select the Scan for Unread check box, Notes drags you through each unread document in your databases each time that you start Notes — including your Inbox, of course.

- **Logout:** Select the Logout (and Lock Notes Display) if You Haven't Used Notes For *xx* Minutes check box if you want to automatically log out (the same as when you press F5) after a specified period of time. Specify the time by typing it in minutes in the Minutes text box shown.

- **Textured Workspace:** To see a pretty, beveled workspace, scroll through the Additional Options list to select Textured Workspace.

In the International tab, take note of these:

- **Unit of Measurement:** Use the Unit of Measurement setting on the International tab to determine whether measurements such as those in the ruler margin dialog boxes are expressed in inches or metric units.

- **Spell Check:** Use the International Spell Check tab to select the language and dictionary (English, French, and so on) that Notes should use when checking your spelling.

Setting Your Notes Password

Every time that you use Notes, you have to enter your password. The fact that you know the password coupled with the fact that no one else knows your password is really one of the foundations of the security that Notes has.

For example, you wouldn't want someone to send an e-mail message with your name on it, would you? What if some merry prankster logs on to your computer and then sends out a message (which appears to be from you) telling your co-worker that he's fired? That would be bad, right?

Or what if you're traveling with your laptop computer, and it gets stolen? What stands between the thief and all that sensitive, confidential, and valuable corporate information that's in Notes?

It all comes down to your password. In fact, passwords are such serious business that there's a pretty good chance that your company or organization has a lot of rules, policies, and procedures that tell you exactly how your passwords should work — how many characters your password should have, how often you should change it, and so on.

Check with your administrator or organization's security expert before messing with your password — play by the rules!

In general, here are a few suggestions regarding passwords:

✔ **Use some variety:** Don't use the same password in Notes that you use in other places, such as your network password, ATM card, and so on.

✔ **Mix it up:** Choose a password that balances easy with hard. You want something that's relatively easy for you to type and remember but also hard for someone else to guess. In other words, your husband's, wife's, or children's names are probably not a good idea to use.

✔ **Don't broadcast it:** Don't write your password on one of those little yellow sticky notes. Even if you do (argh!), don't plop that yellow sticky note to your computer monitor. That sort of defeats the whole purpose, don't you think?

✔ **Change it regularly:** Changing your password once in a while — like every three months or perhaps twice a year.

Changing your password

Changing your password is so easy to do that you really have no excuse not to change it once in a while. You may even find yourself forced to change it on a regular basis — your administrator may have set you up so that you are required to change it, say, every six months.

When the time has come, for whatever reason, here's how to set a new password:

1. **Choose File⇨Security⇨User Security.**

2. **In the Notes dialog box that appears, enter your current password to confirm for Notes that you really are who you say you are.**

   It stands to reason that you have to know your current password in order to change it, right?

   The User Security dialog box opens with the Security Basics tab active, as shown in Figure 16-10.

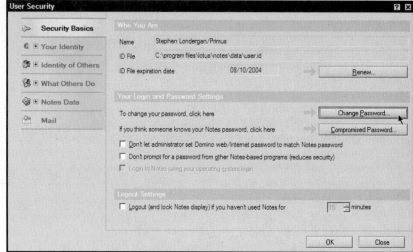

Figure 16-10:
After you
confirm your
password,
Notes
presents
you with this
dialog box.

3. **Click the Change Password button.**

4. **Enter your current password again.**

   The Change Password dialog box opens, as shown in Figure 16-11.

Figure 16-11:
Change
your
password
here.

In the Change Password dialog box, you have to enter your new password twice — once in the Enter New Password field and again in the Re-enter New Password field — to make sure that you typed your password right the first time.

5. **Click OK and then click Close.**

Forgot your password?

If you forget your password, there ain't much that Notes can do to help you — again, that would sort of defeat the whole point of having a password, wouldn't it?

Getting your password reset in Notes isn't something that you do — it's something that you have done for you. And the only way to do that (seeing as you forgot your password and are consequently locked out of Notes and your e-mail) is to pick up the phone and call someone — more specifically, your administrator. (You could call your mother, but she won't be able to help you except maybe bake you cookies and tell you that everything's going to be okay.)

Renewing your certificate

Another one of the Notes security credentials that you have in addition to your password is a *certificate*. This little bit of technology is actually pretty complicated — you'll just have to trust me that without it, you can't access any of the Notes information at your company or organization.

And, like your password, your certificate is set to expire every so often — like every five years or so.

When the day comes — and you'll know when the day is approaching because Notes tells you — do the following to get a new certificate:

1. **Choose File⇨Security⇨User Security.**
2. **In the Notes dialog box that appears, enter your current password to confirm for Notes that you really are who you say you are.**

   The User Security dialog box opens.

   It stands to reason that you have to know your current password in order to change it, right?

3. **Click the Renew button on the User Security dialog box.**
4. **Click the Send button.**

   Sit back and wait for the administrator, who sends you a new certificate via e-mail.

5. **Open the mail message and choose Tools⇨Accept Certificate.**

You can't access any of your organization's Domino servers without a valid certificate, so make sure that you request a new one when the one you have is about to expire.

Part V
Worldwide Notes

The 5th Wave   By Rich Tennant

"I like getting complaint letters by e-mail. It's easier to delete than to shred."

In this part . . .

We can't all stay in our offices, do the daily routine, and punch out at 5 p.m. Some of us just have to zip into the fast lane of life. If you're such a person, you're probably aching to know how to take Lotus Notes 6 with you on your business trips and also how to get Notes to interact with other programs.

Okay, hotshot. You asked for it. This part of the book is devoted to the Notes features of interest to a person like yourself.

Chapter 17

Data In and Data Out

In This Chapter

▶ Copying data to your Notes document with the Clipboard

▶ Copying Notes data to a non-Notes document with the Clipboard

▶ Moving data into Notes by importing

▶ Moving data out of Notes by exporting

▶ Embedding data in Notes

*U*sing Lotus Notes 6 has many advantages over your average, run-of-the-mill, do-only-one-thing programs. You're probably already aware of many of these advantages. For example, Notes works in different operating systems and on different kinds of computers. No matter what the environment, however, you can take information of all sorts from another application (Microsoft Word, for example) and use it in Notes.

In this chapter, I explain how you can bring information from other programs into Notes and use Notes information in other programs. The business of getting the information from one application into another varies from the simple to the complex. Here are your choices:

✔ Copying to and pasting from the Clipboard

✔ Creating attachments

✔ Using the File➪Import and File➪Export commands

✔ Creating links

✔ Embedding

Where's the Glue?

Back in the good old days, when you wanted to include a picture, some text, a graph, or a table full of information in something that you were typing, you began the process by pulling the paper out of the typewriter when you finished typing. Then you used scissors to cut out the picture or text or graph or table and found a bottle of glue to paste it into the blank space in the typed copy. This system was certainly very un-high tech, definitely messy, and also made it pretty hard to jam that piece of paper back into the type-writer when you needed to type some more.

But this is the age of automatic bread machines, hands-free cell phones, always-on Internet connections, and (with the advent of the personal com-puter) cutting and pasting without using scissors or glue. You can use your friendly Clipboard to add objects — such as a graph from Microsoft Excel, a paragraph from Microsoft Word, or a chunk of a Web page — directly to your Notes documents. (The *Clipboard* is a temporary please-hold-this-thing-for-me-until-I-tell-you-what-to-do-with-it area.) Here's how:

1. **Open the thing (document, spreadsheet, Web page, whatever) that contains the information that you want to snag for your Notes document.**

   Technical types sometimes call this program the *home program* or the *source application*.

2. **Highlight (select) the desired information and (usually, depending on the program) choose Edit⇨Copy or press Ctrl+C to put this selection on the Clipboard.**

3. **Switch to Notes, position the cursor where you want the information placed, and choose Edit⇨Paste or press Ctrl+V.**

   Unless the original information was too big to fit on the Clipboard (for example, if you tried to copy 3,000 cells from a worksheet), you see a copy of the original data in the Notes document.

This system is preferable to the scissors-and-glue system because the page with the pasted item doesn't stick to all the other pages. It's also faster and seamless, and it gives you the ability to move the pasted object around or delete it if you change your mind. Besides that, you can edit the information that you paste into Notes.

This copy-and-paste system works fine as long as the source application sup-ports the use of the Clipboard and you're able to open the source application to get at the information that you want to copy. Keep in mind that if the data in the source application changes, Notes can't update its copy of the data. After you copy and paste something into Notes, Notes has no way to know what goes on in the source application.

Unlike most of the other techniques that I describe in this chapter, you can use the copy-and-paste method to copy data from one Notes document into another. Most other techniques work only with data and files created outside Notes.

Throwing Out Your Paper Clips

What if you can't use the Clipboard? Your next weapon in the arsenal of using non-Notes data is to attach files to documents. Think of using a paper clip to attach one document to another. (Hmmm . . . maybe that's why you see a paper clip icon when an e-mail bears an attachment.) It doesn't matter whether Notes knows the file format, or whether the original application has ever heard of the Clipboard, or what kind of laundry detergent you use. In a rich text field, you can attach any file — Word document, Excel spreadsheet, JPEG graphics file — to any Notes document.

Place the cursor where you want the attached file to appear and then choose File⇨Attach or click the Attach button (shown in the left margin) from the toolbar. The Create Attachment(s) dialog box appears. You can either browse for (in the Look In drop-down list) or type the name of the file (in the File name text field) that you want to attach. Click the Create button and, voilà, an icon for the attached file — the whole, intact file — appears in your Notes document.

An attached file is shown by an icon for what kind of file it is. A Word document, for example, has a big blue W, and an Excel spreadsheet has a big green X icon. Attached files also bear their file name. Figure 17-1 shows an attachment called `contract.doc`.

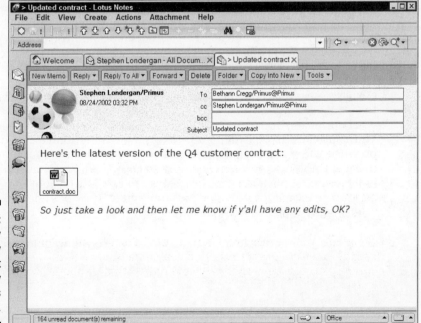

Figure 17-1:
Attach any file in any rich text field in any Notes document.

When a Notes document contains an attached file, all that the reader sees is an icon representing the file, not the data itself. The icon must be double-clicked on to open the file. Remember that the main reason for using an attachment in the first place is simply to give that file to others . . . not to use the data in your Notes document.

Although you or your document's reader can usually use the Notes View option in the Attachment dialog box to see (or print) what's in an attachment, making any changes to an attachment requires the program (such as Microsoft Excel) that was used to create the original file.

Importing and Exporting

Sometimes you want to include information from another source in your document, but the original application doesn't support the Clipboard, so you can't use copy and paste. And perhaps you don't want to attach the file because you want the reader to actually see the information rather than having to deal with that little icon. Your next option is to import the file from its native format and program directly into Notes. By the same token, if you can't copy Notes information to the Clipboard to paste it into the other application (maybe there's too much?), you can export the Notes info.

Importing from non-Notes programs

Imagine that you're composing a Notes document and you need to include a bunch of pages that you've already typed in Microsoft Word. You could use the Clipboard to copy/paste information, but for the sake of this little story, you decide that there's too much material to use the Clipboard or perhaps the file that contains the information doesn't have a copy/paste menu.

What do you do? You import the Word file. Similar to copying and pasting, *importing* converts a file from its original format (Microsoft Word, in this example) right into the Notes document that you're composing and right into the rich text field in which you're typing. You can convert (import) files from many other programs, such as Lotus 1-2-3 and Microsoft Word (among others).

Here are the steps to import something:

1. **Place your cursor in the rich text field where you want to insert the file.**

   By the way, don't even think about importing a document into any kind of field other than rich text.

2. **Choose File⇨Import.**

   The Import dialog box appears, as shown in Figure 17-2.

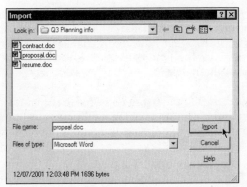

Figure 17-2:
Import files
from here.

3. **In the Look In drop-down list box, navigate to the drive and directory where the file to be imported is located.**

4. **In the Files of Type drop-down list box, select the type of file that you're importing.**

5. **Either highlight the filename, double-click on it, or type it in the File name text field, and then click the Import button.**

   Tah-dah! The file appears inside your Notes document.

When you import a file, Notes converts it to regular text, so feel free to subsequently liven it up by changing the fonts, making some of the words bold, or whatever.

Choosing File⇨Import to include a foreign (non-Notes) file in a rich text field is your technique of choice if the file's source application either isn't installed on your workstation (maybe someone else gave you a Word document, but you don't have Word installed on your computer) or can't be copied and pasted with the Clipboard for some other reason.

Here's a list of the types of files that you can import into a rich text field:

- ✔ ASCII text file
- ✔ Binary with text
- ✔ BMP, CGM, GIF, JPEG, PCX, and TIFF 5.0 image files
- ✔ Microsoft Word and Excel
- ✔ Microsoft RTF (Rich Text Format) files
- ✔ HyperText Markup Language (HTML) files
- ✔ Lotus 1-2-3 Worksheet and PIC files
- ✔ WordPerfect 5.x, 6.0, 6.1, 7, and 8 files
- ✔ Lotus WordPro files

If you need to import a file that's not on this list, see whether the originating program can save the file in one of the formats that Notes supports. For example, if you need to import a Quattro Pro spreadsheet, you can use Quattro Pro to save the file as a Lotus 1-2-3 worksheet and then import the converted Lotus 1-2-3 worksheet into Notes.

Although you can import information, using copy/paste is almost always easier.

Exporting: A document leaves home

Just like you can convert documents from other programs into Notes (importing), you can also convert a Notes document into a file that can be used by a different program (exporting). Perhaps you have a Notes document that you want to give to a few colleagues who don't have access to Notes. (Do they know what they're missing?) You can convert the Notes document into a Word document and then deliver the new Word file to your colleagues through e-mail or (perish the thought!) on a floppy disk.

To convert a Notes document into another format, follow these steps:

1. **Find and open the Notes document that you want to export.**

2. **Choose File⇨Export.**

    The Export dialog box opens, as shown in Figure 17-3.

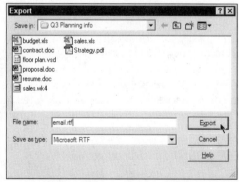

Figure 17-3:
Export a file
from here.

3. **In the Save In drop-down list box, navigate to the drive and directory where the file to be exported is located.**

4. **In the File Name text box, type the name of the file.**

5. **Use the Save as Type drop-down list box to tell Notes what type of file you want it to be.**

6. **Click the Export button and you're finished.**

   Now you (or your friends) can open the new file in the appropriate program.

Here's the list of file types to which you can export a Notes document:

✔ ASCII text file

✔ CGM and TIFF 5.0 image files (for creating images)

✔ Microsoft RTF files

Just as with File⇨Import, use File⇨Export only when you can't use the Clipboard to transfer the Notes document to the other program.

Documents come into view

You can also bring information into Notes by importing lots of documents at the same time. For example, this method is an appropriate choice if you have a Lotus 1-2-3 worksheet and you want to import it in such a way that each row in the spreadsheet becomes a separate document in a Notes database. If your worksheet has 4,362 rows worth of information, you get 4,362 new documents in your Notes database.

First steps . . .

First things first: You have to use Lotus 1-2-3 to set up the spreadsheet in a very particular fashion. Most importantly, remove all the fancy formatting and blank rows in the worksheet. The following are two specific rules for preparing a spreadsheet to import to Notes:

✔ The column headings for the worksheet must be in row 1 of the worksheet, and they must be the same as the field names in the Notes database. This is important, so call the person who created the database if you're not sure what the exact field names are in the Notes database. Don't mistake static text next to the field for the actual field name.

✔ The rows of spreadsheet information must begin in row 2 of the worksheet and must be in a solid block. If you include any blank rows in the middle of the spreadsheet, you end up with empty documents in your database.

If your goal is to convert every row in a Microsoft Excel worksheet into a separate Notes document, you first have to use Excel to save the file as a Lotus 1-2-3 worksheet because that's the only kind of worksheet that Lotus Notes understands.

If you need to import any other kind of file, such as a big text file or an Excel worksheet, it's probably also best to first convert that file into a Lotus 1-2-3 worksheet and then import the Lotus 1-2-3 worksheet into Notes. It should come as no surprise that the easiest type of file to import into Lotus Notes is Lotus 1-2-3.

Second steps . . .

After you get the worksheet all shipshape, use Notes to open the database into which you want to import the worksheet and then choose File➪Import.

When you choose File➪Import, just open the database without opening one of the documents or trying to compose a new document. Otherwise, Notes thinks that you want to put the worksheet into just one document.

Use the Import dialog box (as shown in Figure 17-4) to indicate where to find the file (Look In) and the type of file (Files of Type). Then select the file or type the name in the File Name box. In Figure 17-4, I chose a 1-2-3 worksheet.

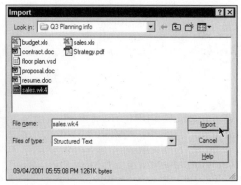

Figure 17-4: Convert rows in a Lotus 1-2-3 worksheet into Notes documents.

After you finish making your selections, click the Import button. Notes presents you with yet another dialog box, the 123 Worksheet Import dialog box, as you can see in Figure 17-5. The goal now is to tell Notes how to import the rows of the spreadsheet. You need to decide whether you want Notes to import all rows or only selected rows as documents, as well as whether you want Notes to include the column heads in the new spreadsheet.

You have five questions to answer:

✔ Are the new documents main documents or responses?

✔ Which form from the database should Notes use to display the new documents?

✔ How should the fields (columns) be named? Follow my advice from the earlier section "First steps . . ." and be careful to make the spreadsheet column heading match the field name: Select the Defined by the WKS Title check box.

✔ Which range should be imported from the spreadsheet? You can enter either the cell coordinates (such as **A:A1 . . A:D341**) or a range name, if you have one.

✔ Should Notes calculate field formulas defined on the form for each document as it is created? If that's what you want, select the Calculate Fields on Form During Document Import check box. If you're not sure whether you should check this box, consult the person who created the database.

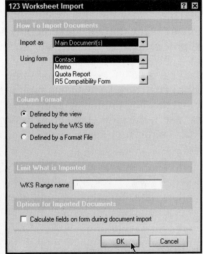

Figure 17-5:
Determining
how the
whys and
hows of the
worksheet
import.

After answering these questions, click OK and you're in business. Notes imports the worksheet and converts each row into a new document for your database.

As with most tasks in computerland, you can import documents in a number of ways. I only discuss importing a Lotus 1-2-3 worksheet because it's the most common type of import and because the other types of view-level imports are complicated. If you're convinced that you need to import a file that's not a Lotus 1-2-3 worksheet, I recommend that you seek help from the person who created the database or from your local Notes guru.

Hey, view, make me a spreadsheet

Exporting from a view is even easier than importing into a view. The idea behind a view-level export is that you want to create a spreadsheet based on the columns in a view.

Exporting a view to a spreadsheet is the most common type of view-level export. You can also export a view to any of the following file types:

- ✔ **A Lotus 1-2-3 worksheet,** compatible with any version of Lotus 1-2-3 and also accessible by most other spreadsheet and database programs, such as Excel, Access, and so on

- ✔ **A structured text file,** which is an ASCII file that would then be imported into some other program

- ✔ **A tabular text file** (ASCII text arranged in rows and columns, separated by tabs), which is easy to import into other spreadsheet and database programs

You can export Notes view data into structured text files, tabular text files, and Lotus 1-2-3 spreadsheet files. Depending on the type of export you select, you may export either the visible text in the view (tabular text) or the text and field data inside the documents (structured text).

Exporting from a view does not remove documents from the view, but simply copies the data into a new file.

To export view data into a 1-2-3 spreadsheet, structured text, or tabular text files:

1. **In a view, select the documents that you want to export.**

2. **Choose File⇨Export.**

   The Export dialog box shown in Figure 17-6 appears.

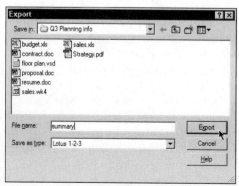

Figure 17-6:
Export a
Notes view
from here.

3. **Select Lotus 1-2-3, Structured Text, or Tabular Text in the Save as Type list box.**

4. **Type a filename in the File Name text box.**

5. **Click the Export button.**

6. **Select to export All Documents or Selected Documents from the dialog box that appears.**

7. **To include the view titles in the exported file, select the Include View Titles check box.**

8. **Click OK.**

When you export a view, Notes exports only the fields that are in the view. If you need to export fields that are *not* in the view, you have to negotiate with the person who designed your database to add a column or two to display the additional fields that you need.

When you intend to export data from a view to a program other than Lotus 1-2-3, you should still export the view to a Lotus 1-2-3 worksheet and then use that other program to further convert the worksheet. (For example, Microsoft Excel can open a Lotus 1-2-3 worksheet.) Take it from me: Using Lotus 1-2-3 is a lot *(a lot)* easier than using the structured or tabular text formats.

A new feature in Notes 6 makes it easy to convert a view into a table that you can easily paste anywhere, such as an e-mail message, Notes document, or a whole different program. Just open the view in question, select the docs you want (by clicking to the left of each line until a check mark appears), and choose Edit⇨Copy Selected as Table. I did that in Figure 17-7. As you can see in the figure, the cool thing is that you also automatically get a DocLink in the table that corresponds to each document. (Read more about DocLinks in Chapter 16.)

What's a DocLink?

Cuff links for your favorite doctor? Sausages for physicians? Not in Notes-speak. A *DocLink* is an easy-to-use connection between one document to another.

Suppose that you're sending a message to an associate about a report in another database. Rather than saying, "Find the document for yourself, you lazy bum," you can put a little icon of the report in your memo. When that

aforementioned lazy bum receives the message, a mere double-click of the DocLink icon opens the document.

Of course, the recipient must have access to the database and the document that you're linking in your message. (An error message appears onscreen if someone clicks a DocLink and he or she doesn't have the rights to access the document or the database itself or doesn't have

(continued)

(continued)

access to the server that contains the database that contains the document that lives in the house that Jack built.) One of the databases to which others don't have access is your own mail database, so you wouldn't even think of linking to one of your mail messages, right?

To create a DocLink, you first need to open (or highlight in a view or folder) the document to which you're creating a link and then choose Edit⇨Copy as Link⇨Document Link. Then switch to the document that you want to contain the DocLink, make sure that you're in a rich text field, and choose Edit⇨Paste.

Recipients receiving this message can simply double-click the DocLink. The document itself

opens before their very eyes. Sure beats typing the whole report all over again, doesn't it? Just for the record, you need to be in edit mode to add a DocLink to a document, but you don't need to be in edit mode to open a DocLink. And even though the example that I present here is a mail message, you can paste a DocLink into any Notes document in any Notes database.

Here's a tip: When reading a document that has a DocLink in it, choose View⇨Document Link Preview to see a little bit of the linked document without actually opening it. It's just like previewing a document in your mail database.

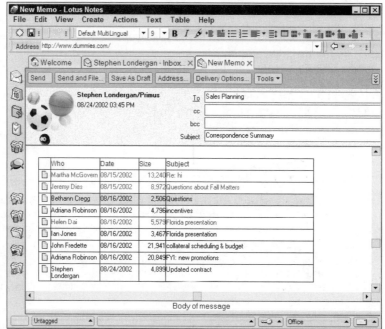

Figure 17-7:
Use a new feature in Notes 6 to copy/paste an entire table.

If You Can't Link 'em — Embed 'em

To the person reading your document, an embedded object looks and acts almost the same as a linked object. Either one can be an icon or data, depending on the complexity of the data in the server file. The difference between the two is that a *linked object* is a pointer to data in a source file; when data in the source file changes, the changes are reflected in Notes. However, an *embedded object* is a copy of data, so changes made to the original file are *not* reflected in Notes.

Suppose, for example, that you want people to enter expense reports in a spreadsheet format into a Notes document for storage in a Notes database. You could embed a Lotus 1-2-3 spreadsheet in a Notes form containing the text and formulas that users need to enter data. When users create an expense form in Notes, the embedded spreadsheet kicks into action, and users find themselves in 1-2-3, where they fill in the data. When they save the work in 1-2-3, they return to Notes, where the data is in the Notes document, but not in the original file.

To embed information in a Notes document, follow these steps:

1. **Open the original file in its original program.**

2. **Copy the information to the Clipboard by choosing Edit⇨Copy or by pressing Crtl+C.**

3. **Open the Notes document and position the cursor in a rich text field.**

4. **Choose Edit⇨Paste Special.**

5. **Choose the format from the As list.**

6. **Click Paste or press Ctrl+V.**

Embedding doesn't require that the readers of the Notes document have access to the original file because they have their own copy of the file. However, if they want to edit the original data, they must have the *server application, access to the source file, and have the same directory mapping to the source file on the file.* Double-click the embedded data: This opens both the server application and the file. Any changes made to the embedded file on one user's version of a document might not be reflected in other users' copies of the document, depending on whether the documents are replicated to all other users.

Searching Notes for text is a valuable tool. Both linking and embedding enable your readers to search for text, as long as you follow two rules:

✔ **You must link or embed the data as text or rich text.**

✔ **The data must be visible; it can't be represented by an icon (like an attachment).**

This business of embedding and linking used to be called OLE and DDE (and still is by people who speak in abbreviations and use pocket protectors). OLE (pronounced Spanish style: *o-LAY*) stands for *Object Linking and Embedding;* DDE stands for *Dynamic Data Exchange.* Don't lose any sleep over which one you're using. It doesn't matter. That's something for Notes to worry about behind the scenes.

Chapter 18

Notes and the Web

This chapter is all about how you can use Lotus Notes 6 with Web pages. Whether you're talking about pages on your company's intranet, or material that's out in the wide, wide world of the Internet, Notes has a role to play.

Opening Web Pages in Notes

Certainly the most direct path to a Web page is to enter its URL in the Address field of the Toolbar, as you can see in Figure 18-1.

Here's a bit of technojargon for you: *URL* is a term used to refer to a Web page address. This acronym stands for *Universal Resource Locator*. That said, you can now forget those fancy words: A URL is just a Web page address.

You can also access Web pages in a couple of different ways:

 ✔ **Bookmarks:** The bookmarks that you keep in the Bookmark bar can be a mix of Notes databases and Web pages.

- ✔ **Links:** Any time that you see a URL (`www.dummies.com`, for example) in a Notes document, you can click it to open that Web page.

- ✔ **Document:** You may sometimes encounter Web pages in Notes applications. Even your mail can have Web pages because it's very easy to forward Web pages to people as e-mail.

- ✔ **Welcome Page:** You can have your Welcome Page show a combination of information, such as your Inbox or Calendar, right alongside your company's intranet home page.

In most cases, you won't use Lotus Notes to open Web pages, even if it feels like you are. In addition to Lotus Notes, most people have a Web browser installed on their computer, such as Microsoft Internet Explorer (IE) or Netscape Communicator. Typically, Notes is set up to work with such programs, so even though you're perhaps clicking a Web page link in your Notes Inbox, it's actually your Web browser software that does the work to go get the page and display it for you.

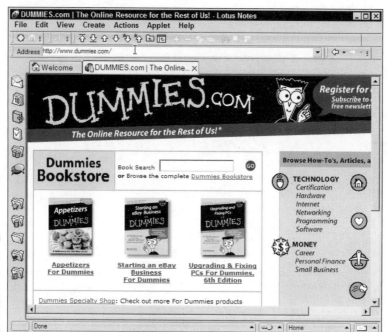

Figure 18-1:
You can open Web pages right from Notes.

Configuring Notes to use your Web browser

Notes decides how to interact with your Web browser based on a setting in your location document, which (as I discuss in Chapter 19) is stored in your Personal Address Book.

As is usually the case, you should be wary of making any configuration changes to your workstation without checking with the powers that be — unless, of course, *you* are the powers that be.

To change the way that Notes retrieves Web pages, you need to edit the location document in question — which is usually accomplished by first choosing File⇨Mobile⇨Edit Current Location and then clicking the Internet Browser tab. In the row labeled Internet Browser, you see a field displaying the method Notes currently uses to access the Web, with a down arrow button next to it. To change the method Notes uses to access the Web, click the down arrow, which brings up the Select Keywords box, as shown in Figure 18-2.

Figure 18-2:
Change how Notes accesses Web documents with the Select Keywords box.

As you can see in Figure 18-2, you can choose from five possibilities in the Select Keywords list:

- ✔ **Notes:** Choose this if you do *not* have a separate Web browser installed on your computer and you want to use the relatively simple Web browser that's built into Notes.

- ✔ **Notes with Internet Explorer:** This is the best choice, assuming that you have IE installed.

✔ **Netscape Navigator:** Choose this if you have Netscape (Communicator or Navigator) installed.

✔ **Microsoft Internet Explorer:** This choice is similar to Notes with Internet Explorer, but it doesn't store the pages you retrieve locally.

✔ **Other:** This is the best choice if the browser that you use isn't included in the list, such as Opera, Mozilla, or some other.

Which keyword you choose, of course, depends on which (if any) Web browser that you have installed.

Browsing while disconnected

The most interesting choice in Figure 18-2 is probably the second, Notes with Internet Explorer. When you use this setting, Notes and Internet Explorer *really* work together. For example, when you open a Web page, IE gets the page, but Notes is also involved — Notes actually (optionally, of course) stores a copy of the page for you in your computer.

Why is that cool? Because it means you can use Notes to browse Web pages even when you aren't connected. Imagine that your company's Human Resources department has updated your intranet with new policies about sick days and so on. By using this feature, you could have Notes (with Internet Explorer) save the pages in question so that you can read them on the train home or while flying at 38,000 feet on your way to Europe.

So, if you select the Notes with Internet Explorer option, the pages that you view are stored by default in a database on your computer called *Personal Web Navigator*. This is the database that you'd use in the plane because it will have the Web pages in it.

Although your system is probably set up to automatically save every Web page that you visit, you can ensure that a particular Web page is saved for you later by choosing Actions⇨Keep Page.

To see the pages in your Personal Web Navigator, choose File⇨Database⇨Open (or press Ctrl+O) and then choose Personal Web Navigator.

You can use the Personal Web Navigator only if you select *Notes with Internet Explorer* in the location document.

You can also configure Notes to automatically monitor certain Web pages for you and then automatically save a new copy into your Personal Web Navigator if/when the page changes. Ask your administrator whether your company supports the use of Notes *Page Minder* and *Web Ahead* if this appeals to you.

Forwarding a Web Page in Notes

Suppose that you find a Web page that you need to share with a colleague. The easiest way to do that is to forward it to your colleague as an e-mail message. Sure, you could start a new message, copy and then paste either the page or its address, but here's an easier way.

First, open the Web page and then choose Actions⇨Forward, as shown in Figure 18-3. The Forward Options dialog box opens.

You have to tell Notes what it is that you want to forward, so select either the Forward Bookmark to Page or Forward Copy of Page radio button. In either case, you get a new e-mail message with either the page itself or a link to the page, ready for address and delivery.

- ✔ **Forward Bookmark to Page:** Select this, and your recipients get just a link to the Web site; they then click this link to open their Web browser and retrieve the page. This choice is usually best if the page in question is likely to be changed between the time that you send it and when your recipients read it — imagine a Web page with stock prices, for example.

- ✔ **Forward Copy of Page:** Select this and your recipients actually get the page itself, right in the e-mail message. An advantage here is that your recipients don't have to be connected to the Internet to see the page because the whole page ends up in their Inbox.

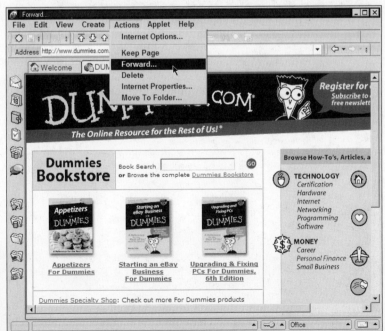

Figure 18-3:
Forward a
Web page
from here.

Sometime you might want to include a Web page in a database that's not your mail, such as a discussion. You can just copy/paste the page from your browser window into the Notes document.

Making a Link to a Web Page

The last thing that I have for you in this chapter is a special way to make a link to a Web page.

If you need to include a link to a Web page (either in an e-mail message, or any other Notes document), the easiest way to do it is to just type the Web page's URL, such as `http://www.dummies.com`.

The good news is that this is very easy and probably very obvious to the person receiving your e-mail. Most people in this day and age recognize and know that an `http://` link is clickable. The bad news is that some URLs are messy — they can be really long and ugly, particularly if you want to put one in the middle of a document.

That's where Hotspots come in because they're short, and pretty. A *Hotspot* is a way to make any word clickable, related to a particular Web page. Check it out in Figure 18-4.

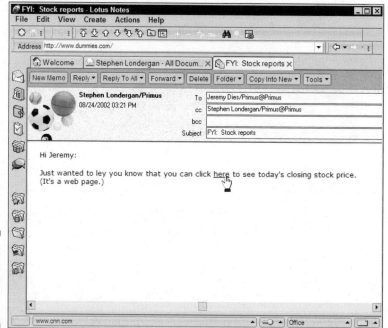

Figure 18-4:
You can use Hotspots as Web page links, too.

The idea is that even though the URL that the document refers to is long and messy, the way that it's presented in the document is nice and neat and consistent with the other format (fonts, bold, italics, and so on) that are used in the document.

Use the steps to make a Hotspot that will take your reader to a Web page.

1. **Open the Web page in question.**

2. **Copy the page's Web address to the Clipboard by highlighting its URL in the Address field and choosing Edit⇨Copy, or pressing Ctrl+C.**

3. **Switch back to Notes and select the word that your reader will click to go to the Web page.**

4. **Choose Create⇨HotSpot⇨Link Hotspot.**

   The HotSpot Resource Link dialog box opens.

5. **Click inside the Value field.**

6. **Click the paste button, press Ctrl+V, or choose Edit⇨Paste to enter the Web page URL. Select the check mark that appears to the right of the Value field.**

7. **Close the HotSpot Resource Link box by selecting the small X in the upper-right corner.**

Figure 18-5 shows what it looks like when you create a URL-based link Hotspot.

Figure 18-5: Create a Hotspot link to open a Web page.

You can attach a Hotspot link to almost anything — any bit of text with any font, or even a picture.

Chapter 19

Notes for Road Warriors

You know that old expression *You can't take it with you?* Well, it's not true, or at least it's not true in Lotus Notes 6, anyway. You *can* take it with you. More specifically, one of the wonders of Notes is that you can work while you're disconnected from the network.

Just because you have to travel doesn't mean that you can't read your mail, use your databases, and generally stay plugged into what's going on back at the office. In this chapter, I explore what you have to do to use Notes on the road. And even if you aren't headed to the airport anytime soon, read this chapter anyway. No matter why you need to work away from the company's network (maybe you just want to work at home?), this chapter will hook you up with all things replication.

What Exactly Is Replication?

Suppose that your company has Domino servers in Boston, New York, and London. On each, your administrator has placed a copy of the Notes application that your company uses to discuss marketing strategies for the coming year. Of course, you want the documents that your colleagues in England post to show up in New York and Boston. And, if someone in New York edits a document, you want those changes to appear in Boston and London, right? But what if someone in Boston deletes a document? You'd most likely want that document to be deleted in both New York and London, too.

Replication is the process that Notes uses to keep databases synchronized with each other. Your administrator first gets a copy of the database(s) in question on each server and then schedules connections between the servers. For example, the Boston server may connect with the New York server at 8 a.m. and then the English server at 9 a.m. Then it's another connection to New York at 11 a.m., England again at 1 p.m., and so on throughout the day and night.

That's nice, but why do you care? Because you may need to replicate your corporate and personal data, too, especially when you work away from the office.

Notes R5 users should pay particular attention because replication is different in Notes 6 in a couple of big ways — all for the better, of course!

Why do you need to replicate?

Try this story on for size. You have your laptop all set up and ready to go. You grab a cab to the airport, check your bags, and then it's down the jetway and onto the plane. Now that you're trapped in your seat for the next 14 hours, why not use the time productively? Wouldn't you like to catch up on some of your e-mail? By the end of the trip, you have 11 new e-mail messages to send and maybe you've even composed a few documents in the Notes databases that you most often use.

Now fast-forward the story to your arrival at the hotel. You're all checked in, you've hung your suits in the closet, checked out the honor bar, and paid off the bellhop. How are you going to send those e-mail messages, post those documents that you composed on the plane, and see all the e-mail messages and Calendar invitations that were sent to you while you were cruising at 35,000 feet? You guessed it — you replicate the databases on your laptop with the Domino server back at the office.

Or how about this scenario? You work from home. In your home office, you have a computer with Notes installed, and you have a modem. You can work from the databases on your system and then dial in to replicate. Even if you're down in your cellar, you can still read your mail and use Notes databases.

Understanding how replication works

The four parts to replicating between your computer and a Domino server are

- A way to connect to the server, such as a modem
- A Location document
- A copy of the database(s) that you'll use while disconnected
- The Replicator

Connecting to the server

In order to replicate, you need a physical connection to the server and a way to let Notes know that you have this connection.

Maybe the physical connection to your server travels from your computer via a cable modem in your home office, then through the Internet to your company's network, and then on to the server in question. That's usually the best kind of connection because cable modems are fast, fast, fast.

But maybe your physical connection uses a modem, which is particularly likely when you're in a hotel room. Then your connection would go from your computer over to that modem in the hotel room, then through the Internet to your company's network, and then on to the server in question.

Or, here's another twist on that: Your company might have its network (or even the Domino server itself) set up so that you dial into it directly. Your connection runs from your computer to the modem to your company's network to your server, in other words.

Odds are pretty strong that it's not your job to sweat the details of how this connection works. This is a serious undertaking; just think of the security implications involved in letting people connect through the Internet to your company's network. Most companies have entire departments to handle the essential details of how remote access works.

After you establish your physical connection, you need a *Connection document*, which is essentially the thing that tells Notes what kind of physical connection you have. Figure 19-1 shows a sample Connection document.

Using a Location document

If you're a road warrior, you probably use the same computer all the time. If so, sometimes you and your laptop are at the office, connected to the network; sometimes you're disconnected altogether, like when you're on an airplane or on the Acela Express between Boston and New York; and sometimes you're connected from afar, such as via a modem in a hotel room somewhere.

All that moving around and connecting/reconnecting the network cable from day to day could get a little confusing for Notes. How would it know where you are and, more important, which method of connecting it should use?

You tell Notes where you are through a Location document. In the above scenario in which you work in three different places (office, plane, hotel room), you'd have three Location documents: one for each place.

Even if you only work from one location all the time — whether that's your office at work or even a home office — you'll use at least one Location document. Some people, on the other hand, have several. (Read more about creating and using Location documents in Chapter 18.) Figure 19-2 shows a sample Location document.

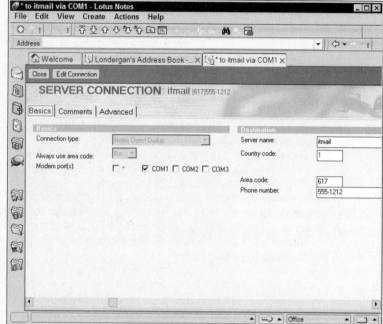

Figure 19-1:
Connection
documents
tell your
copy of
Notes how
to connect
to a server.

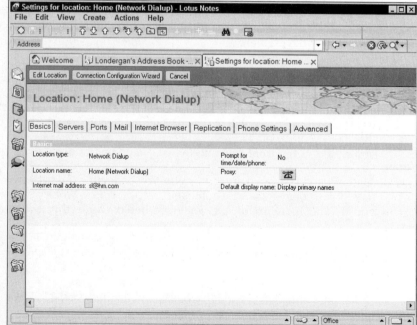

Figure 19-2:
Location
documents
tell Notes
how to
connect to a
server from
a particular
place.

Bringing along a copy of the database(s)

This is the most obvious part of the working offline equation. You need a copy of the database in question (your mail, as a prime example) on the computer that you'll be using while you're away. You normally use Notes databases that are on a server, but if you're on an airplane, you won't be connected to the server. Hmm . . . so you better bring that database along with you on your computer. Although you'd probably want to bring along your Mail database, you can bring as many as you want. For example, if your organization has a discussion database that you use regularly, or perhaps a Notes-based system for filing expense reports, you could bring those, too.

Synching up with the Replicator

The top of the replication pyramid is the Replicator itself. This is the part of Notes where it all comes together — where Notes uses the Location documents, Connection document, and databases that you bring to synchronize what's in your computer with what's on the server(s). Take a gander at Figure 19-3 to get a glimpse of the Replicator.

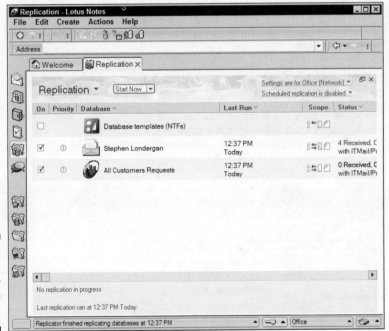

Figure 19-3:
The Replicator brings it all together.

Taking a Copy of the Database with You

You usually want to make a copy of a database to bring along on your trip. Disk space permitting, you can bring any database that you want with you. At the very least, you probably need a copy of your Mail database.

The three steps involved in making a brand-new, first-time-ever replica copy of a database are

1. **Open the database in question.**

2. **Choose File⇨Replication⇨New Replica.**

3. **Click OK in the Create Replica For Database dialog box that appears (see Figure 19-4).**

Figure 19-4: Take a database with you.

You could also use the Create Replica For Database dialog box to change the location and filename for your copy, but you probably shouldn't do that because the default settings are usually just fine the way they are, and changing them can cause more headaches than it's worth.

Click Replica Settings in the dialog box to expand the options in the Create Replica For Database dialog box, as shown in Figure 19-5.

Figure 19-5: Create a replica here.

Use these entirely optional settings to

- ✔ **Encrypt the Replica Using:** Selecting this check box secures your copy of the database by encrypting it. This is such a good idea that some companies have a policy requiring that any database you take has to be encrypted. If you do decide to encrypt a database, you also have to choose the level of encryption from this setting's drop-down list box: Strong Encryption, Medium Encryption, or Simple Encryption.

- ✔ **Create Full Text Index for Searching:** Select this check box if you want to be able to search the database, as I discuss in Chapter 13.

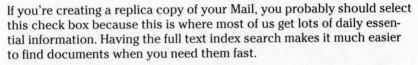

  If you're creating a replica copy of your Mail, you probably should select this check box because this is where most of us get lots of daily essential information. Having the full text index search makes it much easier to find documents when you need them fast.

- ✔ **Create Immediately:** Leave this check box selected so that the copy of the database gets created and replicated right away.

Click the More Settings button in the Create Replica For Database dialog box, and the Replication Settings For dialog box appears, as shown in Figure 19-6.

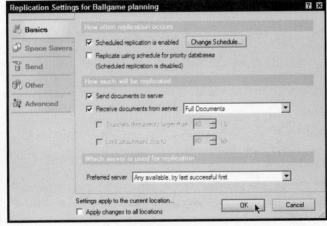

Figure 19-6: Refine replication settings here.

Use these (entirely and totally optional) settings to make more decisions about the database, such as how often it's going to be replicated and whether replication is a one-way or a two-way undertaking. I cover the important parts of this dialog box later in the upcoming section "Deciding which databases to replicate."

All these extra settings and buttons aside, most times when you need to create a new replica copy of a database (which you do altogether infrequently, of course), just follow those three steps: Open the database, choose File➪Replication➪New Replica, and then click OK. It's that easy.

Replicating

The Replication page is your first stop when you want to connect to your Domino server and send/receive the updates that have happened since the last time you replicated. The Replication page lists all the databases that you have to replicate, and it also tells you when each was last replicated.

You open the Replicator, as shown in Figure 19-7, by clicking its bookmark (which you can see in the left margin of this page).

The real action on the Replication page is the Start Now button (top left), which you click when you're ready to replicate. The databases on this page are replicated in the order in which they're listed. You can re-order this list by dragging any one of the databases higher or lower in the list. I recommend putting your Mail at the top because it's probably your prime concern.

Figure 19-7:
Begin replication here.

When you click the Start Now button, things start happening. Notes starts replicating the databases, first sending the updates that you've made to the server. Then Notes gets the updates on the server and then puts them in your local database. You get a real-time indication of the progress — what database is being replicated at the moment, as well as an overall assessment of how much more time Notes needs to finish, as you can see at the bottom of Figure 19-8.

Deciding which databases to replicate

Sometimes you might want to skip replication of a particular database. Perhaps you're in a hurry and you only want to send and receive e-mail messages — leaving replication of your other databases for later.

The easiest way to temporarily suspend the replication of one of the databases on your Replicator is to deselect (clear) the check box in the On column of the Replication page. (Read the previous section for more on this page.) Notes will only replicate the databases that you select in this column, but don't worry — you can always change your mind.

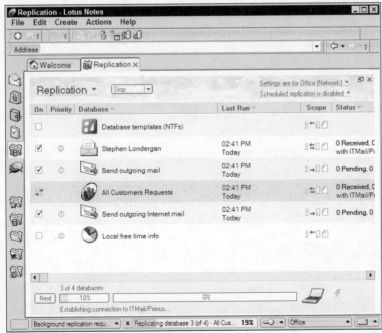

Figure 19-8:
Follow the Replicator's progress.

Remove a database from the Replicator altogether by selecting it on the Replication page and then pressing Delete. Or, right-click it and then select Remove from the drop-down menu that appears.

For more replication options, click the arrow next to the Start Now button in the Replication page. A drop-down list appears, as you can see in Figure 19-9.

You have three choices from this drop-down list:

- ✔ **Start Now:** Selecting this starts the process, replicating all the databases that are on the Replication page and bear a check mark in the On column.

    Selecting this is exactly the same as clicking the Start Now button.

- ✔ **Start Mail Only Now:** Select this to start replication but only send and receive your e-mail messages.

- ✔ **Start High Priority Databases Now:** Select this to start replication but only for the databases that are marked as High Priority in the Priority column.

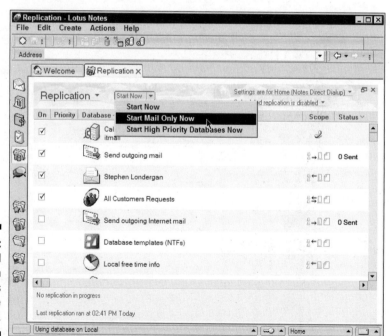

Figure 19-9: Control which databases will be replicated.

You mark a to-be-replicated database as High Priority by right-clicking in the Priority column for the database. Then select High Priority from the pop-up menu that appears, as shown in Figure 19-10.

Databases that are High Priority show an icon with two clocks in the Priority column. All the rest (regular status) show a single clock.

Refer to Figure 19-10 to see that each database on the Replication page has a Scope setting (right-side column). This column is used to determine what the replication settings are in a given database at replication time. For example, you might want to schedule automatic replication so that it happens every hour or so without you having to remember to click that Start Now button. Or perhaps you have a database in which you only receive documents but never send them. Maybe you want to set up your Mail so that it only replicates messages that you've received within the last 90 days. To change these settings, click the icon in the Scope column for a database, and the Replication Settings For dialog box appears, as shown in Figure 19-11.

Chances are pretty good that you'll never, ever have a need to mess with the Replication Settings dialog box.

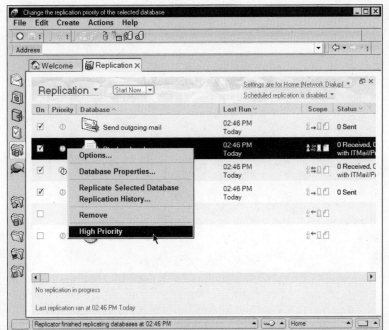

Figure 19-10: Set a database's replication priority.

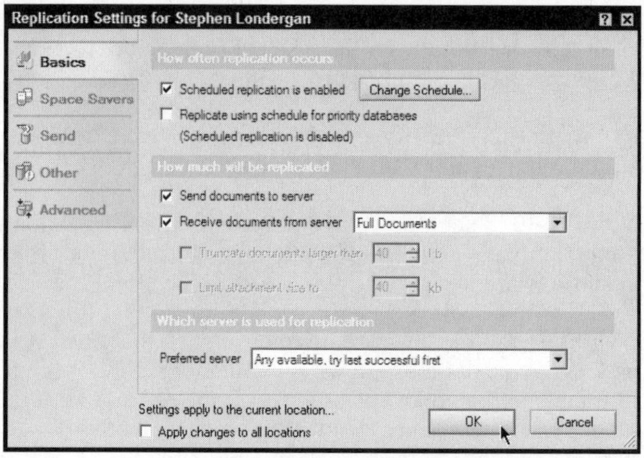

Figure 19-11:
Control how
and how
often a
database is
replicated.

Scheduling automatic replication

As you can see in Figure 19-11, scheduled replication isn't automatic. You
have to enable this feature by first selecting the Scheduled Replication
Is Enabled check box. Then click the Change Schedule button, and the
Replication Schedule for Home (Network Dialup) dialog box appears. (See
Figure 19-12.) You set when your computer will connect to the server from
this dialog box.

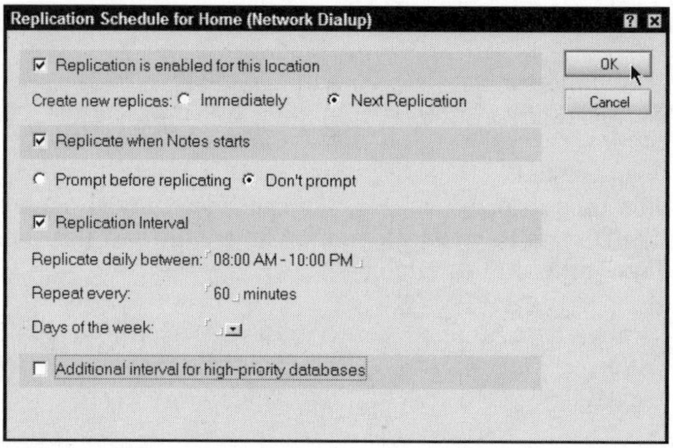

Figure 19-12:
Determine
when and
how
automatic
replication
takes place.

As you can also see in Figure 19-12, you can set up automatic replication
when Notes starts, at prescribed intervals, and at special intervals for High
Priority databases.

Replication tips and tricks

Refer to Figure 9-11 to see the Receive Documents from Server check box. This feature can be particularly useful if you have a slow connection (such as a modem) between your computer and the server. For example, you can choose *Partial Documents* from the companion drop-down list to have Notes retrieve portions of the documents on the server.

If you regularly find yourself waiting to download big attachments that you don't even need while traveling, using this feature is for you.

Another way to save time when replicating is found on the Space Savers tab of the Replication Settings For dialog box, as shown in Figure 19-13.

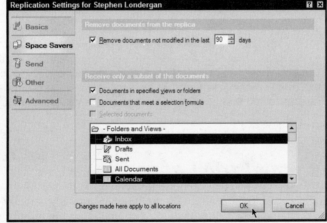

Figure 19-13: Use a Space Saver to make replication go faster.

If you're only interested in recent updates, such as messages that you've received within the past three months, select the Remove Documents Not Modified in the Last *nn* Days check box. Then use the text box there to enter how many days you want as a timer.

Be careful! Removing documents from a database can be a dangerous undertaking because *the documents are deleted from all copies of the databases —* NOT just the copy on your computer.

The fields in the Receive Only a Subset of the Documents section are a less-dangerous way to reduce replication times because you can use these settings to be very specific about what you receive when replicating the database. For example, in Figure 19-13, I select to receive only new documents in my Inbox folder and in my Calendar. The folders and views that you get to choose depend upon the database in question, of course.

Using Your Computer away from the Office

Most of the time, you use Notes while you're at work and plugged into the network. Notes knows that you're connected to the network, so when you dash off an e-mail, Notes knows to whisk it off to the server through that wire snaking out of the back of your computer and into the wall.

But what if you're *not* connected to the network? What if you're working at home, or you've taken your computer on a trip and you're in a hotel room? Notes has to know that when you send a mail message, it shouldn't try to send it through the network because you ain't got one. Instead, Notes needs to let the mail messages that you compose at home pile up so that it can send the messages later when you replicate with the server.

The most important thing to do when you first turn on your computer at home (or in the hotel room) is choose File⇨Mobile⇨Choose Current Location and then choose the appropriate Location document. Or, click the Location tab located in the bottom-right corner of your screen and select your location that way. I discuss this in more detail in Chapter 18. This command tells Notes where you are and what it should do with any outgoing messages that you create.

Sending mail from afar

With two small differences, composing and sending e-mail when you're remote is no different than composing and sending e-mail when you're on the network. Those differences are

- ✔ E-mail is delivered later when you replicate with the server. This can take some getting used to. When you're connected to the office network, your messages are delivered more or less instantaneously. If you're working remotely, though, you don't dispatch messages until you connect and replicate with your Domino server.

- ✔ If you're a fan of the Action bar Address button, you're in for a big letdown. Clicking the Address button at the office enables you to peruse your company Public Directory, which is located on your Domino server. Click the Address button while you're disconnected, and you can't see your company Public Directory — you see only the people and groups in your Personal Address Book. If you want to send an e-mail to folks who aren't in your Personal Address Book, you have to type their exact e-mail addresses in your message.

If you absolutely, positively must have all the people in the Public Directory put into your Personal Address Book, contact your administrator.

Composing documents from afar

More good news: Like when reading a document, composing a document in a local database isn't any different when you're on the road. Of course, when you compose a document in a database on a Domino server, other people can see it and read it the minute that you save it. But if you're composing documents while disconnected, those documents aren't accessible by your co-workers back in the office until you replicate your database with the server's database.

Enough Talk! Call That Server and Replicate!

When you're ready to replicate a database — you've added some documents to your database, you want to see whether any new documents have been added to the database back at the office, or you want to dispatch the 15 e-mail messages that you just composed — click the Replicator bookmark and then click the Start Now button on the Replication page.

Notes connects to the server and synchronizes the databases on your computer with the databases on the server. You can see the progress right at the bottom of the Replication page.

If you're calling from home or from a hotel room, you might hear the modem clear its throat and dial the server. Then, when Notes finishes replicating, it tells you on the Replication page what happened during the call. You see exactly how many documents you sent, how many you received, how many databases were replicated, and how many mail messages were sent.

Using Replication Remotely

Here's a running scenario for a practical use of replication on a daily basis — and how you would use Notes in each.

Working remotely

Suppose that your company has a Sales discussion database, and that's one of the databases that you bring with you on your laptop while you travel to a meeting. While you're cruising at 35,000 feet (business class, of course), you decide to kill some time by reading documents in this database. You turn on your computer, start Notes, and switch to a Location document named Island so that Notes knows that you can't connect to your server back at the office while you're in the air.

You open the database and start reading. You see a document that you want to respond to, so you use the Create menu to add a document to the database. The document that you just added is now saved in the copy of the database that you have with you on the plane, but it's obviously not saved in the copy of the database on your company's Domino server back at the office. Not yet, anyway.

When your plane finally arrives, you have to

1. **Get to your hotel.**
2. **Check in at the hotel.**
3. **Plug in and turn on your computer.**
4. **Start Notes.**
5. **Choose File⇨Mobile⇨Choose Current Location to switch to your travel (Notes Direct Dialup) location settings.**
6. **Go to the Replicator, make sure that the database you worked in is selected in the On column, and deselect those that you don't need.**
7. **Click the Send Now button.**

When your computer finishes replicating with the server back home, two things have happened. First, the document that you created and saved while you were on the plane is now in the database back at the office. Second, any documents that your colleagues posted in the database at the office are now in your copy of the database on your laptop.

Updating remotely

Your co-workers have been busy back at the office sending you memos and also adding, deleting, and editing documents in other databases. To reflect these changes on your local copies of the databases, follow these steps:

1. **Open the Replicator.**

2. **Select all the databases that you want to replicate.**

   All marked databases will replicate, so select the appropriate check boxes in the On column of the Replication page for the databases that you want to replicate. Likewise, deselect (clear) those same check boxes to remove the databases that you don't want to replicate.

3. **Click the Start Now button.**

Replicating back at the office

You're back home after a successful trip — ten new orders, plus treats and gifts for the kids. You plug your laptop into your office docking station, excited at the prospect of using the oh-so-fast network instead of your ever-so-slow modem.

But first, you have to

1. **Choose File⇨Mobile⇨Choose Current Location to switch to your Office (Network) profile.**

2. **Click the Start Now button on the Replication page one last time.**

   Be sure that all the databases you worked in and need are selected.

   Now your workstation can synch up any documents that you added while you were on the plane flying home.

Part VI
The Part of Tens

The 5th Wave   By Rich Tennant

In this part . . .

You have ten small toes to wiggle in the sand, ten idle fingers snap at your command. The chapters in this part also contain sets of (roughly) ten things that I thought you'd find useful or interesting or perhaps even necessary.

Don't consider these chapters to be frills, icing on the cake, or lace on the shirt front of life. No, these chapters are the result of hours and hours of listmaking on the part of your earnest *Lotus Notes 6 For Dummies* author, who likes to think that you'll be glad that he included all this information. You will indulge me, won't you?

Chapter 20

Ten Things You Should Never Do

. . . .

In This Chapter

▶ The ten worst things you can do when using Lotus Notes 6

▶ The reasons why you should never, ever do them

. . . .

*U*sually, I encourage you to be adventurous, try new things, check out menus that you've never used before, and generally live life on the edge and in the fast lane. But, just as the nascent mycologist has to learn to eschew a few dangerous and poisonous mushrooms in favor of the edible ones, you need to know about the ten things in Lotus Notes 6 that you should never, ever do.

Never Change Your Notes Name

Maybe you just changed your name. Perhaps you just got married and you're going to start hyphenating your name with your spouse's — from now on, it's *John Deer-Doe*. Or maybe you have to change your name because you got a new job at your company — instead of *George Parker/Consulting/Acme*, now your name/title is *George Parker/Support/Acme*.

You want your name in Notes to change, too, so that the new messages that you send and the new documents that you compose reflect your new name.

As tempting as it may be, you should never, ever try to change the name that's contained inside your user ID. If you did (and you won't, because I just told you not to, right?), you'd lose all your certificates. Bad, bad news.

If you've never even heard of *certificates* before, prepare to find out about them quickly if you change your name. Check back in Chapter 16 to read more about them. Without a certificate, you won't be able to access *any* of your company's Notes/Domino servers.

In other words, changing your name runs the risk of totally locking you out of Notes.

If you really want to change your Notes name and you have legitimate reason to do so, you need to talk to your network administrator about it. Choose File➪Security➪User Security and then enter your Notes password to access the User Security dialog box. Click the Your Identity button on the left of the dialog box and then click the Name Changes button. As you can see in Figure 20-1, the Notes Name Changes dialog box lists whom you need to contact to get your name changed. You can press Esc a few times (to leave the dialog box) and then send this person an e-mail message explaining your plight, or you can (preferably) just click the Send Mail button here.

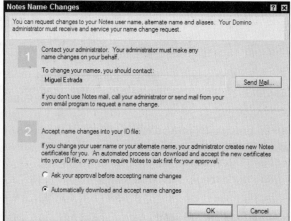

Figure 20-1:
Check the
Notes Name
Changes
dialog box
to find out
whom to
contact to
change your
name.

Never Delete Your E-Mail Database

You may have Manager-level access to your e-mail database. That's good because you may want to be able to customize your mail forms, change the way your folders work, and generally do anything that you want to your e-mail database. However, having Manager access can be a little treacherous if you're not careful.

As a Manager, you can use the File➪Database➪Delete command to completely, totally, irreversibly, forever — I'm not kidding here — delete your *entire* e-mail database. And when I write *entire database*, I mean it. Using this command deletes every last e-mail message, every folder, every Calendar Appointment, *everything*!

If you've already (gulp) deleted your e-mail database, call your administrator. Be prepared to grovel, and you better hope that your administrator has a back-up copy. Otherwise, your administrator has to register a new account and generate a new Notes ID — which means that you have to start your e-mail database over from scratch.

Never Save or Send a Message Without Checking Spelling First

As the olde saying goze, yOu onley have one chanse to maik a good furst impresssion — so don't blow it by e-mailing or posting documents that are full of typos. What excuse do you have for sending e-mail with spelling errors when you can always choose Edit⇨Check Spelling to correct your errors? Shame on you! Better yet, enable automatic spell checking. See Chapter 15 for more details on spell checking.

Never Remove Your Password

Passwords are important in Notes for two reasons:

✔ First, you don't want anyone else to read your e-mail, and you don't want the casual passerby to sit down at your desk and compose a few messages (full of four-letter words) under your name.

✔ Second, you have an obligation to your company not to let anyone use your user ID. If someone from your company's closest competitor gets his or her hands on your user ID, that person can act as you — in fact, as far as Lotus Notes would be concerned, that person *is* you. Thus, that nasty person can read all the company's confidential information that only you are supposed to be able to access.

Don't even consider removing your password. As long as your user ID has a password, even if someone steals your computer, you (and the rest of your company) don't have to worry about the thief getting any unauthorized access.

If it's too late and your (un-password-protected) user ID has been compromised, you should contact your administrator *immediately*.

Never Forget to Press F5 When You Go to Lunch

If you haven't already done so, skip back and read the preceding section about passwords. Taking similar security precautions apply to your leaving a Notes workstation unattended. To thwart any scoundrel who tries to use your computer in your absence, press F5 to enable a password-protected state for Notes. After you press F5, Notes asks you for your password the next time that you try to do anything. Potential no-goodniks won't be able to get in on your workstation if they don't know your password.

Before you leave your computer unattended, *always* press F5.

Never Let Temp Files Pile Up

Notes puts temporary (temp) files on your hard drive whenever you launch an attached file. That can result in a hard drive full of temporary files. Sometimes Notes remembers to delete these files when you're finished with them and sometimes it doesn't.

Every once in a while — maybe once a month — look in your Windows program directory, your Notes data directory, and your TEMP directory for files with names that begin with a tilde (~) or that end with .tmp extensions. If you find 'em, delete 'em to recover valuable hard drive real estate.

Never Forget to Consult the Manuals

I know, everyone hates to read computer manuals, but the Lotus Notes manuals aren't as bad as some. They're not the most exciting things that you'll ever read, but they do contain useful, even vital, information about how to use the program.

So when you're stumped, consider a perusal of your nearest set of Notes documentation. As they say in the computer business, when all else fails, RTFM. (That stands for *Read The Flippin' Manual*.) If you need a copy of the manuals, download them free from the http://notes.net/notesua.nsf Web site in either Notes database format or Adobe Acrobat reader format (.pdf).

Never Forget to Save Early and Often

Notes is like any computer program; unexpected power interruptions can be tragic. I can't stress enough how important it is to get into the habit of saving your work *early* and *often*. Just choose File➪Save or press Ctrl+S.

Never Forget to Switch Back to the Proper Location When You Return to the Office

If you use your computer in many different locations — at the office on the network, at home on a modem, or on a plane without any external connection, for instance — you need to choose the current location to have Notes properly manage your outgoing e-mail and connect with databases.

For example, if you go from the hotel to the office and forget to choose the proper location in the status bar, you may see a series of prompts on the screen telling you that Notes can't find things. You might wind up storing your e-mail locally because Notes doesn't know that it's okay to send it. Or you might not be sending to the server the changes that you made to local copies of your databases. Not good. Make sure that you select the proper location so that these tasks and many more are handled behind the scenes by Notes. For more information, peruse Chapter 19 to find out how to be reminded to change your location.

Never Write Something You Don't Want Everyone to Read

If your temper flares and you're dashing off a hot and hasty retort, wait 24 hours before sending it. If you want to make a pithy comment about someone's ridiculous behavior in a meeting, hold that thought. If you just heard the funniest joke in the world and want to share it via e-mail with a colleague, reconsider whether it could be potentially offensive.

At the end of the day, always remember: You never know where something you write will end up. And anything sent through e-mail leaves an electronic paper trail that could prove disastrous to your career and your company. Ugh . . . the stuff nightmares and lawsuits are made of.

Chapter 21

The Ten Most Common Lotus Notes Problems

In This Chapter

▶ The ten most common problems that you might encounter while using Notes

▶ The ten easy ways to avoid the ten most common problems

Hey, you can't expect everything to work perfectly all the time, and Lotus Notes 6 is no exception. In this chapter, I discuss the ten most common problems that you might encounter when working in Notes. Then I counter with their ten matching solutions. (Bonus points will be awarded to those observant readers who notice that I really discuss 11 potential problems with 11 matching solutions.)

Your Laptop Doesn't Connect to Your Server

Problem: Every time that you try to use Notes remotely, you get an error message reading `Modem could not connect dial tone`.

Solution: Did you know that two kinds of telephone lines exist? One is *analog*, and the other is *digital*. Although you don't need to know the difference between the two, you do need to know that Notes — and any computer program, for that matter — can use only analog lines with its modem. If you get the aforementioned error message when you try to dial in, the problem may be that the phone line that you've plugged the modem into is digital instead of analog. Most offices (and many hotel rooms) are equipped with digital lines, and that causes all kinds of problems for Notes, not to mention your computer and modem.

You must find an analog line to use your modem with Notes. You probably can't tell the difference between an analog line and a digital one just by looking at the jack in the wall, so you'll probably need to ask someone familiar with the facility where you're at.

If all else fails, you can plug your modem into the phone line being used for the closest fax machine because fax machines use analog lines, too.

If you still have problems, check the current location. Look for this in the status bar, which you can find under File⇨Mobile⇨Edit Current Location. Then make sure that the Location document in effect has correct information.

To check the contents of the Location document currently open, click the Location section of the status bar at the bottom of the screen and then select Edit Current from the drop-down menu that appears.

You Can't Edit a Field

Problem: You're trying to compose or perhaps edit a document, and you can't edit a particular field. You've tried the arrow keys, the Tab key, and even the mouse, but you can't even get the cursor into the field.

Solution: You need to be in edit mode. The easiest way to enter edit mode is to double-click anywhere in the document. Of course you need the proper access to the database and the document to edit. If you don't have the proper access, that's a problem for your network administrator (less likely) or the database designer (more likely) to solve. Notes has many security features, and they're all under the control of the designer and administrator. Call one or the other of these folks and explain the problem.

To find out who is the designer or manager of the database, choose File⇨ Database⇨Access Control, scroll up and down the list, highlight a name, and then check the access granted to that person in the upper-right corner of the Access Control List dialog box.

You Can't Use a DocLink

Problem: You double-click a DocLink icon, but you can't open the target document. (Read more about DocLinks in Chapter 16. A pundit once said that a DocLink is to Notes what a bookmark is to your Web browser.)

Solution: Tell the person who composed the document that access to the target document is frozen. Most likely, that person created a DocLink either to a document that's in a database on a server that you don't have access to, or to one that you can't connect to at the moment. (This same kind of problem can also happen with a bookmark.)

Your Server Isn't Responding

Problem: You double-click a bookmark — maybe even your e-mail — but in response you see the error message `Server (servername) is not responding` or `Network operation did not complete in a reasonable amount of time` or perhaps `Remote system is no longer responding.`

Solution: Each of these error messages indicates a network problem over which you have no control. (*Your* job isn't to keep the servers in good working order!) As is often the case, the solution to this problem begins with a call to your administrator.

You Don't Have the Right Certificate

Problem: Whenever you try to access a server, you see the error message `Your ID has not been certified to access the server.` Chapter 16 contains more information about certificates.

Solution: Call your administrator and explain the problem.

You Can't Open a Database

Problem: Whenever you try to use a certain bookmark or particular database, you see the error message `You are not authorized to access that database.`

Solution: Again, call your administrator and report that the Access Control List is incorrect for the database in question.

Refer to the Access Control List as the *ACL* when you talk to your administrator. That way, you'll sound like you know what you're talking about.

You Can't Search

Problem: You're trying to find something, and it's taking way, way, too long.

Solution: If the database that you're trying to search is on a Domino server, the problem is usually that your administrator hasn't set up the server (or database) for searching. Bottom line: You need to contact your administrator if you want searches to go faster.

You Can't Delete a Document That You Composed

Problem: You composed a document and now you want to delete it but you can't, no matter how many times you press Delete.

Solution: Call your administrator or the database designer to check: one, that the database is properly recording author names in the documents; and two, that the Access Control List enables you to delete documents.

You Can't Open an Attachment

Problem: You double-click an attachment but you can't get its affiliated program to start.

Solution: To *open* an attachment, you must have installed on your computer the program that was used to create the object in the first place. For example, if the attachment is a Microsoft Excel worksheet but you don't have Excel installed on your computer, you cannot open or edit that file. (You might also need to install a newer version of Notes; contact your administrator, who knows what the answer is.)

Even if you don't have the program necessary to launch an object, you should be able to view it — just select View instead of Open in the Attachment infobox.

You Don't Know Who Your Network Administrator Is

Problem: As you read this book, it seems that every time that I discuss a potential problem, I use the *Call your administrator* cop-out. The problem is that you don't know who that person is!

Solution: Ask your manager or someone else in your office, or consider changing jobs so that *you're* the administrator — and then call yourself.

You Can't Remember Your Password

Problem: You forgot your password.

Solution: Call your administrator, who will

 ✔ Be mad at you

 ✔ Quite possibly laugh at you

 ✔ Finally tell you what you need to do to get a new password

Chapter 22

The Ten New Things You Should Know about Lotus Notes 6

. . . .

In This Chapter

▶ The desktop is gone

▶ Your e-mail is different

▶ The Calendar is different

▶ Replication is easier

▶ Attachments are better

▶ Notes is easier than ever to use

. . . .

Lotus Notes has been on the market since 1989 — and as the saying goes, "You've come a long way, baby." Here, in no uncertain terms, are the Most Important New Features in Lotus Notes 6, which will be of particular interest to people who have upgraded from a previous version. If you're new to Notes — if you haven't used any other releases of this software — some of this chapter may not be of much use.

There are actually a *lot* more than 10 (okay, 11) new things in Lotus Notes 6, but here are the most important.

Desktop, Oh Desktop, Wherefore Art Thou?

Bye-bye, Notes database icons! The first thing that you'll notice when you open Lotus Notes 6 is that the old, familiar desktop is gone; it's been replaced by the Notes Welcome Page. (Don't worry, all your database icons are still there, in the Bookmarks bar.) In fact, Notes 6 sports a new (and, some would argue, much better) interface. It's prettier and easier to use. The toolbar buttons as well as the browser-like Forward and Back buttons make Notes easier (and more fun) to use than ever.

Rest assured, though, that you can do everything that you're used to doing in previous versions of Notes. And although it may take a day or two to acclimate yourself to the new menus and buttons, it's worth it.

The ins and outs of the Welcome Page are covered in Chapter 2, if you're interested in discovering more.

Your E-Mail Is Different

Probably the biggest difference that you'll notice when you upgrade and start using your e-mail is that when you delete a message, it gets deleted right away. Imagine that. In other words, you don't have to refresh by pressing F9 any more. This may or may not be true in the other databases that you use, but it's definitely the case in your e-mail.

You'll notice other cool things in your e-mail, too — like the fact that folders now list how many documents they contain, and also that it's now much easier to customize and choose what exactly is shown in your Inbox. You can also have messages from certain people highlighted in special colors, and you can even customize your Inbox to look *exactly* the way you want it.

To discover even more updates, read the chapters in this book concerning e-mail: Chapters 3 through 7.

New and Improved Calendar

As you poke around in your new copy of Notes, sooner or later you'll find the new and improved Calendar. Your new Calendar is prettier than ever, with new features and things that you can do. For example, you can now color-code entries so that meetings always show up in a different color than, say, appointments. The coolest thing by far is that you can now edit a Calendar item right in the Calendar view without having to open the document at all. Chapter 8 will get you jump-started on how to use the new Calendar features. Oh, by the way — your Calendar is easier to print, too. (Finally!)

Better Attachment Management

The way that Lotus Notes 6 handles attachments is better than ever before. For example, when you choose to save an attachment from Notes onto your own computer, you can go on about your (Notes) business while the file is copied — no more waiting for the file to be downloaded! It's also easier to attach and remove files, which you can read more about in Chapter 6.

Lotus Notes 6 also enables you to forward or reply to an e-mail message without (necessarily) including the attachment(s). That'll save you a lot of time and effort.

Dragging and Dropping

Lotus Notes 6 has lots of what IBM calls *usability enhancements*, which is a fancy way of saying that it's easier to use. Chief among the reasons that it's easier is that you can do a lot of dragging and dropping — whether dragging an attachment from your Inbox to your desktop, dragging a new database to the Replicator, dragging a vCard right into the Contacts folder in your Personal Address Book (Chapter 11), or perhaps dragging a document from your Inbox to your desktop to make a new bookmark.

Cool New Letterhead

Ever since the days of Notes R4, you've been able to choose your own letterhead — those cool graphics that appear at the top of the e-mail that you send. Letterhead is back in Notes 6, but it's better than ever. (Pony Express is still my favorite, however.) To select the image that appears at the top of the e-mail that you send, open your mail and then choose Actions⇨Tools⇨Preferences⇨Letterhead.

No More SmartIcons

SmartIcons are now called toolbar buttons. Who cares what they're called? Those buttons at the top of the screen, such as Print and Expand, just make it easier to do the things you need to do. Chapter 2 is the place to be if you want to read about these new buttons.

New and Improved Replicator

If you're one of those so-called Road Warriors who use Notes away from the office (and network), you'll find it easier than ever. For example, you can now drag and drop a database on to the Replicator page to take it with you — no more learning how to make a replica copy, initiating the first replication, and so on. You can also drag individual documents and folders on to the Replicator page when you want to take just certain parts of a database with you. (See Chapter 19 for more info.)

Document Locking

In certain databases, you can now *lock* a document so that no one else who has access to the document can edit it until you unlock the document. This is great because it means no more replication conflicts!

Quick Notes

The Notes Welcome Page now has something called Quick Notes — look for a little blue arrow at the right side of the screen. When you click it, you get a quickie little window that enables you to very quickly and easily send a new e-mail message, add a person to your Personal Address Book, add a Personal Journal entry, or add a reminder to your Calendar. Because it's so easy to use Quick Notes, you don't have to go find your e-mail, open the Inbox, and so on.

F5

You use F5 to lock (password-protect) your desktop so that you can go to lunch and not have to worry about anyone using your computer while you're away. In Lotus Notes 6, your screen is now also automatically cleared until you return and log back in.

Part VII
Appendix

The 5th Wave   By Rich Tennant

"Someone want to look at this manuscript
I received an email called, 'The Embedded
Virus That Destroyed the Publisher's Servers
When the Manuscript was Rejected.'?"

In this part . . .

What would a computer book be without arcane terminology? This part contains a glossary to help you make sense of it all.

Glossary

• •

@Function: A formula element containing preprogrammed calculations that make writing a formula much easier. Examples are @Sum, @UserName, @Now.

Accelerator key: A keystroke combination used to accomplish the same thing as choosing a menu item. Ctrl+Z is the accelerator key for Edit⇨Undo.

Access Control List (ACL): The part of every Notes database that determines who can do what in that database. See also *No Access; Depositor; Reader; Author; Editor; Designer; Manager.*

Actions: Tasks that normally involve several keystrokes and that are assigned to buttons or a special menu and then associated with views, forms, and folders so that you can easily perform them. Actions are what happen when you click buttons in the Action bar that some databases have, such as the Reply button in your Inbox.

Administrator: The person in charge of running the servers at your company and to whom you should turn if you have questions or problems.

Agent: A mini-program or set of instructions that automates tasks in Notes. For example, the Out-of-Office agent sends a message to all who e-mail you, informing them that you are unavailable.

Alarm: A visual or audible reminder of a scheduled event in your Calendar.

Application designer: The person at your company who created the database(s) that you use. Also known as a *database manager* or an *application manager.*

Application server: A Domino server only used for application databases — in other words, it doesn't have anyone's e-mail on it.

Archive: A compressed storage of old messages that you're unlikely to need but don't want to delete permanently. Your administrator may ask you to archive some of your old mail in order to free up space on the server.

Archive criteria settings: These settings determine the criteria for which documents should be put in an archive. For example, your archive criteria settings can be set to copy all documents not modified after 365 days to your archive database and then delete these documents from this database.

Archive log: A summary of the documents that have been put in an archive.

Attachment: A file (such as a Lotus 1-2-3 worksheet or a Microsoft Word document) that has been included in a Notes document. You can put attachments only in a rich text field.

Author: 1. The person who composed a document and (usually) the only person who can edit it or delete it. 2. A level of access that you can have to a database. As an author, you can read documents, compose new documents, edit your own documents, and delete your own documents. 3. Someone like the upstanding individual who wrote this book.

Bookmark: A pointer shortcut to a Notes item (a database, or a document, for instance) or a page on the Web or on your company's intranet.

Browsing: The official, more dignified term for surfing or cruising the Internet or looking at pages on your company's intranet. Call it what you want; it means you're looking for information or just wandering around (electronically, of course) to see what there is to see.

Button: A picture or text resembling a button that launches some action or task when clicked with the mouse.

Calendar: A section of your Mail database that contains time-related documents, such as appointments, meetings, or birthdays.

Category: A line in a view that doesn't represent a document but rather represents data in a given field that's the same in all documents listed below the category. All documents with Nebraska in the state field, for instance, could be listed below a line containing *Nebraska*.

Certificate: A special stamp for your user ID that your administrator gives to you. You have to have a certificate specific to your company to use the servers at your company.

Client: Another term for *workstation*; the version of Notes installed on computers that people use to do their work. Not to be confused with servers, which are computers that store information.

Clipboard: A section of your computer's memory used to hold something that you've copied or cut and plan to paste somewhere else.

Collaboration: The act of working together with other people.

Common name: The part of your Notes user name that sounds like what your mother calls you. For example, if your User Name is Stephen Londergan/IBM, your common name is just Stephen Londergan.

Connection document: A special document stored in your Personal Address Book that tells your workstation when and how to connect with the Domino server. Connection documents are especially important when you use Notes while away from the office.

Contact: One type of document in your Personal Address Book. You compose a Contact document in your Personal Address Book to give one of your friends an e-mail nickname or to help you remember someone's complicated e-mail address.

Database: In Notes, a collection of Notes documents, folders, views, agents, and other design elements. In general, any organized collection of information.

Database template: A shell of a database that you use as a starting point to create your own database: a real time-saver.

Default: A preset or preferred value that users can change. The default text color, for instance, is black.

Delivery report: A return message that tells you when a message that you sent was delivered to the recipient's mail database.

Depositor: A level of access that you can have to a database. As a depositor, you can only add documents to a database: You can't read, edit, or delete them.

Designer: A level of access that you can have to a database. In addition to having all the rights that editors have, designers can change a database's forms and views.

Designer client: Separate, special, Notes software that allows users and designers to modify database elements.

DocLink: An icon in one document that you can double-click to quickly go to a different document.

Document: 1. An individual item in a Notes database. In other database programs, a document is called a *record*. 2. A piece of paper with stuff written on it.

Domain: 1. All the Notes servers at your company. 2. What a king or queen is in charge of.

Domino: The aspects of Notes that relate to servers.

Edit mode: The status of an onscreen document in which you are able to change the contents of fields.

Editor: A level of access that you can have to a database. Editors can compose documents as well as read and edit documents, even if they didn't compose the documents in the first place.

Electronic signature: A special numeric code added to a document to prove that it really was written by the person who sent it.

E-mail: An electronic mail message.

Encryption: A procedure in which a document or part of a document is scrambled until opened by a person who has the proper decryption key.

Encryption key: The numeric code used to scramble and unscramble a document or part of a document.

Error message: A dialog box that Notes shows when you make those all-too-frequent mistakes.

Export: A way to turn Notes documents into files for use in other programs, such as Lotus 1-2-3 or WordPerfect.

Field: A place in a database form for specific individual pieces of information. *First Name* might be a field in a personnel data form.

Folder: A database element that lists documents in a database. You put documents in and remove documents from a folder. See also *View.*

Footer: Text that appears at the bottom of every printed page that can provide additional details such as page numbers, a document's title, date, and so on.

Form: What you use to compose, edit, and read documents.

Frameset: A design element of a database containing the rectangles that designers use mainly to display different pieces of information on the Web.

Full-text index: Part of a database that locates words and phrases in all documents in a database so that you can later search for text in those documents.

Full-text search: A feature a database needs to have for you to be able to search for text or phrases in documents.

Fuzzy search: Command issued before executing a search in which you tell Notes to look for variations in or phrases similar to the text you're searching for.

Group: Collection of users' names, defined in either the public directory or your Personal Address Book. Using group names saves you from having to type the individual names of people in a group when sending them e-mail.

Header: 1. Text that appears at the top of every printed page. 2. What you take when you fall over something.

Headlines: Database that you configure to remind you of the most important new e-mail messages, calendar events, tasks, and modified Web pages.

Help document: Special collection of tips about how to use a database.

Hierarchical name: User name that includes not only your common name but also your organization and the level or department in that organization.

Home page: 1. See also *Welcome Page.* 2. A main page on the Web from which you can navigate to other Web pages.

Home server: The one and only Notes server that has your e-mail database on it.

HotSpot: 1. A place where you shouldn't sit. 2. A location in a form or graphic that, when clicked with the mouse, does something.

HTML: HyperText Markup Language. The text and code used to create information in Web pages.

Icon: A graphic used to represent a database, a program, or an action.

Import: What you do when you want to turn a foreign file, such as a Microsoft Word document, into a document in a Notes database.

Index: Shorter name for the *full-text index.* Full-text indexing a database makes finding documents faster and more accurate, and gives you access to features, which allow you to refine or expand your search and to sort your results. This term also refers to the background process by which views are updated to be sure that they display current information.

Infobox: Now more frequently called *properties box.* A dialog box that usually contains several tabs that enable you to change many aspects of the selected item at hand, such as font size and color, alignment, paragraph spacing, and so forth.

Input validation formula: A formula included in a form that checks to be sure that you entered data in a field and that it's the right data type.

Install: A process or a program that places a usable copy of a program on a hard drive.

Internet: A huge collection of computers all connected in a vast global network, which was invented by former Vice President Al Gore.

Keyword field: A special kind of field that presents you with a list of choices for data input. You can make selections by clicking, rather than typing, an entry. Keywords fields can display in several formats, including a drop-down list box, a check box, and a radio button.

LAN: Local Area Network. LAN rhymes with *man*. It's really just a bunch of wires that connect your computer to other computers.

LAN workstation: A computer that has Notes installed on it and is plugged into the network.

Letterhead: Fancy graphics that you can include at the top of your mail messages.

License: The right to use Notes. You need one of these.

Link: A graphical representation in one document of another document, database, or view. Click the link to open the other document, database, or view.

Location: A name and accompanying data that define the places where you use Notes, such as on the LAN at the office, on a modem at home, or not connected at all in the shower. Locations are defined in location documents in your Personal Address Book.

Lotus Notes 6: The program that this book is about.

MAIL.BOX: A special kind of Notes database that holds messages that are pending delivery.

Mail database: The database that holds all your incoming and outgoing e-mail messages. No one but you can read the documents in your Mail database.

Mail server: A Domino server that has mail databases on it.

Manager: The highest level of access available for a database.

Modem: Hardware that enables you to use your Notes workstation to place a phone call to your Notes server. Useful if you need to read your e-mail and other Notes databases when you're at home or on a business trip.

Modem command file: A special ASCII file that Notes needs to use a modem. Every brand of modem has its own modem command file.

Mood Stamp: Not to be confused with mood rings. A picture that you can put at the top of a message so that your reader knows what frame of mind you were in when you sent the message.

Mycophile: A fungus fancier.

Navigator: A database element that substitutes graphics and associated commands for normal menu items, making the use of a database more user-friendly.

Network: A collection of computers that are connected by wires and that use a network operating system.

Newsletter: A special memo that is automatically generated to notify users of new documents in a database.

No Access: A level of access to a database. If you have No Access to a database, you can't use that database. Period!

Notes data directory: The directory on your computer's hard drive that has your local Notes databases in it.

Notes data folder: The folder on your Macintosh that has your local databases and DESKTOP.DSK.

Notes log: A special Notes database that keeps track of all the phone calls that you've made from your remote workstation — if you've made any, that is.

NOTES.INI: An ASCII file on every Notes workstation that holds configuration information for that workstation.

Page: In Notes, a screen full of database-related information generally used as an opening screen. On the Web, a page is a screen full of information.

Page break: A code that you insert in a long document that instructs Notes to print subsequent text on a new sheet of paper. Normally, page breaks are not visible.

Pane: A section of a Notes window (window pane, get it?) The number, name, and purpose of the pane vary depending on the context.

Password: A secret code that you have to enter every time you use your user ID.

Permanent Pen: 1. A unique font used to make editorial comments in a document. 2. A writing implement specifically designed to stain your clothes.

Person document: One type of document in your Personal Address Book. The Public Directory has a Person document for each user at your company. You can also compose a Person document in your Personal Address Book to give one of your friends an e-mail nickname or to help you remember someone's complicated e-mail address.

Personal Address Book: A database on your computer's hard drive in which you can enter person, group, and connection documents.

Platform: Computer-ese meaning the same as *operating system.*

Policy document: A document that describes the purpose of a database and the rules for its use. Also called the *About This Database document.*

Pop-up: A part of a Notes document that has hidden text associated with it. You view this hidden text by clicking the word.

Port: The name for the part of your computer where your network or modem is plugged in. Some computers have more than one port; yours might have one port for the network and one port for the modem.

Power tie: A knot tied around the neck symbolizing extreme corporate fealty but mistaken for a symbol of corporate authority.

PowerBook: A portable Macintosh computer.

Preferences document: The Macintosh equivalent of NOTES.INI, which stores system settings.

Private key: The part of your user ID that's used to decrypt your encrypted mail messages.

Private view: A view that's on only your workstation.

Properties box: 1. A place to keep your childhood treasures. 2. In Notes, a series of dialog box pages, each represented by a tab, and each relating to features (properties) of a given item. Also called ***infobox.***

Protocol: A techie term for the part of your network operating system that's used to connect your Notes workstation with your Notes servers. You may hear about protocols called NetBIOS, SPX, or TCP/IP. Then again, you may never hear protocols mentioned.

Public Directory: The database on the Notes server that defines all the Notes users, servers, groups, and connections at your company.

Public key: The part of your user ID that other people use to encrypt mail messages for you.

Query Builder: A dialog box that you fill out that makes it easy to define criteria for a full-text search.

Query by form: A way to enter the criteria for a full-text search, using the same form that was used to enter the document in the first place.

Read Access List: A way to control which people can read a document that you compose. You set a document's Read Access List in the Document infobox, on the page with the key tab.

Reader: A level of access that you can have to a database. As a Reader, you may read only the documents that other people have composed; you cannot compose your own.

Relational database: A database program that allows the full sharing of data between databases and between forms within databases. Notes is not a true relational database.

Remote workstation: A Notes workstation that's not connected to a Notes server by a network. Instead, remote workstations often use a modem to talk to the Notes server.

Replica ID: A special serial number that every database has that identifies it as the same database, even if copies of it exist on other servers.

Replication: The process used to synchronize two copies of a database between two servers or between a server and a workstation.

ResEdit: The program that you use on a Macintosh to edit your User Preferences document.

Return Receipt: A special kind of e-mail message that tells you when a recipient opened an e-mail that you sent.

Rich text field: A special field type that can include more than one font and formatting (such as bold and italics) and can contain embedded objects and attachments.

Ruler: The part of the Notes screen that you can use (if you choose to display it) to set margins and tabs in a rich text field.

Search bar: The dialog box at the top of the screen (if you choose to display it) that you can use to specify the text to search for and rules for the search.

Section: Part of a Notes form or document with its own fields. It can be collapsible, meaning that the user can choose to display or conceal its contents; it can also have restricted access, which means that only designated people can edit its fields.

Selecting: 1. Designating text or data to be deleted, copied, or changed in some way. 2. Choosing documents in a view for such group treatment as categorizing, printing, or deletion.

Selection formula: A Notes formula usually used to designate which documents will be replicated.

Server: A shared computer that stores Notes databases.

Server-based mail: A setting that you use that causes Notes to send off your messages immediately; the opposite of *workstation-based e-mail.*

Signature: Also called an *electronic signature.* A way for you to guarantee to the recipient of a message that it really, honestly, absolutely came from you.

Sort: 1. To put items in a list in order. 2. To match your socks.

Spam: Junk e-mail, or e-mail sent to too many people. Examples are hysterical notices that you are asked to send to everyone you know about Web-based viruses that eat hard drives for lunch and e-mails from Hot Stuff who has a personal message for you at his or her Web site.

Static text: Text in a form that doesn't change. The title of a form is an example of static text.

Stationery: A template of various types of mail messages that you might send. You can create stationery with text or graphics, letterhead, and a recipient list that you can reuse. This is convenient when you frequently send a message, such as a status report, in the same format to the same people.

Status bar: 1. A line of information at the bottom of the Notes window, part of which you can use to change parts of your document. 2. A drinking establishment on Main Street where they have cold beer and hot tunes. Closed Sundays; shoes and shirt required.

Styles: Named collections of paragraph attributes that you can assign to a paragraph all at once.

Subform: A section of a form with its own fields, text, graphics, and design, which designers can use in multiple forms.

Subscription: An instruction that you issue to Notes to send you a memo listing new information in Notes and Web locations that you specify.

Tables: 1. Small spreadsheets that you can insert into Notes documents. 2. A place to put your cold beer while you're listening to the hot tunes at the status bar.

Task button: Buttons above the work area of a Notes window; each one represents an open window in Notes and contains a short name of the window plus an X, which you use to close the task.

Template: A special kind of Notes database used to create other Notes databases.

TLA: Three-letter abbreviation for *three-letter abbreviation*. No, it is *not* a three-letter acronym unless you can pronounce the abbreviation as though it were a word. Although you may have heard HTML described as a three-letter acronym, it certainly isn't: Aside from the fact that it has four letters, you can't pronounce HTML.

Toolbar: A part of the graphical interface located near the top of the Notes window that contains buttons that help you to perform tasks.

Typeahead: The capability in Notes to start typing the name of an addressee of a memo and have Notes finish it for you.

Unix: An operating system that you can use on Notes workstations and servers.

Unread marks: Stars or colored text used in views to show you which documents you haven't read yet.

URL: Uniform Resource Locator. The address of any particular Web page.

Vacation profile: Also called the *Out of Office agent*. A special mail setting used to reply automatically to messages that you receive when you're on vacation.

View: A summary of the documents in a database. Most databases have more than one view. See also *Folder.*

WAN: Wide Area Network. A bunch of computers connected in some other way than by network cables. Most frequently used are phone lines, satellites, broadcasts, and tin cans with string.

Web page: A document on Web servers that can contain graphics, links to other documents or pages, text, attached files, and multimedia features.

Web server: A computer somewhere in the world with Web pages on the Internet.

Welcome Page: The opening screen in Notes containing tasks that you can perform and locations to which you can navigate.

Window: One of the *Workspaces* that you might have opened in any program. Each Notes window represents a separate Notes document, view, Web page, or other task you have performed. Each Notes window is represented by a task button near the top of the Notes screen.

Windows: An operating environment that you can use on Notes workstations and servers, such as Windows 95, 98, 2000, Me, and XP.

Workflow: Features added to a Notes database that allow users to assign tasks, notify others of assigned responsibilities, and track the completion of tasks.

Workspace: 1. The first Notes screen that you see; it contains the tabbed pages and database icons. 2. Any Notes window. 3. The place where your boss lets you work when you're good.

Workstation: The computer at your desk or (if you have a laptop) the computer in your briefcase. It's the computer you use to work with Notes.

Workstation-based e-mail: A setting that you use when your computer is not connected to a LAN, which causes Notes to queue your outgoing e-mail until you place a phone call (using a modem) to a Notes server, which allows you to send your queued messages.

World Wide Web: WWW. A collection of computers on the Internet that have special pages (see *Web page*) you can use.

Index

Attachment infobox, 79–82
attachments
  definition, 346
  editing, 81, 288
  icons for, 78, 287–288
  including with e-mail message, 77–78, 79, 83
  opening, 79, 80, 82
  opening, not being able to, 336
  from other applications, 287–288
  printing, 82
  removing from e-mail message, 82, 340
  in rich text fields, 200
  saving, 81–82, 340
  temporary files resulting from, 330
  viewing without opening, 79–80
author, level of access, 204, 346
author of document, searching by, 215

• B •

Basics Plus, Welcome Page, 267–268
Basics tab
  Mail tab, Preferences dialog, 273
  User Preferences dialog, 278
Basics, Welcome Page, 266
Basics with Calendar, Welcome Page, 266
bcc field, e-mail message, 53
binary files, importing, 289
birthdays, in Personal Address Book, 166
blind courtesy copy (bcc), 53
BMP files, importing, 289
bold font. See font, style
Bookmark button, Open Database dialog, 175
bookmarks
  creating, 27–29
  creating for database, 32, 33, 175–176
  creating for Web page, 33
  definition, 22, 25, 346

deleting, 29
displaying hint for, 26
folders for, creating, 29
folders for, deleting, 30
folders for, slide-out tray displaying, 27
forwarding Web page as, 303
moving, 30
opening, 26–27
border
  paragraphs, 227
  table, 250
  table cells, 248–249
browser, 300, 301–302
browsing, 32–33, 299–302, 346
buttons. See also specific buttons
  definition, 346
  in documents, 201–202
  task, 22, 30–31, 355
By Category view, To Do List, 148

• C •

calculated fields. See computed fields
Calendar
  adding to Welcome Page, 269
  advantages of using, 109
  all day events, adding, 123–124
  all day events, displayed, 118
  anniversaries, adding, 120–121
  anniversaries, displayed, 118
  appointments, adding, 118–120
  appointments, displayed, 118
  definition, 15, 346
  To Dos, blocking display of, 154
  To Dos, displayed in, 112–113, 118
  double-booking in, 117
  editing items in, 124, 340
  free time slots, displaying, 118
  free time slots, setting, 143
  Group Calendars, 124–126

Notes

Notes

FOR DUMMIES®

The easy way to get more done and have more fun

PERSONAL FINANCE

0-7645-5231-7

0-7645-2431-3

0-7645-5331-3

Also available:

Estate Planning For Dummies
(0-7645-5501-4)

401(k)s For Dummies
(0-7645-5468-9)

Frugal Living For Dummies
(0-7645-5403-4)

Microsoft Money "X" For Dummies
(0-7645-1689-2)

Mutual Funds For Dummies
(0-7645-5329-1)

Personal Bankruptcy For Dummies
(0-7645-5498-0)

Quicken "X" For Dummies
(0-7645-1666-3)

Stock Investing For Dummies
(0-7645-5411-5)

Taxes For Dummies 2003
(0-7645-5475-1)

BUSINESS & CAREERS

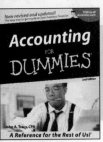

0-7645-5314-3

0-7645-5307-0

0-7645-5471-9

Also available:

Business Plans Kit For Dummies
(0-7645-5365-8)

Consulting For Dummies
(0-7645-5034-9)

Cool Careers For Dummies
(0-7645-5345-3)

Human Resources Kit For Dummies
(0-7645-5131-0)

Managing For Dummies
(1-5688-4858-7)

QuickBooks All-in-One Desk Reference For Dummies
(0-7645-1963-8)

Selling For Dummies
(0-7645-5363-1)

Small Business Kit For Dummies
(0-7645-5093-4)

Starting an eBay Business For Dummies
(0-7645-1547-0)

HEALTH, SPORTS & FITNESS

0-7645-5167-1

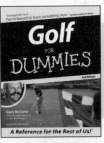

0-7645-5146-9

0-7645-5154-X

Also available:

Controlling Cholesterol For Dummies
(0-7645-5440-9)

Dieting For Dummies
(0-7645-5126-4)

High Blood Pressure For Dummies
(0-7645-5424-7)

Martial Arts For Dummies
(0-7645-5358-5)

Menopause For Dummies
(0-7645-5458-1)

Nutrition For Dummies
(0-7645-5180-9)

Power Yoga For Dummies
(0-7645-5342-9)

Thyroid For Dummies
(0-7645-5385-2)

Weight Training For Dummies
(0-7645-5168-X)

Yoga For Dummies
(0-7645-5117-5)

Available wherever books are sold.
Go to www.dummies.com or call 1-877-762-2974 to order direct.

FOR DUMMIES®

A world of resources to help you grow

HOME, GARDEN & HOBBIES

0-7645-5295-3

0-7645-5130-2

0-7645-5106-X

Also available:

Auto Repair For Dummies
(0-7645-5089-6)

Chess For Dummies
(0-7645-5003-9)

Home Maintenance For Dummies
(0-7645-5215-5)

Organizing For Dummies
(0-7645-5300-3)

Piano For Dummies
(0-7645-5105-1)

Poker For Dummies
(0-7645-5232-5)

Quilting For Dummies
(0-7645-5118-3)

Rock Guitar For Dummies
(0-7645-5356-9)

Roses For Dummies
(0-7645-5202-3)

Sewing For Dummies
(0-7645-5137-X)

FOOD & WINE

0-7645-5250-3

0-7645-5390-9

0-7645-5114-0

Also available:

Bartending For Dummies
(0-7645-5051-9)

Chinese Cooking For Dummies
(0-7645-5247-3)

Christmas Cooking For Dummies
(0-7645-5407-7)

Diabetes Cookbook For Dummies
(0-7645-5230-9)

Grilling For Dummies
(0-7645-5076-4)

Low-Fat Cooking For Dummies
(0-7645-5035-7)

Slow Cookers For Dummies
(0-7645-5240-6)

TRAVEL

0-7645-5453-0

0-7645-5438-7

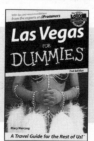

0-7645-5448-4

Also available:

America's National Parks For Dummies
(0-7645-6204-5)

Caribbean For Dummies
(0-7645-5445-X)

Cruise Vacations For Dummies 2003
(0-7645-5459-X)

Europe For Dummies
(0-7645-5456-5)

Ireland For Dummies
(0-7645-6199-5)

France For Dummies
(0-7645-6292-4)

London For Dummies
(0-7645-5416-6)

Mexico's Beach Resorts For Dummies
(0-7645-6262-2)

Paris For Dummies
(0-7645-5494-8)

RV Vacations For Dummies
(0-7645-5443-3)

Walt Disney World & Orlando For Dummies
(0-7645-5444-1)

Available wherever books are sold. Go to www.dummies.com or call 1-877-762-2974 to order direct.

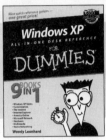

FOR DUMMIES®

Helping you expand your horizons and realize your potential

INTERNET

The Internet FOR DUMMIES
0-7645-0894-6

The Internet ALL-IN-ONE DESK REFERENCE FOR DUMMIES
0-7645-1659-0

eBay FOR DUMMIES
0-7645-1642-6

Also available:

America Online 7.0 For Dummies
(0-7645-1624-8)

Genealogy Online For Dummies
(0-7645-0807-5)

The Internet All-in-One Desk Reference For Dummies
(0-7645-1659-0)

Internet Explorer 6 For Dummies
(0-7645-1344-3)

The Internet For Dummies Quick Reference
(0-7645-1645-0)

Internet Privacy For Dummies
(0-7645-0846-6)

Researching Online For Dummies
(0-7645-0546-7)

Starting an Online Business For Dummies
(0-7645-1655-8)

DIGITAL MEDIA

Digital Photography FOR DUMMIES
0-7645-1664-7

Photoshop Elements 2 FOR DUMMIES
0-7645-1675-2

Digital Video FOR DUMMIES
0-7645-0806-7

Also available:

CD and DVD Recording For Dummies
(0-7645-1627-2)

Digital Photography All-in-One Desk Reference For Dummies
(0-7645-1800-3)

Digital Photography For Dummies Quick Reference
(0-7645-0750-8)

Home Recording for Musicians For Dummies
(0-7645-1634-5)

MP3 For Dummies
(0-7645-0858-X)

Paint Shop Pro "X" For Dummies
(0-7645-2440-2)

Photo Retouching & Restoration For Dummies
(0-7645-1662-0)

Scanners For Dummies
(0-7645-0783-4)

GRAPHICS

PowerPoint 2002 FOR DUMMIES
0-7645-0817-2

Photoshop 7 FOR DUMMIES
0-7645-1651-5

Macromedia Flash MX FOR DUMMIES
0-7645-0895-4

Also available:

Adobe Acrobat 5 PDF For Dummies
(0-7645-1652-3)

Fireworks 4 For Dummies
(0-7645-0804-0)

Illustrator 10 For Dummies
(0-7645-3636-2)

QuarkXPress 5 For Dummies
(0-7645-0643-9)

Visio 2000 For Dummies
(0-7645-0635-8)

Available wherever books are sold. Go to www.dummies.com or call 1-877-762-2974 to order direct.

FOR DUMMIES®

The advice and explanations you need to succeed

ELF-HELP, SPIRITUALITY & RELIGION

0-7645-5302-X

0-7645-5418-2

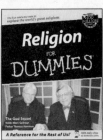

0-7645-5264-3

Also available:

The Bible For Dummies
(0-7645-5296-1)

Buddhism For Dummies
(0-7645-5359-3)

Christian Prayer For Dummies
(0-7645-5500-6)

Dating For Dummies
(0-7645-5072-1)

Judaism For Dummies
(0-7645-5299-6)

Potty Training For Dummies
(0-7645-5417-4)

Pregnancy For Dummies
(0-7645-5074-8)

Rekindling Romance For Dummies
(0-7645-5303-8)

Spirituality For Dummies
(0-7645-5298-8)

Weddings For Dummies
(0-7645-5055-1)

ETS

0-7645-5255-4

0-7645-5286-4

0-7645-5275-9

Also available:

Labrador Retrievers For Dummies
(0-7645-5281-3)

Aquariums For Dummies
(0-7645-5156-6)

Birds For Dummies
(0-7645-5139-6)

Dogs For Dummies
(0-7645-5274-0)

Ferrets For Dummies
(0-7645-5259-7)

German Shepherds For Dummies
(0-7645-5280-5)

Golden Retrievers For Dummies
(0-7645-5267-8)

Horses For Dummies
(0-7645-5138-8)

Jack Russell Terriers For Dummies
(0-7645-5268-6)

Puppies Raising & Training Diary For Dummies
(0-7645-0876-8)

EDUCATION & TEST PREPARATION

0-7645-5194-9

0-7645-5325-9

0-7645-5210-4

Also available:

Chemistry For Dummies
(0-7645-5430-1)

English Grammar For Dummies
(0-7645-5322-4)

French For Dummies
(0-7645-5193-0)

The GMAT For Dummies
(0-7645-5251-1)

Inglés Para Dummies
(0-7645-5427-1)

Italian For Dummies
(0-7645-5196-5)

Research Papers For Dummies
(0-7645-5426-3)

The SAT I For Dummies
(0-7645-5472-7)

U.S. History For Dummies
(0-7645-5249-X)

World History For Dummies
(0-7645-5242-2)

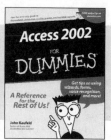

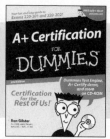